Praise for *The Purpose Reset*

"Much has been written about purpose, but *The Purpose Reset* is the first book to offer an integrated, practical view on how to make your purpose part of every facet of your work life. Beyond that, it's a road map to evolve your purpose as you grow and move through life's stages. It's an essential guide for anyone who wants more meaning, impact, and love in their lives."

—Laszlo Bock, former Senior Vice President, People Operations at Google; Cofounder and CEO, Humu; and Cofounder, UC Berkeley Transformative CHRO Academy

"In a world where people are searching for more meaning, *The Purpose Reset* is a timely and invaluable guide. It offers practical steps to realign purpose at every level—individual, team, and organizational—transforming workplaces into more compassionate, engaged, and high-performing environments."

—Arianna Huffington, Founder and CEO, Thrive Global, and Founder, *The Huffington Post*

"Reset your mind, reset your heart, reset your outlook on life—how many apps, life coaches, and shaman types promise that very thing? And how many actually help you get there? Part of the problem is we try to do it alone, when alone is not how we live, and not how we thrive. Grounded in science and hard data, *The Purpose Reset* offers case studies and actionable tools to help you activate your purpose—not in a silo, but as part of a team and larger ecosystem. What's the point of a North Star if it doesn't lead to ongoing, world-changing collaboration?"

—Elizabeth Koch, Founder and CEO, Unlikely Collaborators

"The search for purpose is one we all share, though we often lack clarity on what it truly means. *The Purpose Reset* introduces purpose as a 'What-Why-Who' process, offering a beautifully simplified yet actionable guide. This approach transforms purpose from a distant goal into a practical way of being, inviting us to make the pursuit of purpose a meaningful, everyday practice."

—Scott Kriens, Cofounder, 1440 Foundation, and Chairman and former CEO, Juniper Networks

"Connecting to our heart's purpose can sometimes feel out of reach, as it takes patience and a willingness to listen deeply. The combined experience and wisdom of Fernandez, Lasso, and Stern illuminates a path for self-discovery at individual and organizational levels, providing concrete guidance to help us each identify and live from our own unique sense of purpose. A worthwhile exploration for businesses and individuals alike."

—Sharon Salzberg, *New York Times* Bestselling Author, *Real Happiness*, *Real Happiness at Work*, and *Lovingkindness*

"*The Purpose Reset* is a powerful call to action for leaders looking to make a lasting impact. By showing how to gain deeper purpose alignment at every level of an organization, this book offers a clear path to creating workplaces and lives that are not only more successful but also filled with significance and fulfillment."

—Nichol Bradford, Executive in Residence, Human and AI Enablement, Society for Human Resources Management (SHRM); Chair and Cofounder, Transformative Tech Lab; and Adjunct Professor, Stanford University

"This wonderful book is written with head and heart (and purpose, of course). Rich, Carolina, and Steph bring together a useful collection of insightful business case studies, mixed with touching personal stories, to present purpose in a way that can be understood and executed on a business level, but also felt and embodied on a personal level. I also really appreciate their insight that the experience of working with purpose is one of love."

—Chade-Meng Tan, *New York Times* Bestselling Author, *Search Inside Yourself,* and Founding Chairman, Search Inside Yourself Leadership Institute (SIYLI)

"Purpose is essential for both personal fulfillment and organizational success. *The Purpose Reset* offers valuable insights and actionable steps to help you align your work with your deeper values, building purpose-driven teams and workplace cultures that thrive. A must-read for anyone committed to living a life in alignment with their values."

—Ronnie Haas, Senior Advisor, former Director of Strategic Talent Management, Massachusetts Institute of Technology

"*The Purpose Reset* offers a powerful guide to redefining purpose and aligning vision for success. Written by seasoned experts in corporate and personal development, the authors approach purpose with compassion, creating alignment across individuals, teams, and organizations. By inspiring meaningful goal-setting at every level, this work can create an organizational culture of unified direction and impact."

—Vicente Gracias, MD, Senior Vice Chancellor, Rutgers Behavioral Health System, and Vice President, Health Affairs, Rutgers University

"*The Purpose Reset* is more than just a book—it's a movement. It redefines what purpose looks like in today's fast-changing world of work, offering practical tools, relatable stories, and deep reflections. If you're ready to move away from just climbing the ladder and start living with greater meaning and purpose, this book is for you."

—Soren Gordhamer, Founder, Wisdom 2.0, and Cofounder, Wisdom Ventures

The
Purpose
Reset

Also by Rich Fernandez

Memory Makes Us

Also by Carolina Lasso

The Path to Flourishing

The Purpose Reset

How Reconnecting to What Matters Most Drives Fulfillment and Success

Rich Fernandez,
Carolina Lasso,
and Steph Stern

Matt Holt Books
An Imprint of BenBella Books, Inc.
Dallas, TX

Matt Holt is an imprint of BenBella Books, Inc.
8080 N. Central Expressway
Suite 1700
Dallas, TX 75206
benbellabooks.com
Send feedback to feedback@benbellabooks.com

BenBella and *Matt Holt* are federally registered trademarks.

Printed in the United States of America
10 9 8 7 6 5 4 3 2 1

Library of Congress Control Number: 2024052030
ISBN 978-1-63774-670-7 (hardcover)
ISBN 978-1-63774-671-4 (electronic)

Editing by Katie Dickman
Copyediting by Michael Fedison
Proofreading by Denise Pangia and Karen Wise
Indexing by WordCo Indexing Services, Inc.
Text design and composition by PerfecType, Nashville, TN
Cover design by Morgan Carr
Printed by Lake Book Manufacturing

Special discounts for bulk sales are available. Please contact bulkorders@benbellabooks.com.

To everyone dedicated to creating a positive ripple effect in this perfectly imperfect world.

CONTENTS

PART IV: THE ORGANIZATION RESET

FOREWORD

In modern times, Purpose has become a possession. We've all heard people say, "I can't find my purpose" as if it's a handbag they left in a roadside gas station bathroom. We feel a bit naked if we don't have a purpose, as if we're the only one without the "big P."

As a noun, Purpose is something you possess—a valued asset in your grasp that you can show to others. But, as a verb, it's a deliberate and conscious way of being: to be purposeful. You don't have to obtain or clutch your purpose as an object that might slip through your fingers. You show up being purposeful and, magically, you become a magnet for the possibility that your purpose may come to us rather than us having to track it down. It's much like happiness: always better when it arrives organically and on its own time, rather than being pursued. Acting in a purposeful manner may be more important than discovering your purpose. You can't have the noun if you don't live the verb.

Over the course of my long career, when I feel like my purpose has eluded me, I ask the questions, "How could I show up purposeful and optimistic today?" or "How might I serve someone beyond myself?" When I move into that action-minded, verb-focused approach to purpose, I soon find unexpected gifts coming my way. It's those questions that led me to creating the world's first midlife wisdom school, the Modern Elder Academy, focused more on a new form of ROI, Ripples of Impact, instead of Return on Investment. One of our MEA faculty members, Dan Buettner, the author of the "Blue Zones" set of bestselling books, has found that having a purpose can add eight years of longevity to your life. And, those are likely happy and healthy years since purpose positively impacts one's life satisfaction.

It is with this context that I fell in love with *The Purpose Reset* as it's perfectly timed for exactly what so many of us need right now. This book is a unique take on the topic of purpose: it's a practical guide to align individuals, teams, and organizations around purpose. At a time when it's easy to fall into cynicism, *The Purpose Reset* is a breath of fresh, hopeful air along with a holistic, prescriptive model that any person, team, or organization can adopt.

The book elaborates a "3-domain model" of purpose—the "What" (strengths and capabilities), "Why" (values and intentions), and "Who" (impact on people, community, and the world around us)—as different but interrelated component parts of purpose. Rather than seeing purpose as some rugged individualist way of showing up in the world (full of unhelpful comparisons with others), the authors contemplate the individual (specifically, working people) as part of a larger ecosystem that includes that person's team and the organization of which they are a part. And, it features numerous personal stories, business case studies, "Purpose Reset Exercises," and micro-practices all on the topic of purpose. It is both supremely readable and practical.

Over the course of my 40-year entrepreneurial career, I've been fortunate enough to be a pioneer boutique hotelier disrupting the staid hotel industry, the "modern elder" to the young Airbnb founders helping them grow their little start-up into the world's most valuable hospitality brand, and the founder of a whole new category, midlife wisdom schools dedicated to "long life learning." Over and over again, I've found that clarifying our purpose—both personally and organizationally—provided the roadmap and the fuel to enable us to navigate all the inevitable obstacles we encountered along the way. I hope this insightful book will be your guide to fulfillment and success as well.

—Chip Conley
Santa Fe, New Mexico
Autumn 2024

INTRODUCTION

Several years ago, I (Rich) had the opportunity to teach *Search Inside Yourself*, the mindfulness-based emotional intelligence program born at Google, at the Bombay Stock Exchange (BSE) to a group of people who didn't know one another. What started as the usual training I'd delivered scores of times became a moment of reset that continues to stay in my mind as a reminder of my purpose, our organization's purpose, and the ripple effect it can have on people around me and the world at large.

One section of the program focuses on the scientific foundations of empathy and practical ways to develop it as a skill, at work and in life. For a particular interactive exercise called "Seeing Similarities," I asked participants to sit in front of a stranger, close their eyes, and reflect on a series of verbal prompts. I heard my voice reaching every corner of that silent room: "This person sitting in front of me has experienced pain and suffering, just like me . . . This person wants a life filled with happiness and well-being, just like me . . ."

As soon as the exercise ended, one of the participants raised his hand and stood up to share his experience. With tears in his eyes, he said: "When my partner introduced himself, I realized he was from a place and culture that I was taught to hold in very poor regard. I was taught to distrust people like him, just because of his place of origin and religion. He said he was Pakistani and a Muslim. I am Indian and Hindu. But as we did this exercise, I realized that I was holding tension and animosity toward him simply because of his external identity. That immediately melted away and what was present for me instead was the fact that he was a person, a human being, just like me, with all of the joys and struggles that I also have. And that tension and animosity as a learned behavior was replaced by kindness and goodwill toward him. I even experienced love, even though we just met a few minutes ago. I can see now that I would consider him as a brother!" The audience broke out into spontaneous applause, and a few tears, as the two participants hugged.

Standing on the stage witnessing these two men and the entire audience coming together to connect with the threads of our common humanity, expressing true empathy and compassion, I, too, felt deeply touched. I was completely absorbed in the moment. Observing the room, I remembered we were practicing the skill of empathy while sitting in a business center, which can often symbolize greed, competition, and separation. Smiling, I felt in complete alignment with what I was doing, why I was doing it, who I was doing it with and for, and the type of impact our team wanted to have in the world. I wasn't *thinking* about purpose. I was experiencing it so vividly, deeply, and fully that I felt something shift. It felt like a reset—a Purpose Reset.

As soon as I got back to our office in San Francisco, I made sure to share this story with my team as it aligned perfectly with our mission, vision, and purpose as an organization. We knew that every encounter, every program, every client call, every action we took was created in support of our purpose, the reason behind our existence as an organization, and the fuel that kept us going as teams and individuals, day after day. Ever since then, I have held this story as a reminder of it.

WHY PURPOSE?

Is it utopian or unrealistically optimistic to think of a working environment that would allow individuals to feel a sense of meaning, belonging, purpose, and fulfillment by what they do personally, by what is accomplished in their teams, or by their organization's positive impact? We don't think so. Not only is this thinking not utopian, it's exactly what work is meant to be. It's exactly what work needs to become *today*.

The three of us writing this book—Carolina, Rich, and Steph—feel lucky to be part of the small percentage of people who are aligned with their purpose. We used to work together at SIY Global, a science-based global learning community, partnering with organizations to train human-centered skills such as emotional intelligence, conscious leadership, resilience, belonging, and mindfulness. As such, we've helped thousands of people become aligned with their larger purpose. We know it's possible. We see it happening. We're certain of the impact that purpose at work has on individuals, teams, and organizations. We've been witnesses to many Purpose Resets. That's why we're writing this book to share with you *what* the Purpose Reset is all about, *why* it needs to be a top priority at work today and for the years to come, and *how* to make it happen.

People are stressed, reassessing their life priorities, and feeling a deep desire to be reengaged at work. Research reveals that only about 13% of employees are engaged at work[1] and 49% of people are experiencing burnout symptoms around the world.[2] Individuals are looking for a more profound sense of meaning and engagement; a paycheck, annual benefits, or climbing up a ladder are no longer enough. At the same time, organizations are increasingly aware that they need to account for their impact beyond shareholder results, looking to their impact on the world at large. According to PwC, 79% of business leaders believe that purpose is central to success. Despite this, less than half of employees know what their organization stands for and what makes it different.[3]

The last few years have provided an inflection point for how companies respond to multiple stakeholder needs—including addressing climate change, championing racial equity, responding to a pandemic, and taking a stance on myriad social issues. Clearly defining and acting out purpose—and creating alignment across organization-team-individual—is necessary, not optional, for individuals' motivation, engagement, and well-being, and for long-term business success.

We want this book to be a practical guide for you to deepen your alignment with purpose at the individual, team, and organization level. It is an invitation to press the reset button and shift from primarily focusing on endless achievement and competition to cultivating work based on meaning, broader impact, and well-being. It is a road map to develop a purposeful, compassionate, fulfilling, sustainable, conscious, and humane way to work.

WHAT IS THE PURPOSE RESET?

A Purpose Reset is anything that increases awareness of your (or your team's or organization's) purpose and helps you put it into action. Resets might be almost imperceptible or large shifts. Think of driving a car—your hands on the steering wheel are making constant adjustments as you move forward and occasionally you take on-ramps (or off-ramps) in new directions.

A Purpose Reset starts with a mindset shift. *Search Inside Yourself,* our core training, supports people to *shift from autopilot to aware*—from a default state to one of greater clarity and deliberate action. This is the start of a Purpose Reset too—shifting from our autopilot to a crisper awareness of the strengths and values that feed into our sense of purpose.

The Purpose Reset starts with the process of aligning the **awareness** of three domains:

1. What: our strengths and skills
2. Why: our values and intentions
3. Who: the impact on people, community, and the world around us

From this greater clarity, purpose must then be lived out through ongoing **action**. We believe that purpose is not a destination or an achievement but is lived through aligned actions and behaviors in an ongoing way.

While much has been written for individuals finding their purpose and passion, to truly live this out at work and to create workplaces and organizations that support individuals to thrive, purpose needs to align at all levels of an organization:

- **At the Individual level:** Aligning unique strengths, skills, and interests with values and meaning, and with a sense of where each person wants to contribute to their community and the world.
- **At the Team level:** Finding the intersection between how the organization's purpose cascades down, and how the team supports individuals to align with their purpose. This requires teams to have a strong sense of belonging and trust for individuals to fully contribute and for teams to operate as more than the sum of their parts.
- **At the Organization level:** Ensuring that stated values and mission are acted out in the world, using the strengths of the team, founders, and culture of the organization, and aligning these values with the actual impact in the industry, on all stakeholders touched, and on the broader world.

> *The Purpose Reset* challenges you to answer
> this question: How can you align your life
> with your individual purpose, and that of
> your team and your organization, to make
> your unique contribution in the world?

Our team has worked for more than 10 years developing skills that lead to more purpose-driven individuals, teams, and companies, impacting more than 250,000 people worldwide. *The Purpose Reset* consolidates key lessons we've learned over the past decade, from our interactions with teams across industries and regions, from the thousands of people we work with in more than 60 countries, and from our own personal experiences. While purpose can take many, many forms, we'll focus on purpose in working environments. We hope you find it practical, relevant, and deeply inspiring.

WHAT'S LOVE GOT TO DO WITH IT?

We'll be using the word *love* throughout this book. When undergoing a Purpose Reset, love becomes a key part of the process. As each of us has connected more and more with our sense of purpose, the experience of working with purpose is one of love. It often feels like enthusiasm, devotion, taking pleasure in many moments throughout the day, and ending most days with a sense of satisfaction. Each of us often feels a profound sense of gratitude that we get the opportunity to do our work in the world.

We know the word *love* might feel odd when talking about work and our professional lives. Some might even find it too "touchy-feely" or taboo. The three of us feel strongly that it's time to shift that mentality. Indeed, we believe that it is imperative to talk about love as a critical element of work.

> Deepening our connection with our sense of purpose, we should aim to love what we do, do what we love, and love who we are while doing it.

Connecting with our purpose, of course, means **doing what we love**. Purpose is essentially about both working toward goals that we care about and that feel meaningful, and doing the tasks that bring us joy. Hopefully, we also get to do these tasks with other people (peers, family, community) we care about and love being around.

Love is also about devotion, and that devotion can work in the other direction as well, and can in turn impact the growth of our love. The more attention and care we give to something, the more potential we have to **love what we do**. The more we understand about a topic, the more skills we gain; and the greater sense of mastery we can feel at work, the easier it becomes to love it as well.

Finally, at the deepest level, purpose should lead us to **love who we are**. Doing what we love means understanding what that is and determining how we choose to spend our time. As we deepen our understanding of our unique strengths and preferences, we also come to accept and love who we are, what drives us, and what makes us unique. We develop a sense of pride in our work and in our contribution to something larger than our own selves. As we include our values and our impact on others in our sense of purpose, we can also appreciate who we are in the world.

If more people around the world could increase their connection to love at work, even in small, gradual steps, if a greater number of individuals and organizations had a strong sense of meaning and purpose, if more of our hours were dedicated to what brings us joy and allows us to contribute to the world, then we believe that we would see a huge shift in our culture. Fewer people would be depressed or in a state of languishing; suicide rates would decrease; teams would be able to accomplish more, collaboratively; more people would feel fulfilled, productive, and happier; and more of humanity would flourish. We are overdue in accomplishing this shift, and in this book, we'll show you how to make it happen.

Throughout these pages you will find interactive practical exercises, vignettes featuring inspiring real-life stories, business case studies, and tool kits. Rich personal stories are woven throughout, especially to emphasize the clarity, well-being, and impact that aligned purpose has made possible for people in organizations, ranging from large multinational companies to small nonprofits to government agencies. Each chapter includes short *Micro-practices* that can be done in one to two minutes without putting down this book, as well as practical exercises we call *Purpose Reset Practices* for people at all levels of an organization to reflect and deepen their understanding of their own purpose and of how to put that purpose into action at each level: individual, team, and organization.

In **Part I** we begin with a definition of *purpose* for each of the three levels and present the latest research findings about why it matters for personal and organizational flourishing. **Part II** dives into understanding purpose on an individual level and how to take action to align with it. **Part III** explores ways to sharpen a sense of purpose for a team and how a shared sense of team-level purpose helps as a middle step to align individuals and organizations. We share research about high-performing teams and organizational cultures and suggest ways to clarify and cultivate a sense of purpose at the team level. **Part IV** discusses the ways in which purpose can be cultivated for an organization as a whole and how to bring that purpose to life. We recognize that people will fall back into default patterns and need future resets, so each section also includes a bit about pitfalls and suggestions for ways to build resilience during challenges and reset again.

We believe that transformation happens from the inside out: from the individual to the team to the organization. Similarly, each organization has a ripple effect on its stakeholders, cities, countries, and the world at large. We are certain of the positive impact that a Purpose Reset can make, and we're beyond excited to share the insights we've learned with you. Thank you for taking one more step in aligning your life with your purpose, which is one of the biggest contributions you can give to our planet. Let's begin our journey together.

MINDSET SHIFT: FROM LADDER TO LOVE

by Steph

When I joined the Search Inside Yourself team in 2015, I made a conscious decision to shift from "ladder to love." I had grown up assuming that success equated to climbing up a career ladder, aiming for promotions, increases in title and salary, and greater responsibility. This worked while I navigated my first few jobs and earned a prestigious master's degree. But when I graduated without a job, I felt ungrounded and questioned what I was working for. For the first time, I deeply reflected on what was most important to me, what I most enjoyed, and the impact I wanted to have. I quickly realized that what I'd been most excited about during my master's program was a mediation training that had nothing to do with the environmental policy work I had been studying!

I realized how much I liked to work with people and deepen my emotional awareness and theirs, and create a sense of connection. I shifted my mindset to give up driving for achievement and working my way up a career ladder to instead finding work that felt like love. I wanted to follow what was exciting, even when it didn't seem to make sense. This was the beginning of my own Purpose Reset.

I decided it was worth it to take a big pay cut to join the SIY team. To remind myself why I'd made this decision, I wrote myself a note that I've kept on my desk that reads: "Ladder to Love." At its core, the Purpose Reset is about exactly this shift.

A **ladder mindset** is the default of the past: it is achievement-focused, doesn't consider the impact of our actions beyond ourselves and the organization's bottom line, and tends to be both driven by and measured by external, tangible metrics like salary, title, sales or revenue, profit, size, and market share. While all these metrics are beneficial and important, they have little to do with well-being, sustainability, or deeper thriving.

In contrast, shifting to a **love mindset** is about focusing on a deeper purpose, aligning individual and organizational strengths with desired impact within and beyond the organization. It is driven by an internal experience of love and wholeheartedness. Purpose becomes highly individual and unique to you, while acting on it is in service to the larger collective. While profit and financial sustainability remain important, a greater sense of purpose and impact is the driving motivation.

When announcing during an all-staff meeting that after seven years with the organization I was leaving my role with Search Inside Yourself to be an independent coach and facilitator, I told this story of the "ladder to love" note and it sparked the idea for the book you're holding now.

MICRO-PRACTICE

Take a moment to reflect on what ideas or beliefs you might be starting out with:

- What comes to mind when you think about purpose?
- What do you already know about that gives you a sense of purpose?
- Do you identify with the "ladder mindset"?
- What messages have you received about purpose from your family or upbringing? From your work experience? From the culture at large?

PART I

ON PURPOSE

CHAPTER 1
Defining Purpose

We can hear the questions running through your mind: What am I meant to do with my life? Who am I as a person, as a professional, and as a leader? How can I add value to others, to this planet? What am I here for? What even is "purpose"?

Though purpose can seem elusive, daunting, or even privileged, we are certain that you, as well as each person on planet Earth, is meant to live a life of purpose and meaning. Decades of research show that people with a strong sense of purpose report greater work and life satisfaction, are more resilient, and have greater well-being. We're meant to move beyond simply going through the motions of life, climbing up a ladder on autopilot, or following "shoulds" imposed by who-knows-who, who-knows-when. Instead, we can choose to use our drive, talents, and passion to follow the wisdom stemming from our hearts—the irreplaceable intelligence that comes from love.

WHAT IS PURPOSE?

The Merriam-Webster dictionary's simple definition of purpose is "something set up as an object or end to be attained."[1] However, when it comes to our life's goals and what gives us meaning, we take a radically different view of purpose.

Our definition of purpose is: Purpose is the ongoing process of understanding and connecting strengths, values, and desired impact with aligned actions to unlock your full potential and be of service.

To unpack this a bit more, let's look at key parts of this definition:

Purpose as Process—*Purpose is the ongoing process . . .*
Purpose starts with intention and becomes an ongoing and unfolding process. We see purpose not as a destination or an achievement to be obtained. Instead, it is the light that illuminates our path, pointing us in a direction so we can arrive more fully into our vision of the self, our life, and the team, organization, and world we truly want to create with our whole hearts. Your purpose is not something you figure out quickly or all at once. It's an intention that you set and that evolves over your lifetime as you grow and as the world around you changes.

Purpose Comes from Awareness and Aligned Action—*of understanding and connecting strengths, values, and desired impact with aligned actions . . .*
We develop clarity of our purpose from our awareness of ourselves, our teams, and our organization. We must know and understand our own strengths, talents, and values (for us as individuals, teams, and organizations), and align these skills with the desired impact we want to make. Importantly, we live out our purpose when our behaviors and decisions are congruent with our purpose. This becomes a virtuous cycle: actions feed into greater awareness, and we can then choose to continue or adjust, and take new aligned actions. If our purpose is not lived out, if our actions are misaligned, we create inner tension and resistance. At an organizational level, we risk harm to the company's reputation and employees feeling disengaged and mistrustful.

Purpose Is Motivating and Self-Directed—*to unlock your full potential* . . .
The outcome of purpose is in your lived experience of being at your best.
Living according to your full potential will leave you with a sense of meaning and fulfillment in your unique way. These metrics are self-directed and self-assessed. Only you will know if you are living according to your sense of purpose. Metrics of status, salary, title, or other accomplishments could be by-products but are not the goal of living out your purpose. At a team and organizational level, enacting the desired impact for your stakeholders, in your industry, and the world is the key outcome; business metrics will follow.

Purpose Accounts for Impact—*and to be of service.*
Our definition of purpose ends with the phrase *of service.* Why is this? Why is it not enough to just live a good life for yourself? We believe that our individual, team, and organizational purposes must account for the impact that we have on those around us and on the greater, interconnected world.

The world needs us to include our impact on others in our definition of purpose and how we think about our work. We live at a time of unprecedented interconnection among people, and unprecedented extinction among other species. It's a time of revolutionary technological development and incredible wealth disparity. Put simply, we need to create our individual and collective futures holding one another in mind.

In this way, finding our purpose is not a selfish endeavor, though it does require a bit of navel-gazing. It will be up to you, however, to decide how you want to be of service. One SIY participant recently shared that her current vision of service and the purposeful life she wants to lead is to be home from work in time for dinner with her family; that's so meaningful! We're not asking you to grandly take on all of the world's challenges, but simply to consider how you want your time, energy, and life to impact others beyond yourself.

CULTIVATING PURPOSE

Given our definition of purpose, the Purpose Reset becomes a formula. It's not a mathematical formula with one unchanging correct answer; instead, it's one to recalculate again and again throughout our lives. Purpose is brought to life through the combination of building awareness and taking action. We visually summarize it as:

Purpose =

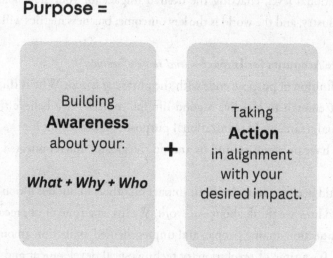

Awareness

The critical first step in developing or resetting your sense of purpose is to deepen your awareness of who you are (as an individual, team, and organization) and what you have to contribute.

Purpose is born from awareness of what's at the intersection of three spheres of influence (which we'll talk about in great detail throughout the book): the what, why, and who.

WHAT
Our strengths and skills.

WHY
Our values and intentions.

WHO
The impact on people, community, and the world around us.

When we think about our work and jobs, we tend to focus on *what* we are doing—our role and the tasks we spend our time doing all day. It is essential to align our strengths and skills with our work. From there, we also need to include our motivating drivers: Why do we work? The *why* includes examining what we value and our intentions for our lives. This alignment with our deeper sense of meaning brings us closer to living according to our purpose. Finally, it is critical to acknowledge *who* our efforts impact. It is only at the intersection of our what, why, and who that our true and aligned purpose lives.

Aligned Action

From this awareness, we put purpose into aligned action. It is through our actions that we really create the Purpose Reset and can shift from operating from the ladder mindset to operating and acting out of love.

It is tempting to focus on purpose for us as individuals. Indeed, this focus on our own individual purpose is critical, and where it is often easiest to understand and take action and to see and feel the effect of greater alignment. However, we believe that awareness of individual purpose is necessary but not sufficient for lasting transformation. Most of us work with teams and organizations. We believe that organizations—and the people in them—thrive when purpose resonates across levels and functions.

This resonance is like sound waves. When sound waves align, they amplify each other in magnitude. When they are not aligned, they cancel each other out, like an out-of-sync orchestra. This alignment and amplification is what makes for successful, sustainable, and high-performing workplaces where individuals can thrive.

There is a positive upward cascade of purpose. Individuals can use the best of their strengths and talents and work in alignment with their values to contribute to their team's success. Doing so supports them to feel engaged and motivated. At the team level, high team performance is built on a sense of individuals feeling safe to contribute and being clear and aligned around goals. This sense of trust and alignment of individual strengths and interests and team needs is what makes for high-performing teams that are more than the sum of their parts. When an organization has many engaged employees and high-performing teams, that, of course, cascades up to the success of the whole.

And vice versa—organizational purpose will be an empty set of statements if it does not cascade downward. People leaders, in particular, should live out the stated purpose through meaningful actions and thoughtful decision-making. Team goals should also offer their own contribution to the larger purpose of the organization. Top-level direction and clarity can be inspiring and motivating across levels.

For a while in our organization, our sales team felt a lack of alignment until we deliberately made a shift, our own mini–Purpose Reset. Our team was responsible for bringing our flagship training programs to organizations—selling new opportunities and holding ongoing relationships with our corporate clients. These corporate programs were the biggest revenue source, even in years when much of the organization was focused on other forms of impact, like training new teachers and running programs open to the public. Especially in years when increasing the accessibility of our programs and trying to welcome a more racially and socially diverse audience was a big priority for the organization, our client team felt misaligned and out of step with the organization's focus.

This lack of alignment around purpose and impact could be demoralizing; it felt like the team's hard work wasn't being fully recognized or appreciated. To realign and reset, the sales team did two things: They got better at sharing about the impact of the work they were doing (e.g., reporting back to the full organization more often about clients they were working with, the mindfulness champions in those organizations, and sharing participant testimonials from programs they ran). Importantly, as a team, they also redefined their contribution to accessibility. Instead of just thinking about accessibility in terms of the demographics of our participants (including economic privilege, race, and gender), they also thought about who would opt into a personal development program. They started thinking about bringing the program to people at work as a way of connecting with individuals who would not otherwise have sought out this type of personal growth and emotional intelligence program on their own. By bringing the SIY program to their workplace, they were able to participate, which made the program more accessible to a wider range of people. With these two shifts, the team felt a greater sense of purpose and alignment with the organization and an increased sense of motivation.

WHAT PURPOSE IS NOT

When it comes to the topic of purpose, there is a lot of bad or incomplete advice out there. This topic is complex and unique; there are no one-size-fits-all answers. This book you're reading lives in shades of gray. Instead of definitive answers or simple maxims, we'll offer many questions to sit with, ways of considering and reconsidering this central and thorny topic of purpose, and practices and actions that you might take. It may not feel linear or straightforward. However, it will truly help you cultivate a deeper sense of self-awareness, meaning, and alignment over time, from the inside out.

As an example, for Meredith, pursuing her purpose as a writer and advocate has meant becoming a lawyer where she can spend her days writing briefs and providing legal representation to those who couldn't otherwise afford it. For Meiko, pursuing her purpose as a writer meant working at night, after her full-time shift, to complete a novel telling the stories of women in Osaka. For Mario, publishing a children's book required long days as a summer camp counselor followed by many years as a schoolteacher and a three-month sabbatical.

While articulating what purpose is can be complex, there are some aspects we can identify with certainty that purpose is not related to:

Passion Versus Purpose

The reason we don't use the concept of passion in this book is that we believe it can cause confusion when it comes to a Purpose Reset. We see passion as a strong and intense emotional feeling or enthusiasm for something that tends to be temporary or fleeting in nature. You might be passionate about a hobby or cause at one point in your life and later find a different passion. There is nothing wrong with that. We want to see more passionate people enjoying life in the world; yet, while it's energizing (and feels good), it may not be the answer to a deeper reset.

On the other hand, purpose is a fundamental reason for being, a sense of meaning and direction in life. It's about a long-term, overarching goal or principle that guides your actions and decisions. It often involves contributing to something larger than yourself. It serves as a guiding star that can remain relatively constant throughout your life. Purpose looks to the future and provides a sense of direction and vision, whereas passion is often more about a temporary experience in the present.

Thus, this will not be a "follow your passion"–style book. We will not tell you to "just say yes to everything that feels good!" We don't have simple aphorisms, blind optimism, or easy answers for you. This process is about reflection, finding yourself, knowing yourself, and letting yourself grow and change. It's about sensing what the world needs, opening your heart, and aligning what lights you up with what is of service. We also want to invite you to think about your purpose in relation to the teams or communities you work or interact with, and with the world at large; following your passion is not about just your own inner flame, but how it can shine a light to others.

I (Carolina) feel passionate about many topics, including writing, oil painting, teaching, marketing, contemplation, and entrepreneurship. Yet, I found purpose alignment when doing deep inner work after hitting my rock bottom and asking myself, "How can I be of service?" Focusing on my long-term legacy and contribution has shown me the difference between what I do out of enjoyment versus what guides my life and decisions in the long term. I'll share more about this in the coming chapters.

Purpose Is Not a Luxury Good

Though taking some time to reflect on your purpose does require the luxury of time and having basic needs met, we want to be clear that we don't want this book to be just for a privileged few who have the means to make big changes in their lives or be picky about their careers. We are aware of the many systemic issues that create obstacles that often seem insurmountable and unfair, and we also know that the three of us writing these lines may not be aware of all the situations you may be facing.

At the same time, we wholeheartedly believe that anyone can bring more purpose and alignment into their life and that small changes can have a big impact. Even if you are not considering a big change, you might still ask yourself how more of your purpose can come through in your current work.

Purpose Is Not All About Work

Importantly, purpose doesn't have to be borne out through work or career. Since our organization, SIY Global, focuses on organizational contexts, we incorporate a lot of work-related examples in this book, but your purpose may well be primarily as a parent or caregiver, community leader, artist, or citizen.

Greg's a great example of fulfilling purpose outside of work, and yet still using his skills and talents in his job. Having always been passionate about music, Greg earned his master's degree in that discipline. However, early on in his life, he ruled out being a professional musician (too hard to earn a stable income, according to him) or an academic (too theoretical). Greg has also always been clear about his values and priorities in life: family, community, and music. Greg is married with two wonderful kids, and for him, work comes last and serves largely to support his family. His priorities allow him to continue to play music, which he does on his own, with his family, and occasionally performing. Still, it is important to Greg to use his skills and interests at work, which led him to combine his technical and people skills as a customer success manager in various technology companies. Greg is a very empathetic and caring person, and he thrives when he can connect with his colleagues and help his customers. Having crisp clarity about the skills he can bring to his job and how his passion for music and dedication to his family are supported by work gives him a greater sense of motivation and contentment.

Potential for Burnout and Overwork

While pursuing one's passion can be energizing, it also carries the risk of leading to burnout. People who feel passionate about a cause can be more susceptible to overworking, neglecting self-care, and setting unrealistic expectations, even out of good intentions. Striking a balance between passion-driven dedication and the importance of self-care, boundaries, and maintaining a sustainable pace is essential to prevent exhaustion. We'll talk more about how this has an impact on teams in Part III.

Reinforcing Social Inequalities

The notion of finding one's passion can inadvertently reinforce social inequalities by assuming that everyone has equal access to opportunities and resources for self-discovery and the pursuit of a passion. In reality, systemic barriers, economic disparities, unequal access to education, and social biases can limit individuals from marginalized backgrounds in their ability to explore new opportunities.

Affluent groups often have more resources and support to cultivate their interests, while those facing socioeconomic disadvantages may be constrained by the need to prioritize survival over alignment. The pursuit of passion (and sometimes purpose too) can downplay these systemic inequalities and place undue pressure on individuals, particularly those with fewer advantages, to "just find and follow their passion" without addressing the structural barriers that present obstacles along their journey.

For example, only certain parts of the population can wait until their ideal job comes their way, take on unpaid internships, or do volunteer work, without worrying about student loans, paying rent, or how to cover basic needs. Sociologist Erin Cech, PhD, author of *The Trouble with Passion*, explained in an interview with the University of California Press:

> The passion principle was almost tailor-made for wealthy and upper-middle-class young adults . . . They have access to parents' social networks to help them find jobs. The passion principle presumes access to resources and cultural capital that are really only available to middle- or upper-class workers. But it's not just well-off passion-seekers who benefit most from the passion principle. Employers of passionate workers do, too. I conducted an experiment to see how potential employers responded to job applicants who expressed different reasons for being interested in a job. Not only were passionate applicants preferred over applicants who were dedicated to the organization or liked the city where the job was located, but employers preferred passionate applicants because they would work hard at their jobs without expecting an increase in pay. In other words, employers knowingly exploit the passion of the people who work for them.[2]

While the pursuit of passion can be invigorating, we must pay close attention to its complexities and potential drawbacks. Once again, it all starts with awareness: Awareness of ourselves, when a passionate pursuit may lead to burnout. Awareness of others, when we may be unintentionally perpetuating social inequity within ourselves or with others. Awareness of when passion is something exciting but temporary, or when it's a strong signal for long-lasting purposeful living. It's through awareness that we can find clarity, connect the dots, and shine a light on our journey to cultivating our purpose(s).

PURPOSE IS FOR ALL OF US

Howard Thurman, author, activist, and educator, advised, "Don't ask what the world needs. Ask what makes you come alive, and go do it. Because what the world needs is people who have come alive."[3] Figuring out what brings you alive is a core part of this book. We believe that the world also needs people who recognize how their purpose uplifts those around them and contributes to what the world needs.

The Purpose Reset is about turning toward everything that makes you come alive. Looking at your limiting beliefs, your internalized expectations from family and culture, and how your actions impact others around you and those far away. We challenge you to align all levels: How can you align your individual purpose with that of your team, your organization, and what is needed for a more sustainable, compassionate, and equitable world?

THE SEARCH INSIDE YOURSELF INITIATIVE: OUR QUEST FOR PURPOSE

by Rich

"If you are interested in mindfulness and leadership, then you will definitely appreciate what is being built here at Google with Search Inside Yourself," Google's Head of Human Resources at the time, Laszlo Bock, said to me during my final interview for the role of Head of Executive Development at the company. During the interview process, I met with close to two dozen Google leaders and heard all about

Google's strategies and priorities, especially regarding leadership development and capability-building to deliver on their extremely ambitious organizational goals. The idea that across the company there was also rising interest in harnessing neuroscience to develop mindfulness and establish emotional intelligence skills for leaders was possibly the most interesting thing I had heard during those four weeks of interviews (I'm admittedly biased as I had already been a mindfulness meditation practitioner and enthusiast for many years at that point). "What in the world is Search Inside Yourself," I asked, "and how did it come about here at Google?"

In 2007, one of Google's earliest engineers, Chade-Meng Tan, became fascinated by the idea that it might be possible to create the conditions for world peace if people had the right internal tools and mindsets. To conduct the *search* within their own selves to discover the causes and conditions within for happiness, thriving, compassion, and peace. Changing one's mindset and worldview, so the thinking goes, can change the world.

Meng also knew that, Google being Google, the company could play an influential role in helping people develop these skills and driving further adoption of the same outside the company. To make this happen, Meng realized he had to go deep into neuroscience to show how brain changes could occur if people began practicing mindfulness and emotional intelligence skills that would lead to more empathy, compassion, effective leadership, and the conditions for a more peaceful and sustainable way of living and working. He also knew that he had to demonstrate how these skills resulted in sustainable high performance, well-being, and outstanding leadership at Google and beyond because, after all, the training ground for this massive shift in consciousness would be organizations and cultures of high performance.

Meng became the first Google engineer to transition to the company's human resources department to lead the development of the program and convened some of the world's leading experts in emotional intelligence, mindfulness, leadership, and contemplative practices. The group included meditation teachers Mirabai Bush, Norman Fischer, and Yvonne Ginsberg; neuroscientist Philippe Goldin; business leader Marc Lesser; and advisory and guidance from Daniel Goleman, Richie Davidson, and Jon Kabat-Zinn.

The program, called Search Inside Yourself (which started as a joke and then stuck), became, within a short period of time, one of the most popular trainings within Google and aimed to help people develop the skills needed to create the conditions for individual and collective thriving, leading to world peace.

The creation of that program with such a lofty purpose within the walls of a young tech company in Silicon Valley marked the beginning of why this book exists today and how we, the three authors writing these lines, came to meet and work together. I myself became one of the first teachers of Search Inside Yourself within Google, often teaching together with Meng and others and tinkering with the content and models to offer optimal impact and transformation for participants.

Five years after Search Inside Yourself (SIY) was first taught at Google, Meng Tan, Philippe Goldin, and Marc Lesser began to grapple with the challenge of scaling SIY beyond Google. There was huge demand from other companies as SIY had become the single most highly rated and in-demand training within Google, and Meng had recently released a *New York Times* bestselling book titled *Search Inside Yourself: The Unexpected Path to Achieving Success, Happiness (and World Peace)*. Interest in the SIY offering was rising globally. But how to teach an internal Google program externally?

The answer came in the form of Google's ethos of sharing best practices in the people development and culture arena (Google's publicly published coaching study Project Oxygen is an example of this, as was its team effectiveness study entitled Project Aristotle). The Search

Inside Yourself group got permission to offer SIY and its tools and training externally through the structure of an independent nonprofit educational institute they called the Search Inside Yourself Leadership Institute, SIYLI (pronounced like "silly"—the joke continued to keep things light). That change solidified the goal of attaining world peace, one trainee at a time.

For 10 years, SIYLI brought Search Inside Yourself to more than 200,000 people, in 17 languages across 150 cities and 60 countries around the world, working with a community of more than 700 certified teachers. Participants reported powerful transformational experiences after taking the program(s), and today, SIY enjoys a 97 net promoter score across tens of thousands of participants.

Despite the amazing metrics and list of accomplishments, the team at SIYLI began to wonder if they were truly on track to achieve their mission, which was updated to "create a global community working to make mindfulness and emotional intelligence practical and accessible, and working toward a more peaceful world in which all people feel connected and act with compassion."

Was that the right purpose to work toward? How could it be measured? Was it inspiring enough? How to attain such a big goal with a group of fewer than 20 full-time employees and limited resources? How to have a greater impact? What did each individual have as their own personal purpose and how did it align with the greater mission? These were the questions that we confronted at SIYLI despite the success we had experienced over the years.

At that point, Steph, Carolina, and I were working together at the Institute, as Director of Business Development, Director of Marketing, and CEO, respectively. Those questions were key for us both personally and professionally as leaders, and to continue to formulate the organization's strategy for the years to come. Answering them, however, was not an easy task.

Business school management classes, entrepreneurship books, leadership podcasts, and beyond all teach the importance of having a clear vision, mission, and purpose, but they're not always easy to identify, let alone implement.

When we spun off from Google, our initial mission was to "train one billion active practitioners of mindfulness and emotional intelligence in order to create the conditions for world peace." We soon realized that the "one billion" goal, as well as the idea that *we* would be the ones creating world peace through our efforts, was way too focused on us as the doers. In some ways, our original mission mirrored that of Google's, which is to "organize the world's information and make it universally accessible." In that formulation, Google is definitely the doer. We asked ourselves instead how we might focus more on the power of our community and collective human effort to create the outcomes we wished to see in the world.

Our full staff, in consultation with our trusted teachers and some of our key clients, decided to put "community" at the center of our mission and still retain the goal of practicing the internal skills of mindfulness, empathy, compassion, and emotional intelligence to support the emergence of individual and collective thriving.

Our new mission statement reads: "We are a global community working to make mindfulness and emotional intelligence practical and accessible worldwide." Better. More suited to our actual approach and more inclusive.

While that mission continues to guide us, the COVID-19 pandemic made us question many aspects of *how* we'd bring it to life. During a challenging time for a company that focused on in-person programming, our team once again had to follow another Purpose Reset. We'll tell you more about the surprising outcome this led us to in the coming chapters.

MICRO-PRACTICE

Read our definition of purpose again: *Purpose is the ongoing process of understanding and connecting strengths, values, and desired impact with aligned actions to unlock your full potential and be of service.*

What comes to your mind when you apply this definition to your own life? Your team? Your company? Your community?

CHAPTER 2

Why a Purpose Reset?

W hy does purpose matter? Our inner compass tells us that living a meaningful life and thriving is simply the *human* way to live out our time on this planet. Yet, while this reason should suffice, we can't help but pay attention to our outer compasses—intellectual curiosity, analytical side, and business minds—which also encourage us to seek the data that validate that inner knowing. So we'd like to share with you both our experiences and research findings that provide additional evidence that the Purpose Reset will only grow in importance in the years to come.

LEANING IN WITHOUT BURNING OUT

Worrisome levels of stress, anxiety, and burnout continue to exist around the world.[1] Read that first sentence again, please. Chances are, you've read or heard that same statement so many times that it no longer touches you at a deep level.

While burnout is a term that has become part of our day-to-day vocabulary, it should not be normalized. It's *not normal* for human beings to live day after day with such high levels of depletion or exhaustion. It's not okay to accept that work is meant to be a negative experience that drains our energy away, leaving us with nothing for the rest of our lives. It's not acceptable or healthy to have to spend the majority of our waking hours on endeavors that make us anxious, depressed, or sick. Or in jobs that don't fulfill us, bring out the best in us, allow us to unlock our true potential, or bring us at least some level of joy. That is not normal or okay. We must stop accepting this as the status quo.

Addressing the burnout epidemic requires action on all three levels: personal, team, and organizational. It shouldn't be left just to individuals to figure it all out alone. From a company perspective, there's enough data and empirical evidence coming from our own lives showing the overwhelming cost and negative impact of burnout to business operations to ignore it:

- Depression and anxiety disorders cost the *global* economy $1 trillion each year in lost productivity.[2]
- Employees who are not engaged in their work cost their company the equivalent of 18% of their annual salary.[3]
- Burned-out employees are 2.6 times as likely to be actively seeking a different job, 63% more likely to take a sick day, 13% less confident in their performance, and 23% more likely to visit the emergency room.[4]

The World Health Organization (WHO) officially recognized burnout as a workplace phenomenon in 2019 and defined it as a syndrome resulting from chronic workplace stress that has not been successfully managed. According to the WHO, burnout is characterized by three dimensions:

1. Feelings of energy depletion or exhaustion
2. Increased mental distance from one's job, or feelings of negativism or cynicism related to one's job
3. Reduced professional efficacy[5]

Based on our experience working with hundreds of companies from around the world, the main drivers of burnout include:

Drivers of Burnout: The P.T.O. Model		
Personal	**Team**	**Organizational**
"I'm burned out and stressed all the time. My values aren't in congruence with my organization's, and/or my current path isn't in alignment with my purpose."	"I don't feel supported. I can't trust or don't feel that I belong to my team or community at work."	"What I give to my organization is greater than what I can handle or what I receive from it."
• Lack of tools to cope with chronic stress • Lack of resilience-building skills • Values mismatch • Purpose-level misalignment • Personal dreams and longings ignored • Unable to be my true, full self at work • Skills mismatch: my tasks are too challenging or too easy	• Lack of support from manager or peers • Feeling lack of connection and belonging • No sense of trust or safety in the group; inadequate level of autonomy and flexibility • Perception of equity and fairness: thinking others are receiving more than me or what I'm getting isn't fair • Lacking shared purpose in the immediate team • Team doesn't take time for connection, stress relief, or resilience-building	• Compensation, recognition, and rewards that aren't enough for my contribution • Demands and workload that exceed my capacity • Dehumanization: being seen as a number or output-creator • Lack of well-being support, systems, or resources • Lack of organization-wide system to support personal interests and purpose • A culture that emphasizes competition and ego-driven behaviors • Company values and mission are not lived out, leading to disillusionment and disengagement

Burnout is not the same as one step beyond stress. In general, stress is about struggling to cope with pressure and leads to preoccupation with present issues or anxiety. On the other hand, burnout is deeper and more existential. It includes a sense of disillusionment, hopelessness, lack of meaning, low motivation, and difficulty dealing with even small projects. Burnout includes disengagement and withdrawal, and it may even lead to depression and detachment. We can see stress resulting from leaning in so much that one gets tired and out of balance (but can recover when the stressor has passed), whereas burnout is a level of exhaustion that makes us lean back, disconnect, or even collapse.

As you can see in the P.T.O model representing the main drivers of burnout at the personal, team, and organizational level, many of the drivers of burnout are related to purpose: not having a strong sense of meaning, lacking shared purpose, misalignment between the individual's and the organization's values, and feeling unable to be fully oneself. Cultivating purpose can help to address many of these causes of burnout.

ALIGNING VALUES

The P.T.O. Model shows us how purpose is key for well-being and values alignment. Christina Maslach, burnout researcher at the University of California at Berkeley and codeveloper of the renowned Maslach Burnout Inventory (MBI), and Michael P. Leiter from Acadia University, have found that values alignment ties directly to either engagement or lack of motivation, resulting in burnout.

> Values are the ideals and motivations that originally attracted people to their job, and thus they are the motivating connection between the worker and the workplace, which goes beyond the utilitarian exchange of time for money or advancement. When there is a values conflict on the job, and thus a gap between individual and organizational values, employees will find themselves making a trade-off between work they want to do and work they have to do, and this can lead to greater burnout . . . The leveraging of personal

impact is at the heart of the values area. The ideal employee is one with the greatest overlap of values. When individual and organizational values overlap, work furthers both parties . . . When individual values are independent of organizational values, the work is personally irrelevant. The personal commitment to the work rests solely on the exchange of rewards or development opportunities.

As Maslach's work shows, values are essential for engagement and well-being. However, she warns that when values are written and not lived out, they can be depleting.

The strain associated with an enduring mismatch of values depletes personal energy, reduces involvement, and undermines personal efficacy or accomplishment . . . A mismatch reduces involvement in a job as it limits the point at which staff members are confident that their efforts are making an important contribution. Meaningless work encourages indifference, cynicism, and depersonalization. Work without meaning may reduce efficacy by focusing staff members on the inconsequential or detrimental impact of their efforts on the large community.[6]

As more people and organizations seek ways to get to the root of the burnout epidemic at work, it is of absolute importance to authentically assess values congruence and long-term purpose alignment between the two. A job that solely focuses on the achievement of certain projects without a sense of impact, meaning, and values alignment isn't conducive to thriving for anyone involved, and can actually increase burnout.

FULFILLMENT OVER FRILLS, PURPOSE OVER PAYCHECKS

"Meaning Is the New Money" was the title of a 2011 *Harvard Business Review* article.[7] Indeed, a growing number of studies indicate that people are no longer merely motivated by money as it relates to work. People at work are seeking a deeper sense of meaning, and they're even willing to "pay" for it.

A study by BetterUp Labs, with 2,285 professionals across 26 industries in the United States, found that "on average, employees would be willing to give up 23% of their total future lifetime earnings—nearly a quarter of their income—in exchange for work that is meaningful." According to their estimates, this percentage translates to an average sacrifice of $21,100 per year, every year, until retirement, in exchange for work that would always feel meaningful.[8] All three of us can relate to this study: at some point in our careers, we left jobs that didn't provide us with meaning or weren't aligned with our higher purpose, initially giving up a significant percentage of our annual income.

As we write these lines, we're wondering about what's going through your mind as you reflect on that percentage. Are you doing the math to determine what portion of your current salary you'd be willing to give up to do work that you'd find meaningful? Or thinking about your employees and how much they'd be willing to sacrifice, in case their roles aren't meaningful to them? Are you questioning how much one needs to make, how much disposable income one needs to have, or how privileged one needs to be to be able to make such changes?

We've asked ourselves similar questions too. Money is such a personal topic, and we all value it differently. We all have different needs and family commitments. We recognize that not everyone is in a financial position to take a pay cut. This book includes ways to increase your sense of purpose in the job you're in as well. We cite this important study not as an injunction or suggestion, but as a reflection of how much people value having a sense of purpose and meaning at work.

Given this statistic, if you're a leader or manager, or you work in a human resources function, you may be thinking about the impact of meaningful work regarding talent acquisition and retention, one of the top concerns for companies across industries. In Canada, a series of studies led by researchers from the Rotman School of Management at the University of Toronto found that participants reported lower minimum acceptable salaries when comparing jobs they considered to be personally meaningful with those they considered to be meaningless. Participants who experienced more meaningful work lives were more likely to turn down higher-paying job offers elsewhere.[9]

As a matter of fact, research from Great Place to Work indicates the following three questions will predict workplace turnover, regardless of generation or job type:

1. Are you proud of where you work?
2. Do you find meaning in your work?
3. Do you have fun at work?[10]

Pride, meaning, and fun. We have to admit that the last one surprised us. We get it, and love it when we're having fun at work, but for that to be a top topic related to employee retention, out of all possibilities? It brought smiles to our faces to realize the importance of bringing more joy to work—not as a nice-to-have, but as a key driver of talent acquisition and retention.

Now, all three questions have something to do with alignment with higher meaning, impact beyond net income or shareholder value, and purpose. As a matter of fact, it's been found that across generations, employees who score their work as highly meaningful stay at their current job significantly longer than employees who find their work lacking meaning.

The impact of purpose for talent retention is even more pronounced for newer generations in the workforce. Millennials, for instance, believe that business success should not be measured only in terms of financial performance, but also on the impact it has on society. They're motivated more by mission and purpose than paycheck, and they're more likely to leave if a job feels out of alignment with what they find meaningful. According to PwC, millennials are 5.3 times more likely to stay when they have a strong connection to their employer's purpose (versus 2.3 times for people outside that generation).[11]

RETURN ON PURPOSE

In addition to the reasons listed above, there are many other economic factors that validate the importance of a Purpose Reset for business, including the following research findings:

- **Clear Direction and Purpose Leads to Shareholder Value.** According to a Harvard Business School study, "When employees experience a sense of purpose at work and believe their leaders set a clear direction and expectations (purpose and clarity), those companies outperformed the stock market, achieving returns 6.9% higher than the market."[12] (We'll talk more about this topic in Part IV.)

- **Purpose can be a catalyst for innovation.** Great Place to Work research found that a barrier to innovation "has to do with front-line workers experiencing much less purpose than others. And if employees feel they're not sharing in the company's mission and excitement, they quickly feel excluded from innovation as well."[13]

- **Purpose leads to a quantifiable return.** According to a *Harvard Business Review* article, employees who find their jobs meaningful "are 69% less likely to plan on quitting their jobs within the next 6 months, and have job tenures that are 7.4 months longer on average than employees who find work lacking in meaning." In addition, they experience greater overall satisfaction, which translates into increased productivity, which in turn can generate an additional $9,078 per worker, per year, based on established job satisfaction-to-productivity ratios. Researchers also estimated that companies can save an average of $6.43 million in annual turnover-related costs for every 10,000 workers, when all employees feel their work is highly meaningful.[14]

Deepening our individual or collective alignment with purpose is not just a feel-good, nice-to-have idea, but a major factor for people and organizations to thrive. It can help to sustain well-being, foster values alignment, provide direction, and drive innovation, resilience, and performance—all essential ingredients that create prosperous workplaces.

A BIG DEAL: LONGING FOR PURPOSE

by Carolina

"Are you serious? You're saying you're going to quit your seven-year-long marketing career at Google's headquarters, exactly when you're about to be promoted, cut your salary by more than two-thirds, and go to work at a nonprofit organization with just 16 employees? That's a pretty big deal." This was the type of refrain I heard from many friends, former colleagues, and family members when I received an offer to work at the Search Inside Yourself Leadership Institute, right at the peak of my trajectory at Google.

I shared my dilemma with as many friends as I could to gather as many data points and perspectives as possible. I created a pros and cons spreadsheet, and a detailed quantitative analysis of long-term implications, as I usually do in the face of big decisions.

The Excel model's output was clear: quantitatively or rationally, the move didn't make sense. But there was something I didn't know how to add as a variable in the model: my profound longing for purpose.

"Higher Purpose" is how I ended up referring to it. That deep need buried in my chest that I couldn't hide for much longer, the fire in the pit of my stomach I couldn't continue to quench, the desire to use my skills and limited breaths on Earth in a way that aligned with my values and how I wanted to contribute to the world. I wanted Work, with a capital W. Work that would make my eyes spark with passion, my heart beat with excitement, my hands move with determination, and my full body and soul shout a big, loud "yes." I wanted to wake up each day with joy, the type of feeling I know humans are meant to experience daily. I wanted to break free and sprint to where I could do more, in a bigger way, feel a more authentic sense of belonging, and create a greater impact.

So, I scratched the model and the pro/con list and leaped. Deep inside, I knew that my attempt to gather data was meant to convince myself of a decision that a part of me had already made. My inner wisdom knew it was the right next step for me, but my intellectual side needed extra validation, especially on the financial front.

There was a lot of history behind this decision. At the age of 17, I moved from Colombia to the United States with $100 in my pocket. I had to find all sorts of ways to finance my college education—whether it meant babysitting, clerical work, or working at a bookstore. A few years later, I moved to New York City to pursue my master's degree, this time with the heavy weight of a six-figure student loan on my shoulders. Throughout that time, I had to be careful with my budget, study hard to get scholarships, and do all the extracurricular activities recommended so I'd land a solid job after graduation.

I kept on following all the "shoulds" I thought I needed to succeed and flourish: Straight As throughout college. Valedictorian. MBA from a top university. Landing a great job at the World Financial Center in New York City. A promotion, then another one. Working at Google, then ranked as one of the most desired companies to work for. Another promotion. Check. Check. Check.

Checking off all those boxes and working as hard as my body would allow me to led me to burn out. Badly. I felt the need to prove myself constantly, so I followed all the rules, receiving compliments on my work ethic and dedication. After experiencing panic attacks and levels of anxiety I had never felt in my entire life, I ended up needing to take a six-month leave of absence to get to the root cause of my burnout. I traveled around the world, alone (the story I share in my book *The Path to Flourishing*), which gave me the space I needed to "search inside myself" and identify and more deeply connect with my new purpose: to help human beings flourish.

Upon my return, I promised myself I'd follow that purpose within my own team at Google. I wanted to become the kind of leader and coworker I wanted to see in my company and in the world. I wanted to help my direct reports flourish, based on what was within my control. Instead of just focusing on accomplishing my never-ending list of goals, or focusing on my own career growth, I focused on helping whoever was around me with theirs. I became certified to teach the Search Inside Yourself program at Google and gained the knowledge, skills, and embodied practices I needed to align even deeper with my purpose.

What still amazes me to think about is that with that approach, my performance at Google improved significantly, my anxiety disappeared, and I became more creative, empathetic, and innovative. That shift, my Purpose Reset, also allowed me to be a better leader and manager. I built stronger connections, which gave me a deeper sense of belonging. I felt a greater level of meaning and fulfillment.

That's why, when I received the offer to join the Search Inside Yourself Leadership Institute as its Global Head of Marketing, I knew it was the perfect opportunity to take my purpose to the next level—spending all my working hours supporting the mission to build more human workplaces so individuals and organizations can flourish around the world.

Changing jobs seemed like a huge deal to me back then, and it was, but not for the reasons I'd imagined. It was a huge deal for me to be able to align my values and higher purpose with that of my organization, work with the like-minded people I met then, and feel that my Work mattered. I'm now leading my own bilingual human flourishing academy and it continues to be a big deal to cultivate awareness and take action toward living out my purpose, and to be among the people who can spend our time loving what we do, doing what we love, loving who we do it for, and loving who we are while doing it. *That* is certainly a life-changing, big deal.

MICRO-PRACTICE

Take a moment to reflect or write about the following questions:

- What work-related benefits matter most to you? How do they compare to working on projects that bring you a sense of fulfillment and meaning?
- What would you be willing to give up at work to increase alignment with your purpose, interests, and values?

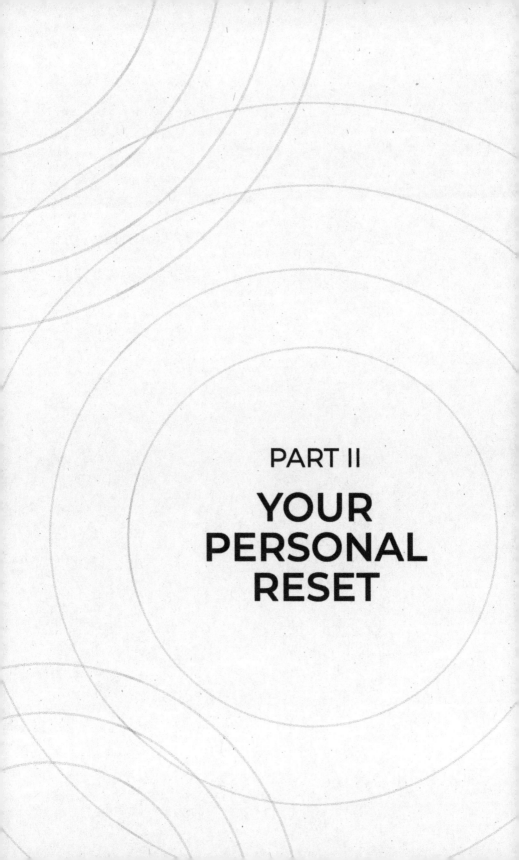

PART II

YOUR
PERSONAL
RESET

CHAPTER 3

Why Purpose Matters to You (Singular)

A few years ago, I (Carolina) attended a retreat on cultivating purpose and meaning in life, where we did a funny, unique, and, ultimately, illuminating exercise. After two days of activities, visualizations, journaling, meditations, and group work, the retreat culminated with a breakfast where everyone was meant to show up and act just how they envisioned their lives to be when filled with greater purpose, five years in the future. As soon as the facilitator went over the idea, I immediately knew what I wanted to "be" the next day: I wanted to be on the other side of that retreat. I wanted to be the facilitator of that transformational personal development experience. I wanted to be the one helping other people connect with their purpose.

Back then I was still working as a marketing leader at a multinational corporation, so that vision didn't match my reality. I spent the rest of the evening wondering why I could so quickly have such a clear picture of *what* would fill me with meaning and excitement, and yet such a blurry sense of *how* I'd get there. The next morning, I decided to just go for it without thinking too much. I wore my favorite dark blue dress and aquamarine earrings, and showed up as myself five years into the future. After initially feeling awkward, shy, and giggly, I started to act like the person I wanted to become. I began speaking, gesturing, and behaving like "her," an assertive, charismatic, wise, confident, and friendly woman. And to my surprise, those behaviors began to flow in an easy and effortless way as if they were already alive within me and just needed to be let out.

During breakfast, I also interacted with other people in the program who showed up, dressed up, and acted like their future versions. Some presented themselves in radically different ways. There were a few others who made just a few life adjustments. A handful more showed up just as they were in the present moment, explaining how they were already living purposefully and wanted to commit to their life pretty much just as it was. Some others realized who they *thought* they wanted to become didn't really *feel* right, viscerally, when acting like them—another important insight.

The activity made us all take a moment to pause, evaluate, and consider what a Purpose Reset could look and feel like for each one of us. The act of embodying—not just thinking about, researching, or planning—presented us with the opportunity to truly connect with our future versions and get a deeper understanding of what we envisioned for ourselves and who we wanted to become, authentically and effortlessly.

In Part II of this book, we want to invite you to dive deep into the impact of a Purpose Reset specifically for you as an individual; we'll cover topics related to teams and organizations in Parts III and IV. To begin, let's revisit our definition of purpose, centering the "you" as a single person:

**Purpose is the ongoing process of understanding
and connecting your strengths, values, and
desired impact with aligned actions to unlock
your full potential and be of service.**

As we've mentioned, purpose is a key driving force that can give your life meaning and direction. It guides us toward something bigger than the self. By more deeply understanding your personal purpose, you'll be able to align your actions, decisions, goals, and aspirations to lead a more fulfilling life.

In chapter 2 we shared the impact purpose can have on decreasing burnout, improving well-being, and aligning with your values. In this chapter, we'll review more reasons why we believe so strongly in a Purpose Reset for each and every person, as an individual.

A FINITE NUMBER OF HEARTBEATS

Adults spend most waking hours working (or studying, which is usually meant to prepare them for work). Someone who works eight hours a day, five days a week, will end up working more than 80,000 hours in their lifetime. That's usually more than the time spent with loved ones, or doing pretty much any activity other than sleeping. We could modify writer Annie Dillard's famous words, "How we spend our days is, of course, how we spend our lives," to "How we spend our working hours is, of course, how we spend our lives."

Now, we don't have unlimited hours in our lifetimes. We have a limited number of heartbeats; we just don't happen to know how many. How do we want to spend those heartbeats?

Every time the three of us ponder that question, something shifts. We gain perspective in a very unique way, opening up space to reflect and then take action on the best way we can live our days. The question makes us wonder about our legacy, the footprints we want to leave behind, and how we want to feel as we work toward that legacy.

The concept of *memento mori*—remembering the inevitability of death—is considered a cornerstone of stoicism and other philosophies. Instead of finding the concept debilitating or sad, the reminder that life is limited can be a catalyst to live life to its fullest.

Australian author Bronnie Ware wrote in her renowned book *The Top Five Regrets of the Dying* the five most common regrets shared by people nearing death when she worked as a palliative caregiver[1]:

1. I wish I'd had the courage to live a life true to myself, not the life others expected of me.
2. I wish I hadn't worked so hard.
3. I wish I'd had the courage to express my feelings.
4. I wish I had stayed in touch with my friends.
5. I wish I had let myself be happier.

Most of these regrets have in common the courage to take action and the ability to behave authentically. They're not related to making more money or acquiring more assets. They focus on what seems to truly matter at the end of our existence. Have you ever considered these wishes? Did any of these cross your mind during the COVID-19 pandemic or as we settled back into life post-pandemic? For many people, they did.

Facing the vulnerability of our human lives is one of the reasons why finding meaning and cultivating purpose became even more poignant during the outset of the COVID-19 pandemic. A 2022 Gartner study found that the pandemic changed employees' feelings about their work: more than 50% agreed or strongly agreed that the pandemic made them rethink the place work holds in their lives, made them long for a bigger change, want to contribute more to society, and question the purpose of their day-to-day jobs.[2] Human beings around the world were indeed reminded of their limited heartbeats and the value of being alive each passing day. The pandemic brought to the surface a deep desire that had been brewing for many decades both at home and at work: the need for a Purpose Reset.

MY MEMENTO MORI

by Carolina

My family and I were getting ready for a road trip to celebrate the end of the year. I had reserved a beautiful Airbnb to host a New Year's Eve celebration with 25 of my closest relatives in one of my favorite small and quaint towns in South America. I hadn't seen many of my family members as a result of the pandemic, so this was going to be a very special way to get together again, in person. As we were getting ready to leave, with the car fully packed with NYE decorations, suitcases, and an exorbitant amount of food, I started to feel unwell.

I thought a short stop at the closest clinic to see a doctor and get some medication would be all we'd need before hitting the road. To my surprise, however, after five long hours at the clinic, I was told I needed to be hospitalized, indefinitely.

What started as an inconvenience and disappointment for missing the New Year's celebration I had helped to organize, and for spending that special beginning of a new year alone in a hospital room, evolved into a quite concerning diagnosis. I ended up being moved to the intensive care unit, where I stayed for many days.

One cloudy morning, a group of six doctors representing different specialties approached my ICU room and gathered around my bed. With a concerned look on their faces, they told me I had a very serious illness that could lead to multiple organ failures and even become fatal. The moment I heard the words "You can die in a matter of days" from a group of medical experts was the most shocking and earth-shattering of my life.

After they left my room, I looked on my phone at a photo of the vision board I had created a few days earlier for the new year that had just started. All my goals, plans, and big dreams now seemed unattainable and suddenly and unfairly disappearing before my eyes. I locked the phone, closed my eyes, and as my chin touched my chest, tears rolled down my cheeks, creating dark wet spots on my light blue gown.

I began to see images from my earliest childhood memories to my most recent events, along with images of my loved ones, one after another, flashing in my mind's eye as if quickly swiping right on a digital album. My past, my present, and my future, all converging into a single point.

As a life purpose coach, I couldn't help but wonder about what would become of my life's mission, and what I could do with the limited time I had, should my health completely deteriorate or should my life come to an end.

I'm fortunate to be writing these lines today, exactly one year after that momentous event. I just underwent the last surgery I needed, once again right before New Year's Eve, and have recovered successfully.

There are many details around this life event that I'm still processing and that are too tender to share. It was such a personal and profound moment in my life that marked a transition and deepening in my sense of purpose.

Being so close to what I momentarily thought would be the end of my life was the catalyst I needed to take actions I had postponed or didn't feel compelled enough to take. I quit my job and launched my own academy, focusing on teaching programs in English and Spanish, all about *purpose* (very meta). I also started facilitating personal and professional development workshops and retreats about human flourishing, well-being, and empathetic marketing, and dedicated more time to conducting research on the topic of purpose for individuals and organizations, informing many of the pages in this book.

I feel an unwavering commitment to do work that is in alignment with my purpose, to increase accessibility to personal development content in Latin America, to create a purpose-driven organization that stands for human and planetary values, and to support social justice causes through my work.

I'm also investing more time and energy in taking care of my physical health, well-being, spirituality, volunteer projects, and personal relationships. Something shifted within me: instead of seeing any of these as activities *I have to do*, I now see them as activities *I get to do*.

As I type these words from the comfort of my home, I feel incredibly thankful for being alive and healthy.

For loving the type of work I do.

For loving who I get to work with.

For loving who I am when I do my work.

For loving the impact I get to witness on a daily basis.

For having the privilege of following my heart's calling.

And for how I get to use its finite beats, one at a time.

MICRO-PRACTICE

Take a moment to write a few lines about the first things that come to your mind as you consider the question, "How do you want to use your limited heartbeats?"

HOW PURPOSE LEADS TO FLOURISHING

Did you know that the word *business* in some romance languages comes from the Latin *negotium*, which also means "lack of leisure" or "lack of ease"? For those of us who work advocating for human flourishing in all areas of life and for work as a source of fulfillment, it's painful to think about work signifying lack of ease. Yet, we bet you can think of at least one person who isn't at ease, let alone who derives meaning and joy, from their work. Are *you* the example that first came to your mind?

The good news is that cultivating a sense of fulfillment and meaning helps to develop greater well-being and flourishing. Research provides evidence that individuals who have a strong sense of purpose and meaning in their lives tend to have better mental health and overall well-being compared to those who lack a sense of purpose.

In a meta-study conducted by the Center for Healthy Minds at the University of Wisconsin, Madison, researchers integrated evidence from well-being research, cognitive and affective neuroscience, and clinical psychology to identify the drivers of well-being. They found four core dimensions:

awareness, connection, insight, and purpose. Specifically, their research concluded the following link between purpose and well-being:

> Purpose is an important component of influential scientific models of well-being and is central to perspectives of human flourishing in the world's contemplative and humanistic traditions. Purpose and meaning in life shape our personal narratives and are associated with a range of outcomes related to psychological well-being and physical health. A strong sense of purpose is associated with improved health outcomes and behaviors, including increased physical activity, decreased incidence of stroke, fewer cardiovascular events, reduced risk of death, lower healthcare utilization, and even better financial health. Purpose is also central to healthy psychological functioning, including memory, executive function, and overall cognitive ability, and also psychological resilience across the life span, including both teens and the elderly . . . On the other end of the spectrum, low levels of purpose are associated with various psychological disorders.[3]

By cultivating a sense of meaning and purpose, people are more willing to establish and maintain routines that support their well-being, including healthy eating habits, exercise, good sleep, and mindfulness-based practices. It makes sense: working toward a cause that's close to their values, interests, or passion gives people yet another reason—quite a meaningful one—to take care of themselves.

Examples of these behaviors abound: A man starting an exercise routine when his grandson is born so he can be healthier to watch his grandchildren grow up. A new entrepreneur establishing a regular mindfulness practice after understanding the importance of mental health in order to accomplish her professional dream. A schoolteacher setting better sleeping habits to have more energy for his students each day. A CEO taking more time off for self-care to be better equipped to lead her team. A newly promoted team lead establishing better time management habits to complete their exciting new projects without burning out. Can you think of any examples from your own life?

ENGAGING WITH PURPOSE

Think about a moment in your professional life when you felt authentically engaged while at work. Great, now think of a second example. And now, try to remember your level of meaning, fulfillment, or sense of purpose in those moments. Was there a connection between your engagement and a sense of meaning? Chances are, there was. When there's significance in what we do, or who we do it with or for, our levels of engagement rise.

American psychologist, educator, and author Martin Seligman examined positive psychology interventions that may be helpful to create a life worth living and cultivate well-being. In Seligman's PERMA model,[4] he outlines five essential elements, each contributing to someone's level of fulfillment and flourishing.

- **Positive Emotion (P):** This refers to experiencing a wide range of positive emotions like joy, contentment, gratitude, and love, which can enhance overall well-being and encourage a positive outlook on life.
- **Engagement (E):** This involves being fully absorbed and interested in an activity, or finding activities that challenge our skills and bring a sense of fulfillment.
- **Relationships (R):** Having a sense of belonging, love, and connection with others is considered to be fundamental for emotional support and personal well-being.
- **Meaning (M):** This refers to having a sense of purpose and direction in life. It's about feeling like our lives have significance and that we're contributing to something larger than ourselves. Having a sense of purpose and feeling that one's life is valuable and worthwhile provides motivation.
- **Accomplishment (A):** This involves setting goals and achieving them, feeling a sense of mastery and competence. Accomplishment can come from big or small achievements, but the key is to experience the satisfaction of completing a task or reaching a goal.

In many ways, we can see how having a sense of purpose may act as a unifying thread connecting and enhancing each of the elements in Seligman's PERMA model. Having a sense of purpose can lead to more frequent and intense positive emotions; when you feel your actions contribute to something meaningful, it can trigger feelings of joy, satisfaction, and fulfillment. Purpose can strengthen relationships by fostering a sense of shared goals and values. Working toward a common purpose with others can create deeper connections and a sense of belonging. Having deep connections to others can give our lives deeper meaning or become the source of our purpose. Our achievements can have greater weight and feel more rewarding when they're aligned with our purpose; it's not just about ticking things off a list, but about progressing toward something meaningful to us. Purpose, of course, is directly related to meaning: a sense of purpose provides an answer to the question "Why?," giving our lives direction and significance and making our actions feel more impactful. When it comes to engagement, purpose can have a direct and positive impact on it by making activities more meaningful, interesting, and aligned with what we truly care about.

> **Work engagement can be defined as involvement,
> enthusiasm, and dedication in a job. It entails
> a deeper emotional connection to work,
> characterized by a high level of energy, focus,
> and intrinsic motivation. Engaged individuals
> are not just passively completing tasks; they are
> actively invested in their work and its end result.**

At a personal level, as you may have experienced yourself, when you're highly engaged you are more likely to experience greater:

- **Commitment.** A stronger alignment between personal and organizational goals may lead to a higher willingness for you to invest your time and effort to help achieve organizational objectives.
- **Fulfillment.** A clearer understanding of how your contributions impact the organization, colleagues, customers, or even the world at large may make your work experience more rewarding, which, in turn, increases happiness, a sense of pride, and satisfaction.
- **Collaboration.** You're more likely to work effectively with colleagues, fostering a sense of teamwork and positive team dynamics when you and your team members are engaged in your work.
- **Continuous Learning.** You're more likely to seek opportunities for growth and development and take on additional responsibilities to enhance your contributions, out of an authentic desire to grow.
- **Flow State.** At the highest levels of engagement, you may be able to experience a state of flow, where you feel fully immersed in your work. This heightened focus and absorption in tasks contributes to a sense of fulfillment and enjoyment.
- **Performance.** When your individual sense of purpose is congruent with your job, projects, or daily activities, you will be more likely to attain higher levels of performance.
- **Intrinsic Motivation.** You may be driven by a stronger *internal* desire to excel and contribute, experience greater satisfaction in your tasks, and derive a higher sense of accomplishment from your achievements. Intrinsic motivation refers to engaging in an activity for the inherent satisfaction and pleasure derived from the activity itself.

Furthermore, when you feel purpose-aligned with your work, team, and organization, the effect can be positive for everyone. The visual that follows shows some of the beneficial ripple effects of purpose alignment across the three levels:

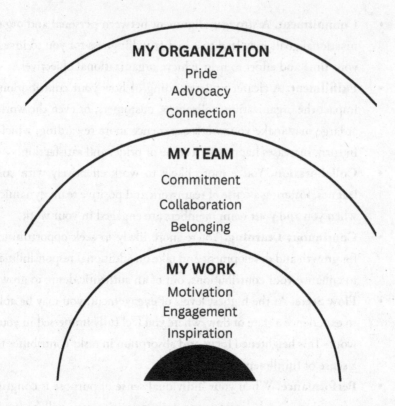

MY ORGANIZATION
Pride
Advocacy
Connection

MY TEAM
Commitment
Collaboration
Belonging

MY WORK
Motivation
Engagement
Inspiration

Having a sense of purpose and fulfillment allows you to see how your unique skills, strengths, interests, and aspirations affect the team's and organization's goals and connects you with something bigger than yourself. That type of impact beyond the self can be a catalyst for motivation, dedication, productivity, and collaboration. Ultimately, purpose can help us shift to the more potent, meaningful, and significantly more sustainable intrinsic desires that leave us feeling engaged, motivated, connected, and proud of our work.

When a sense of purpose is at the core of your job, meaning and engagement become the forces that transform routine into meaningful

actions, duty into dedication, and indifference into commitment. It's the invigorating pull that invites someone to lean in, explore, learn, innovate, create, collaborate, and care about their work out of a true desire to be of service.

MICRO-PRACTICE

Spend a few minutes writing about the two examples of high engagement you thought of at the beginning of this section and consider:

- Which elements in those work projects or jobs made you feel highly engaged?
- How did your project relate to your sense of purpose, impact, or fulfillment at that time?
- What does a sense of purpose feel like in your body? What sensations are present when you evoke it?

HOW YOUR WHY HELPS YOU NAVIGATE YOUR HOW

Life is never made unbearable by circumstances, but only by lack of meaning and purpose.

—Viktor Frankl

Catalina Escobar used to run a successful medical product company in Colombia. In 2000, two tragic events changed her life: the death of her 16-month-old son, who fell from an eighth-story balcony, and the death of another child, a 12-day-old baby who passed away in her arms while she was volunteering at a neonatal clinic. The second child died because the baby's mother had not been able to afford the $30 medical treatment her child needed. Determined that no mother should lose a child for lack of access to medical care, Catalina quit her job in the private sector and dedicated her life to launching and leading a social initiative, the Juanfe Foundation, named in memory of her son. The foundation is committed to breaking the cycle of marginalization, reducing infant mortality rates, and addressing adolescent pregnancies, one of the main factors that perpetuate poverty in developing countries. Her new sense of purpose gave her life a new direction and helped her to navigate losing her own child, one of the hardest events any human being could face.

Catalina's story is certainly an extraordinary example of courage, showing us how a Purpose Reset can become a source of equally extraordinary resilience. Having a sense of direction and purpose can bring out high levels of motivation, resilience, courage, and determination in our day-to-day lives as well. It's a unique strength we get from within to be able to stand up and keep going after a setback or difficult situation.

Consider Anjali, a senior researcher at a pharmaceutical company, who faces strict protocols, failing experiments, employee turnover, and obstacles along her path to developing a new lifesaving medication. Discouragement and a sense of futility could easily set in. However, Anjali's purpose—to save lives—fuels her resilience. Knowing her work contributes to a larger cause gives her meaning and encourages her to find new research strategies and new ways to keep her team motivated. Seeing even small victories reaffirms her purpose. When faced with setbacks or negativity, she remembers the bigger picture and remains committed to her cause.

Research suggests that higher levels of purpose are associated with less emotional reactivity to negative stimuli and stress, and more effective brain-related emotion regulation. A 2020 paper of cross-sectional studies published in the international journal *Anxiety, Stress, & Coping* presents data supporting the idea that purpose may help individuals navigate the stresses of life: "Findings suggest that individuals with greater trait life meaning experience less stressor-related distress and repetitive negative thinking."[5]

When we care deeply about a cause or when we have a strong sense of purpose in a given situation, we're more likely to face setbacks and recover from adversity with greater ease. When we truly care about something, our creativity expands, we become resourceful, and challenges don't seem insurmountable.

MICRO-PRACTICE

1. Think back on a setback you've experienced and compare how you reacted to it in the past with how you'd react to it today, based on two different environments:
    - A situation or environment where you're not vested, engaged, or interested—one that's not aligned with what you care about.
    - A situation or environment you care about deeply.
2. Explore where the drive, energy, or desire to overcome the challenge comes from in your life. How much do your purpose, values, or interests alignment support you through challenges?

HIGHER SUCCESS AND PERFORMANCE

In the prior sections, we saw how cultivating a stronger sense of meaning and purpose can lead to higher levels of well-being, engagement at work, and resilience. It can also lead to higher performance—and success—given that people who are in alignment with their purpose are more likely to be:

- Driven by a genuine passion for what they do, which can lead to higher levels of dedication and perseverance.
- More resilient in the face of challenges, as mentioned in the previous section, which ultimately increases their chances of success.
- More adaptable and long-term focused.
- Better able to set a clearer sense of direction, goals, and priorities.
- Driven by a deep commitment to their mission to put in the extra effort required to excel.
- Able to seek opportunities for personal and professional development to learn and acquire new skills, which can enhance their competence and adaptability.

A study conducted by New York University and Imperative of 6,332 adults in the United States focused on the concept of "work orientation," to describe the way a person sees the role of work in their life.[6] The study explains that people tend to see work in one of two ways: (a) being primarily about personal fulfillment and serving others (a purpose orientation) or (b) about status, advancement, and income. When comparing both groups, researchers found that purpose-oriented employees:

- Are 50% more likely to be in leadership positions.
- Cultivate more meaningful relationships at work.
- Feel they can have an impact through their work.
- Experience greater personal and professional growth in their work.
- Are 65% more likely to experience a high level of fulfillment in their work than their colleagues.

In addition, something we've experienced ourselves and have seen in others is that purpose can be a magnet for like-minded individuals. Purpose alignment can thus help to build strong teams, networks, and communities around a common goal, which is also a key factor to well-being, success, and high performance. When purpose-driven work is focused on making a positive impact, whether on individuals, communities, or the world at large, it can lead to a sense of fulfillment and satisfaction that goes beyond traditional measures of success.

TRANSCENDING INTO SIGNIFICANCE

As a person fulfills their basic needs—for food, shelter, safety, financial security—along with their emotional needs—a sense of belonging, trust, love, and connection—an often inevitable next step is to seek meaning, self-realization, and transcendence.

You may remember this concept from the well-known Maslow's hierarchy of needs, often visualized as a pyramid with five levels, each representing a different need that motivates human behavior. According to this theory, people are driven to fulfill the basic needs at the lower levels of the pyramid before moving on to address the needs at the higher levels.[7] The five levels are:

1. **Physiological.** These are the most basic needs for survival, including food, water, shelter, sleep, and protection. When these needs are not met, it's difficult to focus on anything else.

2. **Safety and Security.** Once our physiological needs are met, we focus on feeling safe and secure. This includes needs for physical safety, such as protection from violence and illness, financial security, and emotional security (stability in relationships, freedom from fear, etc.).

3. **Love and Belonging.** As we feel safe and secure, we start to crave social connection. This includes the need for love, affection, intimacy, friendship, belonging to a group, and feeling accepted by others.

4. **Esteem.** At the next level, we develop a need for self-esteem. This includes the need for achievement, recognition, respect, and a sense of competence. It's about feeling good about ourselves and our accomplishments.

5. **Self-Actualization.** This is the highest level of the hierarchy and refers to the need to reach our full potential. It's the desire to grow, develop our talents, and become the best person we can be. This can involve creative pursuits, self-discovery, connecting with a higher purpose, and leaving a positive impact on the world.

Maslow's theory primarily focuses on what motivates us when our needs are not being met and is not necessarily meant to be a strict, linear progression. People may move up and down the different needs stages depending on their circumstances. This concept may also provide additional insights into what gives you a sense of purpose and motivation, based on what needs have (or have not) been met at a given point in your life.

MICRO-PRACTICE

- Reflect on where you stand in Maslow's hierarchy. Which needs are already met in your current circumstances?
- What might you need to be able to transcend into the self-actualization stage and reach your full potential?

Most people who feel the calling toward a more purposeful life are driven to reach their potential, make a difference, contribute, serve, and perhaps leave a legacy that can last beyond the course of their lives. At the core of this inner longing lies a profound desire to ensure their lives are significant. Uncovering their purpose and aligning their lives with it offers them direction when the unexpected occurs, aspirations to unlock their potential, space to better use their gifts, guidance through uncharted territories, and the fuel needed to sustain daily motivation.

As we've said before, purpose doesn't have to mean a grandiose project for the world, but simply what each person decides to connect with, individually and uniquely, as their *raison d'être*—reason to exist. Without a sense of purpose, we can be left feeling insignificant, lost, and like we don't matter. Even as it changes, evolves, fluctuates, or becomes blurry at times, that sense of meaning is a constant inner longing many of us possess and, sometimes, we simply can't help but follow it.

As we close this chapter, we'd like to invite you to reflect on why purpose may matter to you. How would your life be (or feel) different if you lived from a clear sense of purpose? What difference might it make to your daily experience of work and life? What might there be more of and what would drop away?

CHAPTER 4
Your Purpose Journey

Whatis *my* purpose?" is likely a question you've asked yourself before (we don't think you'd be reading this book if you hadn't). And you aren't alone. A simple Google search for "what's my purpose" generates 6,910,000,000 results as of the time of writing. That's actually very close to the number of adults around the world today. While it's pure coincidence, it's a poignant symbol of how there's likely one distinctive answer for each person. Everyone's search result for "what's my purpose," in the journey of life, is 100% unique.

Chances are, the person typing that query isn't expecting to miraculously find the answer to their unique purpose on the search engine, but instead, *how* to embark on their purpose journey. Specific ways to uncover more about it. Examples of how others have done it. That's what we'll cover in this chapter: *how* to embark on your unique purpose journey.

CLARITY BEGINS WITH AWARENESS

As a purpose coach, many of my clients come to me (Carolina), eagerly wanting to know the answer to their big question, "What's my purpose?," hoping that I hold the key to quickly unlocking the door to their one, meaningful, authentic, and clear purpose. I quite often wish I had those magic powers (I truly do!). Yet, nobody else holds that answer for you, and you already know that. The answer lies within.

Purpose is not something that can just be found, like a pin at the bottom of a catchall kitchen drawer, something that already exists and we just have to be lucky enough to locate it. Purpose is *cultivated*. It requires us, as in gardening or agriculture, to be attentive, to care for the process, and to work on it on an ongoing basis. It needs us to dig deep, plant seeds, care for them, adjust when needed, enjoy the fruit of our labor, and continue the process again and again.

Continuing with the gardening analogy, the first step before being able to eat a fruit from our own orchard is understanding clearly what it is that we want to plant: Which seed in particular do we currently have or want to plant? What's the type of terrain and climate available to us?

Indeed, seeing purpose as *the ongoing process of understanding and connecting your strengths, values, and desired impact with aligned actions to unlock your full potential and be of service* requires starting with **clarity** about what each one of those three aspects means to you, and only you. When we describe your unique purpose, we don't mean that you'll have a job that no one else has. Of course, we may have a similar sense of purpose as other like-minded peers. Unique means that your definition and process of purpose truly and only belong to you. You get to define it and will be the only one to know if you are aligned; it's your unique internal compass.

Thus, the first step toward our unique personal purpose is to cultivate AWARENESS around three components: your what, why, and who.

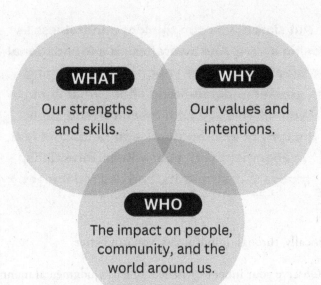

Developing a deeper understanding of these three aspects will be the key to uncovering *how* to better align your life with your purpose. Because this is the basis of connecting with your purpose, we'd like to go step-by-step in this part of the process. This is a good moment to bring out a piece of paper or journal and a pen to begin putting these insights into practice in your own life.

MINDFULNESS LEADS TO SELF-AWARENESS

Mindfulness can be defined as "paying attention to what's happening in the present moment in the mind, body and external environment, with an attitude of curiosity and kindness."[1] It's that ability to focus on the present and everything that is happening at the moment that allows you to develop greater awareness of your own self.

Put simply, you can think of mindfulness as being aware. And awareness is a foundational step to crystallize your purpose, bringing greater understanding about what lights you up, fills you with meaning, and about the type of environments and fields that feel in alignment with your values, intentions, motivators, strengths, and desired impact.

Specifically, through mindfulness, you can better:

- Observe your inner experiences in a less judgmental manner. This means you notice and allow your thoughts, emotions, and physical sensations as they arise without labeling them as good or bad.
- Become more attuned to your moment-to-moment experiences, as opposed to being preoccupied with the past or future.
- Recognize thought patterns that can help you identify beliefs that may be influencing your behaviors.
- Connect with your emotions as they arise, which can lead to valuable insights about what excites you, what triggers you, and what aspects of life matter most to you.
- Gain perspective by taking in a full picture of all of the thoughts, emotions, and external circumstances, which encourages you to see the bigger picture.
- Assess your life using the more innocent curiosity that stems from the concept of a *beginner's mind*, letting go of preconceived notions, while approaching life with a willingness to learn and a readiness to embrace new possibilities.

You can incorporate mindfulness into your life through dedicated sessions—such as seated or walking meditation—or through integrated practices, including mindful eating, mindful listening, or increasing your moment-to-moment awareness throughout your day. A regular mindfulness practice can help you gain deeper insights into your own life, which can lead to greater clarity around your core values, beliefs, inner longings, desires, and motivators. Mindfulness is especially important to gain awareness of how work makes you feel, and what you respond to, in contrast to what others might expect of you or what you think you "should" do. This clarity is the first step in creating alignment toward your unique purpose.

Without taking the space to pause, be present, and become aware of your internal and external circumstances, it may not be possible to have the necessary clarity to understand aspects related to your purpose. That's why we see mindfulness as a prerequisite to developing the type of self-awareness that is needed to cultivate a purposeful life.

As an example, I (Steph) didn't always know that my purpose would be related to helping people connect with their emotions. I grew up in a very logical and intellectual family and expected that my intellectual and cognitive skills would be at the center of my career success. However, mindfulness practice guided me toward greater awareness of my in-the-moment state and helped me see where I *felt* most excited and engaged, in contrast to what I *thought* was important to me. Early in my career, I focused on environmental issues because they were important to me, intellectually. I remember the moment in college when I thought to myself, *If we don't have an earth to live on, then what else could be more important?!* This became my guiding point as I picked biology as a major, found my first few jobs managing environmental programs, and went back to grad school.

Yet, while pursuing my master's degree in environmental policy and planning, I became enthralled with a meditation training I decided to sign up for because a friend of mine was taking it (it wasn't even for credit!). As I deepened my mindfulness and meditation practice and became more and more aware of what was happening in the present moment, I could more easily sort out what I really cared about and was engaged with (specifically, a volunteering role where I coached job applicants) and what I could do, maybe even well, but left me depleted or less engaged (e.g., working on spreadsheets for hours without talking to anyone). It was the experience and feelings, rather than pure cognitive ability, that led me to deeper insights.

After graduate school, as I tuned in to my *experience* of school, work, hobbies, and other parts of life, I realized that I feel most excited about working with people to help them navigate their emotions. Now, more than a decade after finishing my master's program, I feel deeply grateful to spend my days coaching individuals and leading groups to support people to honor their own emotional experiences and grow into who they want to be. This transformative career shift—which has made my life significantly more meaningful, purposeful, and enjoyable—wouldn't have happened if I hadn't developed my ability to be aware of my in-the-moment experiences, emotions, inclinations, and preferences, resulting from my mindfulness practice.

PURPOSE RESET PRACTICE

- Can you think of any activities you have done in the past or are currently doing that feel dull or meaningless? What do you notice when you compare them to activities or projects that energize you and make you feel alive? Try to connect with emotions and sensations in your body as you compare those two experiences.

- Journaling: When you have a moment to journal, use the following questions. We recommend spending no more than three minutes per prompt, writing freely and without editing:
  - Activities that make me feel alive include . . .
  - When I'm at my best, I . . .
  - People come to me to seek my advice on . . .
  - I feel a sense of reward when . . .
  - I'm glad I've invested time to develop my ability to . . .
  - From my family growing up, I learned that work . . .

AWARENESS OF YOUR *WHAT*

WHAT
Our strengths and skills.

WHY
Our values and intentions.

WHO
The impact on people, community, and the world around us.

When we talk about the *what* of your personal purpose, we're referring to your skills, strengths, talents, and interests, defined as follows:

Skills	Learned abilities or proficiencies that you have acquired through education, training, or experience.
Strengths and Talents	Innate or developed qualities or aptitudes that you excel at, often effortlessly, or that come naturally to you.
Interests	Topics, activities, or areas that captivate your attention or that you feel inclined toward, including hobbies, pastimes, or topics that you find yourself consistently drawn to, excited about, or fascinated by.

Even though these aspects are key to a Purpose Reset (and may sound really basic), people don't always have them top of mind. Often, we only think about our set of skills and strengths when choosing a major, or preparing for a job interview, and it's rare for someone to sit down to reflect on their deep life interests. We also can leave a lot of assumptions about what work and life should look like unquestioned, perhaps advice or expectations we took on from our parents, communities, or culture at large. Also, when considering your interests and the topics you are drawn to, you might consider the different scales that you might work on that connect to your interests. For example, if you're interested in health, you might think about becoming a doctor, supporting people individually. But you could also consider healthcare policy, which also addresses health, but on a broader scale, or an administrative position in the field.

When was the last time *you* spent time better understanding your top skills or the topics that sparked your curiosity the most? Whether it was recently or not, it's always a good idea to reconnect with your *what* as it can change with time. In the sections that follow we'll focus on a few practical ways to uncover insights on your what, including finding your state of flow and your flourishing zone. In the micro-practice that follows, you'll have an opportunity to explore it at a more concrete level.

PURPOSE RESET PRACTICE

1. Answer the following questions, based on the first ideas that come to your mind (don't overthink it):
   - What are your top three strengths? Would people you work or live with agree with that list . . . or what other two to four strengths would they add?
   - What makes you the exceptional human being you are?
   - In what areas do you usually have an edge relative to other people around you?
   - What are the topics that interested you most as a kid? What fascinates you the most now? What do you read or pay attention to for fun?
   - How do you like to spend your time? What activities or tasks give you the most energy? Which feels most depleting?
2. Another way to grow your awareness around your strengths and values is to use interactive tools, surveys, or diagnostic assessments

developed by trusted organizations with experience in the field. Consider the following tests, available as of the time of writing:

- The VIA Character Strengths Survey: https://www.viacharacter .org
- The CliftonStrengths Assessment by Gallup: https://www.gal-lup.com/cliftonstrengths/en/home.aspx
- The HIGH5 Test: https://high5test.com/

In addition to your own introspection, you can also have conversations with friends, colleagues, and relatives about what they see in you that may not be as obvious to you. Here are a few examples and ideas of what you could ask them:

1. Consider sending a text message to your closest friends, colleagues, or significant other to gain their insights about your strengths and values. You can share a message such as: "Hi [Name], I'm work-ing on understanding my strengths and values better, and I would really value your perspective and insights. Would you mind shar-ing your thoughts with me?

2. Share your questions:
   - What three words come to your mind when you think about me as a professional? As a person?
   - What are some of the qualities you think I excel at?
   - Can you recall a time when you thought I handled something particularly well?
   - What do you think are my core values based on how I live my life and make decisions?
   - How do you think I contribute most effectively in group set-tings or friendships?

3. Offer different ways for them to share their thoughts, depending on their comfort level. "I'd love to hear your thoughts in whatever way is easiest for you—over coffee, a phone chat, or even just a text or email."

Your Flow

In chapter 3, we briefly mentioned that high levels of engagement at work can lead someone to experience a state of flow, where they are fully immersed in their project, and that this heightened focus and absorption in tasks contributes to a sense of fulfillment and enjoyment. We now want to dive deeper into this state, as it's a key aspect of a Purpose Reset at the individual level.

Chances are, you've probably experienced a flow state before. Flow, often described as being "in the zone," is a mental state of complete absorption and focus on a task. It's characterized by a deep sense of enjoyment, effortless concentration, and a distortion of time. Psychologist Mihaly Csikszentmihalyi, who coined the term, described it as a state where the challenge of an activity perfectly matches your skill level. A few examples of flow could include:

- An artist lost in the creative process, hours flying by while painting an intricate masterpiece, fully immersed in each stroke, paint texture, and color.
- A software engineer solving a complex coding challenge, writing lines of code, losing track of time, engrossed in the logic and problem-solving of the task.
- A cook in the kitchen, preparing a multicourse meal, fully engaged in the process, combining various flavors, aromas, and ingredients with precision and delight.
- A small team, creating a detailed and carefully orchestrated cross-functional project plan for an upcoming product launch.
- A professional athlete during a high-stakes game, making split-second decisions and executing remarkable plays, their every movement aligned with the flow of the match.
- A photographer capturing a moment in time, adjusting settings with precision, fully engrossed in the interplay of light, composition, and emotion to freeze a fleeting instant into a timeless image.

You can enter into a state of flow both at work and in areas outside of your job. You can enjoy this state in multiple areas or in just a few. It's all about the enjoyment and depth of connection to the task and to yourself you find in those moments. For instance, Steph enters a state of flow when deeply engaged in coaching, helping her clients really get in touch with their inner worlds, as well as when writing and drawing. Carolina is in flow teaching a course to a group of people, designing a new curriculum, getting lost in deep conversations, or when painting with her colorful oils and multisized brushes. For Rich, flow is composing original poetry when inspired by nature or deeply experienced emotions, and also while facilitating conversations with work groups or individual leaders who are grappling with complex business challenges.

The state of flow can be a tangible experience that points you in the direction of purpose alignment. In the flow state, time seems to vanish. This temporal distortion highlights the immersion you experience when pursuing something you feel drawn to. To reach a state of flow, you need a balance between the challenge of the task and your skill level. This sweet spot is where you feel both engaged and challenged, at once. You're not bored. You're not overwhelmed or anxious. The feeling is of optimal alignment and engagement. Bringing increased awareness to the moments in time when you experience flow can provide insightful data points to continue to guide you on the *what* of your purpose.

MICRO-PRACTICE

- What are the areas where you often experience flow at work and in the rest of your life?
- In which activities do your skills align with your projects?
- When was the last time you found yourself losing track of time? What were you doing?
- What activities feel effortless and yet engaging to you?
- Reflect on what you were doing and why it mattered to you.

Your Fulfillment Zone

> Everybody is a genius. But if you judge a fish by its ability
> to climb a tree, it will live its whole life believing that it is
> inadequate.
>
> —Anonymous

When I (Carolina) was leading a marketing team at Google, one of my favorite tasks was working together with my team members in a way that allowed them to feel engaged, enjoy their projects, and develop their strengths. Inspired by a theory known as the "skill/will matrix," made popular in *The Tao of Coaching* by Max Landsberg, and other methodologies I came across in a number of leadership workshops, I used a framework that I call the "Fulfillment Zone" and published it in my book *The Path to Flourishing*. This zone is where you can align what brings you joy, your strengths, and your projects to the extent that is possible.

As a people manager, I had a one-on-one session with each member of my team twice a year to identify the four areas, or F zones: frustration, functioning, fostering, and fulfillment.

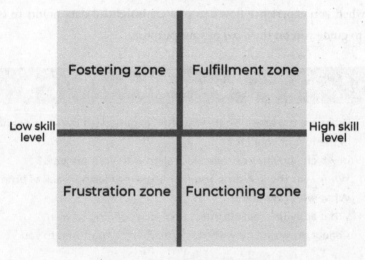

- **Frustration zone.** In this zone, you're working on projects you're not interested in, don't fill you with enthusiasm, and aren't aligned with your skill set. You may be likely to perform poorly and become disengaged when working on such projects. For example, if Hans doesn't like public speaking, and he doesn't have any experience with it, asking him to speak in public can frustrate him, as the name of this zone implies. Hans can easily lose meaning in the project due to overwhelm or even burnout when consistently assigned projects in this zone.

- **Functioning zone.** You can be in this zone when doing something you're very good at but don't feel enthused by it. As an example, let's say Chris doesn't enjoy managing a budget, but they often excel at forecasting, updating, and reporting on financial numbers. While it would be extremely easy to assign more budgeting projects to Chris because they're efficient and effective at them, it's better to see these kinds of tasks as Chris's contribution or service to the team or project, and to the extent that it's possible (we know it's not always feasible in the short term), assign them to other activities that would be better aligned with their interests. It may help to have transparent conversations with Chris about the projects in this area, and even name the fact that the task is part of their functional zone. To keep Chris engaged and support their development, it would also be advisable to consider delegating or outsourcing these tasks to another person or team (especially to someone for whom budgeting is part of their fulfillment zone—win-win!).

    North American tennis player Andre Agassi is a clear example of someone who spent years stuck in the functional zone. In his autobiography, *Open*, Andre reveals that he always hated tennis, even though he was one of the best players in the world and won numerous championships. According to Andre, his father pressured him from an early age to become a star, which he ended up accomplishing. However, his lifestyle led him to drug use and depression. When Andre retired, he decided to pursue activities that aligned with his purpose and inspired him, such as starting up philanthropic projects and sharing his story to help others.

- **Fostering zone.** You're in the fostering zone when working on projects that fill you with enthusiasm and joy, but where there's room for improvement. For example, if Fatima is passionate about graphic design, but lacks practice or doesn't yet know how to use the design software used in the company, she's in her fostering zone. Fatima can develop these skills through classes, books, videos, mentors, and so on so that she can eventually move them across to the fulfillment zone. Having skills for you to build on is quite positive because it can foster motivation to develop your strengths (and interests) and allow you to feel challenged, which is one of the ingredients of being in a state of flow.

- **Fulfillment zone.** In this ideal area, skills and interests are aligned. Being in the fulfillment zone makes you feel in your element. When Soo-Young, an excellent programmer, works on a programming project for a new AI tool she's fascinated by, she's in her fulfillment zone. By working on something she both enjoys and finds appropriately challenging, Soo-Young will tap into her strengths and skills to get great results and feel highly engaged. Over time, she may become known in her company for her excellent outcomes, leading to further growth in that area or receiving rewards, compliments, or compensation that keeps her engaged. When in her fulfillment zone, Soo-Young is more likely to feel vitality, enthusiasm, and high levels of motivation. Furthermore, she will be more likely to embrace a growth mindset and resilience, as her activities will fill her with a genuine desire to improve.

Someone doesn't necessarily need to spend 100 percent of their time in the fulfillment zone. Life and work will always require some function and frustration, and we want to also have periods of fostering. We've met many people who feel engaged and fulfilled while spending about 65 percent of their time in this zone, 20 percent in their fostering zone, 10 percent in their functional zone, and 5 percent in their frustration zone. Even with that allocation, they felt satisfied in their daily lives and still had interesting challenges that motivated them.

Your zones will change constantly, given that your interests, projects, desires, and skills are dynamic and constantly evolving. If you're up for it, use this framework a few times per year to figure out where you're at and, based on that, decide which actions or adjustments may be needed. You may even want to consider sharing this model with your manager, peers, or direct reports. Send a message to Carolina on LinkedIn to receive a downloadable template to complete this exercise.

AWARENESS OF YOUR *WHY*

Your *why* is the deep-rooted reason that gives you meaning, the "what for" that can guide your decisions and fuel your actions. Unearthing the *why* behind your purpose is a journey of self-discovery. While your *what* is more about doing (what are you spending your time on?), your *why* focuses on your emotions and how you feel (why does this matter?). A key aspect of connecting with your why has to do with your values.

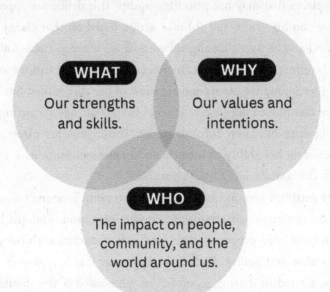

WHAT
Our strengths and skills.

WHY
Our values and intentions.

WHO
The impact on people, community, and the world around us.

Your Values

Values are the core principles and beliefs that guide and heavily shape our behaviors and decisions. Values represent the convictions of what we perceive to be right, important, or desirable. Your values are your answers to questions like "What is truly fundamental for me in life, regardless of the role I'm playing?" or "What are my nonnegotiables?" Your answers can serve as a moral compass and are often deeply ingrained and fairly stable—though not immutable—over time.

For Ivan, an MBA graduate, equity is a core value, involving fair and impartial treatment for all individuals, a principle deeply rooted in personal integrity. During his summer internship, Ivan observed instances of unequal opportunities and treatment, which immediately triggered strong emotions for him. While some suggested accepting these disparities as the norm early in one's career, Ivan couldn't compromise on the value of equity. During his round of full-time job interviews, he proactively inquired about each organization's commitment to diversity, equity, and inclusion, seeking insights into policies and practices that promote a fair and inclusive workplace. By aligning values with career choices, Ivan aimed to weed out potential workplaces that may not prioritize equity. This deliberate approach to (a) be clear on his values and (b) take action based on that clarity helped Ivan to find a workplace that aligned with what's nonnegotiable for him.

For Jazmine, a senior product manager in technology, innovation, agility, and questioning the status quo are some of her core values. She holds a belief that continuous improvement arises from challenging existing norms and seeing situations from different angles. Throughout her career, she has been known for her ability to identify and implement innovative solutions that push the boundaries of what's possible.

After getting a promotion in a new department, Jazmine noticed that product development was often slow, cumbersome, and hindered by inefficient and outdated processes. This inefficiency clashed with her passion for innovation and agility. Badly. She began to lose her passion for the company, started to disengage, and even questioned if she should begin looking for another role elsewhere. Eventually, she was able to understand how to drive change within the culture of her new team, earned their trust, spearheaded a project to update existing processes, introduced agile methodologies, and fostered a culture where team members were encouraged to propose and experiment with new ideas. This shift not only reconnected Jazmine to the company and her purpose within her new role but also prevented her from leaving and supported the launch of a new product faster than originally anticipated.

Have you ever worked in a place where you experienced misalignment with your core values? If so, you know that values alignment at work is not just a nice-to-have. Values are something we hold dear, and misalignment can trigger strong emotions over time. Indeed, as we shared in our P.T.O. Model in Part I, values mismatch is a leading cause of burnout for individuals. What can initially seem like something small can snowball and become a reason for disagreement, conflict, and turnover.

Values play a vital role in cultivating a purposeful life as they guide our behaviors and influence how we approach relationships, challenges, and opportunities. Our actions are often the result of what resonates with our values, not just intellectually or conceptually, but on a more visceral and profound level. When our values are in alignment with our actions, we experience greater authenticity, which can lead to greater fulfillment.

PURPOSE RESET PRACTICE

One methodology we recommend at SIY Global to explore core values is to connect with key attributes of people you admire, following these steps:

1. Think of someone you currently admire.
2. List the qualities or characteristics you admire about that person. Identify as many as possible.
3. Now, looking at the list, pick the top five qualities that resonate with you or the ones you consider most important in your own life.
4. Reflect on those values and identify which ones you would consider part of your "moral compass" in life.

5. Reflect on the following questions:
   - How does it feel to have new insights or clarity around your values?
   - What does your list of values tell you about your current job or personal projects? About your purpose?

MY PURPOSE RESET: WHY VALUES MATTER

by Rich

It's funny to me now, but I definitely took the scenic route in my life and work. I wandered a long and winding road from where I started my career to where I am now. In retrospect, each waypoint in my work and life journey served as a stepping stone toward the work I do today—in which I feel deeply aligned with my purpose and values. But it wasn't an easy, straightforward, or linear journey.

Let's start by saying this: coming out of high school, I had no idea what I wanted to do in or after college. Even in college, I felt a little lost. When I was an undergraduate, I got a job as a cook. After college, I traveled a good deal in Europe and Asia to see the world, while I tried to sort out my purpose and goals. Around this time, I got really interested in social work or psychology as a career because I was volunteering with children in the United Way (a social services agency in the United States) Big Brothers Big Sisters program, mentoring and providing childcare to children in under-resourced homes. I was also taking extension courses in psychology back at my old university.

All this enabled me to get a job as a rehabilitation therapist in a community mental health clinic, part of a county agency in San Diego that served clients who were having severe psychological crises, including patients who were actively suicidal and/or homicidal. The job was hard work, but I also found it quite fulfilling. I deeply cared about that community. It was work that connected me with my values and interests. Eventually, I knew that I needed to get more formally trained, so I applied to graduate school in psychology, and to my surprise and delight was admitted for a PhD in psychology at Columbia University Teachers College, back in New York City where I had grown up.

That's where my career shifted again, almost immediately. I began to learn about the field of organizational psychology, and I was intrigued. Working on "potentiation" (optimizing strengths) of individuals, teams, and entire organizations (optimizing strengths) versus "remediation" (more of a clinical approach to prevent further harm) at more individual or family levels was tremendously exciting for me. I decided to focus my graduate studies in organizational psychology. After graduating, for nearly two subsequent decades, I worked in internal learning, leadership, and organizational development departments in large organizations such as Google, eBay, JP Morgan Chase, and Bank of America. It was interesting work, no doubt, and finally offered me and my young family some measure of stability. Yet even with this successful career in a field of my choosing, it was clear to me that something was missing.

As we describe in the Purpose Reset formula (developing clarity around our what, why, and who), my inquiry began with awareness. I became aware that I felt that I needed something more from my work. Worse, I began to fear that I was misaligned with my deepest values. Back in college, I had volunteered to work with children in need because I hoped to be of service and have a positive, lasting impact in their lives. Being of service, having a positive impact, and creating transformation toward well-being for myself and others were clearly core values for me.

I realized that even though I helped to promote positive learning and outcomes for organizational leaders in my work as an organizational psychologist, most of it only served to further accelerate the business impact of the organizations I worked for but did not necessarily contribute to a more lasting transformation in the minds and hearts of those leaders or the team members and customers they impacted.

Even more importantly, I became aware that I was losing sight of my own personal journey and transformation. I focused most of my time, energy, and attention on business matters that were interesting but not that resonant for me, as I had always wanted to focus more on service and having a positive social impact in the world. I also prioritized and valued time with my family. Where and when, I wondered, did I have time for the personal development and transformation work that I cared so deeply about?

It occurred to me that I needed to reorient the balance of my work to include a focus on personal, leadership, and organizational transformation in the arenas that I cared most about: mindfulness, empathy, compassion, and a more peaceful and sustainable world—key values in my life and the very work that SIY advances.

I decided to commit to taking action that would make mindfulness, empathy, compassion, and wisdom my primary work. I considered that this meant I would be leaving my career to follow my calling after having spent seven years in graduate school and the better part of two decades building my expertise and career in large organizations. The insight was clear, however, and my commitment to it was strong. Six months later, I left Google to cofound Wisdom Labs (a workplace mindfulness and well-being company). At the same time, I helped launch the Search Inside Yourself Leadership Institute, the parent nonprofit organization of SIY Global.

My Purpose Reset continued. A few years after starting Wisdom Labs, the board of SIYLI made a strong effort for me to return to the Institute as its CEO. Ultimately, their message was that SIYLI was at an inflection point in which there was a significant opportunity to scale the mindfulness, compassion, and emotional intelligence practices it offered globally. They believed I was the exact right person to lead that effort. Well, they had me at "scale mindfulness, compassion, and emotional intelligence." So I came back to SIYLI as its CEO.

Personally and professionally, each chapter of my life and work has felt increasingly "on purpose," where today I can say that I've never felt more aligned with my values. I feel blessed to be doing what to me is meaningful and sustainable work. I believe that my own experience is part of the power of the Purpose Reset and the formula of combining awareness each step of the way with aligned action. Often it was a non-linear, doing-as-you-go process of learning from one experience, which pointed to the next experience, and the next. All were stepping stones. All movements toward purpose and fulfillment. I hope your journey is similar, if not more direct! That is why I was so interested in sharing my own story and coauthoring the book you have in your hands.

Your Past: Your Fuel to Purpose

Malala Yousafzai was born in a region with strict and oppressive attitudes toward education for women. Her father, Ziauddin, an educator and an advocate for girls' education, played a pivotal role in shaping Malala's future. Ziauddin ran a school for girls in Pakistan, and was committed to providing his daughter and other girls with an education despite the societal norms that discouraged it. Malala grew up with the strong influence of her father's values, and her upbringing instilled in her a deep appreciation for learning and a fierce commitment to girls' empowerment. In 2012, Malala was shot in the head while on a school bus, due to her advocacy for girls' education. She survived the attack and went on to become an even more prominent global advocate for equity in education, women's rights, and peace. Her past, defined by her father's teachings and her experiences, shaped her unwavering purpose and led her to become a Nobel Peace Prize laureate at the age of 17.

Ashanti Branch was born and raised by a single mother on welfare in Oakland, California. He overcame many obstacles to be able to finish high school, attend college, and graduate as a civil engineer. He then worked as a construction project manager, following what would be expected of someone with his degree. After tutoring struggling students, he realized he had suddenly found the "fire" that was missing in his life and hoped to ignite a similar feeling in young people. He switched careers, became a teacher, and started the Ever Forward Club to provide a support group for African American and Latino males who were not achieving their full potential. The organization has helped 100% of its members graduate from high school and 93% attend college.[2] Ashanti Branch is on a mission to change the way that students interact with their education and the way that schools interact with students.

Silvia Vasquez-Lavado experienced sexual abuse as a child while growing up in Peru. She moved to the United States to pursue her college degree, and after overcoming difficulties as an immigrant, became a successful businesswoman in the Silicon Valley start-up world. While feeling overworked, falling into alcoholism, facing the death of her first love, and still remembering her childhood trauma, Silvia decided to attend a plant medicine retreat in Peru, where she had an epiphany about her life and purpose. A calling propelled her to journey through the Himalayas and become the first Peruvian woman to climb Mount Everest and the first openly lesbian individual to complete the Seven Summits, which comprise the tallest mountains on each continent. Leaving her corporate life behind, Silvia published her memoir, *In the Shadow of the Mountain*, which is set for a film adaptation starring Selena Gomez as Silvia. She also recently founded Courageous Girls, a nonprofit organization dedicated to helping victims of sexual violence find their own sense of peace and closure through trekking. She decided to empower survivors by helping them find inner strength. In addition, through Courageous Girls, Silvia is creating leadership and empowerment educational programs and schools in Nepal and Peru.

Malala's, Ashanti's, and Silvia's stories come from different corners of the world, and they all converge on a purpose to support youth and their education. These three stories also illustrate how one's upbringing and past experiences can profoundly influence their chosen paths and show how someone's deep sense of purpose can be rooted in their personal history, an impactful event, or the values instilled during their formative years.

While these are examples of significant events and world-renowned endeavors, a Purpose Reset doesn't require radical changes; it's deeply personal and can look very different for each person. For some people, it's about reorganizing their schedule to get home in time to have dinner with their children or to walk their dog. For others, it's about signing up for a meetup or class to spend time on their favorite hobby with like-minded people on weekends. For others still, it's related to volunteering in their small community.

> In navigation, shifting directions by just one degree toward a different direction can result in being one mile farther from the original destination, after traveling 60 miles. Even small shifts can add up and have a large impact on the destination and the overall journey toward your purpose. It's not about the grandeur or magnitude of your Purpose Reset, but your ability to gain greater alignment with your purpose, one step, or one degree, at a time.

Our past can provide insight into our values, interests, and the experiences that have shaped us and made us who we are today. Examining past events can highlight recurring themes or patterns in our lives, what truly matters to us, and when we felt most aligned with our core values, all of which can be a helpful guide toward a purpose that resonates authentically with us. In addition, revisiting our past can help us identify achievements that can be a source of motivation and inspiration when we need a reminder of our capacity to overcome obstacles and achieve our aspirations.

It's now your turn. Complete the Purpose Reset Practice on the next page to assess how your past may be having an impact on your purpose journey.

Take a moment to reflect or journal on the following questions:

- **Memorable Moments.** Recall and write about a few memorable moments or turning points from your past. What took place and how did or do they shape your path and what you care about?
- **Challenges and Growth.** Reflect on some of the most challenging experiences you've faced. How did you overcome them, and what did you learn from these challenges that might inform your purpose?
- **Childhood Dreams.** What were your dreams and aspirations as a child? What hobbies or interests did you have? Have any of these childhood dreams persisted into your adult life or resurfaced in different ways?
- **Role Models.** Think about people who have inspired you in your family, school, community, work, or the world at large. What qualities or actions in these role models resonate with you, and how have they impacted your sense of purpose?
- **Regrets and Lessons.** Reflect on any regrets or mistakes you've made. What have these taught you, and how might they shape your future actions and purpose?
- **Achievements.** List some of your proudest achievements, both big and small. What about these achievements brings you a sense of accomplishment and meaning?

Your Present: Your Purpose Gift

As mindfulness practitioners and teachers, the three of us frequently speak (and remind ourselves) about the value of the present moment. We believe that the biggest present (gift) of the present (now) is to be present in (be aware of) moments of enthusiasm, engagement, and joy.

Another beautiful element of present-moment-awareness is using a beginner's mind to embrace what is present with curiosity and openness. A beginner's mind is an attitude of openness, curiosity, and lack of preconceptions, to approach life situations as if seeing them for the first time. Throughout your day, you may go through a variety of emotions ranging from boredom, excitement, dislike, annoyance, joy, engagement, connection, disconnection, frustration, motivation, and so on. What's key is to be proactively aware of those emotions and see into the wisdom behind each one with that type of nonjudgmental curiosity. Just as we did earlier when discussing flow, explore with an open mind the activities or tasks that energize and inspire you rather than drain you. It's equally valuable to be able to pay close attention, with kind curiosity, to identify examples of when you feel disengaged, bored, or frustrated throughout your day.

To practice this type of kind curiosity, it's also helpful to try out new experiences, activities, and roles, and be open to exploration, whether at work or in your personal life. Trying out new activities may reveal new interests and passions that align with your purpose, or shed light on those that are not at all aligned. Both types of knowledge are helpful. For example, how will you know that you find flow when working on environmental causes if you've never done anything directly related to that topic?

Think about the issues or causes you cannot ignore. The topics, problems, or events that continually grab your attention and concern. Those issues that pull you in, like a potent magnet you can't pull away from.

What are the causes that move you, deeply, within? What issues strike a chord with you, today? Which pursuits do you find interesting or compelling? If you could speak with your best friend about a topic you care deeply about, for one hour nonstop, with no preparation at all, what would it be? If you could share a message with the world about something you're passionate about, right now, what message would it be?

As you go through your day, you may also want to reflect on your relationships with others: your interactions with friends, family, colleagues, or community members can provide clues about the roles you naturally play in social settings.

> ## MICRO-PRACTICE
>
> For the next five days, incorporate a daily reflection practice into your routine and take a few minutes at the end of each day to write down:
>
> - The experiences that brought you a sense of fulfillment, joy, or meaning in your day.
> - The experiences that made you bored, frustrated, or disengaged.
>
> Try to do this exploration with a large dose of kind curiosity, without judging your responses, but merely observing what was present in your day, as a journalist or objective consultant providing insights about your emotional states as you go through your day.

AWARENESS OF YOUR *WHO*

Now that we've covered the *what* and *why* behind your personal journey to purpose, let's explore the third step—*who*—which focuses on who you want to become through following your purpose journey, who has had an influence in your life, and who you want to have a positive impact on.

WHAT
Our strengths and skills.

WHY
Our values and intentions.

WHO
The impact on people, community, and the world around us.

Who's Walking Next to You?

> What counts in life is not the mere fact that we have lived.
> It is what difference we have made to the lives of others
> that will determine the significance of the life we lead.
> —Nelson Mandela

Getting to know the group of people you are interested in having a positive impact on can bring additional clarity to your purpose and also provide additional energy and motivation to take action. Oftentimes, when we think about our purpose, we may see it as somewhat self-serving or less important than other tasks we're committed to doing, but shifting our focus to *who* we can help can enable us to prioritize them and take actions to get us closer to our purpose-filled vision.

Do you see yourself having an impact on a specific group of people? Who are you best positioned to help? What are they going through right now? What's their biggest pain point from your perspective? What's something you're uniquely positioned to help them with? How could you contribute to making their lives a little easier or better? How could you support them in solving their needs or achieving their aspirations?

Also, consider who you're interested in collaborating with as part of your vision. In any role, you're going to encounter numerous stakeholders, partners, colleagues, volunteers, collaborators, clients, consumers, investors, or allies. What are some of the characteristics of the people you want to spend time with? What are your nonnegotiables when it comes to who you collaborate with? Who wouldn't qualify as an investor, client, or partner? What would be the ideal qualities of the people you want to hire to grow your current team?

Getting to know, at a deeper level, who you want to serve and who you want to work with, in an ideal situation, can give you more details about ways to cultivate your purpose. Our recommendation is not to stay at a superficial level when you consider those individuals or groups of people, but to go deeper and truly understand them, their motivations, their needs, their aspirations, what moves them, what triggers them, and what would make their lives easier and better. Answering those questions, with depth and authenticity, can give you many insights into the role you can play. Contributing, even if in a small way, to addressing or solving their needs can give you a big sense of satisfaction and can be quite rewarding.

And if you're a leader or people manager in your organization, your own purpose sets the tone for your team and company. Your purpose must be authentic and aligned with the purpose of the organization and lived out in an embodied way. If you are out of alignment, everyone will notice, and it will erode meaning and engagement for the whole organization. We'll discuss more details about this topic in Part IV.

PERSONAL PURPOSE, WITH A MULTIPLIER EFFECT, AT SAP

German industrial engineer Peter Bostelmann joined the global software company SAP in 1999 and has remained with the company since then. However, his journey has evolved over the years into roles he never imagined possible when he first started as a young project consultant.

"For about half of my career, I was in the role I expected to have and on track to grow as a successful program manager, and then as a delivery executive running large-scale software implementations. But then, mindfulness found me," Peter said in our recent conversation. "I like to say I'm a recovered skeptic about mindfulness. I wasn't initially interested, but then I became intrigued, started to develop my own practice, and soon realized how potent the practice is and how this was one of the biggest gifts I had received in my adult life."

Peter continued to deepen his mindfulness and meditation practice as a personal endeavor, without talking about it at all at work. He observed how he evolved into a kinder, more compassionate person who was also able to better regulate his emotions and cultivate greater well-being. Eventually, he questioned how he could use these skills to help others.

"I asked myself, 'How can I be of service?' I remembered hearing a talk by Rich Fernandez, who explained that out of the biggest 150 economies in the world, about half are companies. Realizing that it's easier to shift the culture in a corporation than it is to shift the culture in a country, I felt inspired to start creating a positive impact right where I was, inside a multinational. That's who I wanted to help, starting with the idea of my old self, basically how I'd talk to my past self, and truly help people with similar needs."

Inspired, Peter followed his curiosity to explore the role and benefits of mindfulness-based practices in the workplace, looking at other companies that were starting to implement similar initiatives in the early 2010s. In 2012, Peter attended a Search Inside Yourself program in San Francisco and experienced something unique: during one of the journaling exercises, he was invited to envision his life in five years if everything were to meet or exceed his most optimistic expectations. "I immediately wrote down that I wanted to bring mindfulness programs to my company, speak on big stages around the world, and support people at SAP by transmitting the gift I had received and felt compelled to share with my colleagues. During the exercise, I looked down at what I had written, I spoke about it with a small group, and not only did it feel right, but the other people also responded well to the idea. There was a clear need around me and I was inspired to work on it. It felt amazing to dare to dream big and to have a bold vision at that point, even without having any details on *how* it was going to play out."

Years later, Peter became SAP's Chief Mindfulness Officer, and today speaks frequently at global conferences, having created a large-scale program supporting thousands of people across continents. "Be careful with what you wish for," said Peter to us with a big smile on his face.

Peter first started with two pilot programs at one local branch of his company. He then used the confirming results he got to create a business case and propose a larger program, linking key organizational objectives to the intended outcomes of his vision. "The project aimed at having an impact on organizational culture, so it was important to translate intended outcomes to our broader organizational goals, make them relevant, and receive the buy-in we needed to scale it," shares Peter, also explaining how it took many years and a lot of dedication to make it happen.

He was convinced about the importance of bringing evidence-based and practical tools that could help SAP employees and leaders manage stress, build emotional intelligence, cultivate well-being, and strengthen leadership skills from the inside out. But Peter realized he couldn't continue pursuing his vision and personal purpose alone. So, he cocreated and rolled out a Search Inside Yourself train-the-trainer program to certify SAP employees to become teachers, which was an enriching and purpose-filled experience in and of itself for both Peter as one master trainer and the teachers in training. He then supported other companies, such as Procter & Gamble and Allianz, to follow the methodology he had developed and tested, having an even greater impact beyond his own organization.

The programs Peter and his growing team have developed continue to have high demand, a statistically significant positive impact across multiple behaviors, a positive effect on employee engagement (a robust metric that is measured regularly at SAP), and a positive return on investment. As of the time of writing, Peter and his team have trained 100 teachers, who in turn have offered the program to 17,000 employees at SAP. "Seeing our teachers have such a multiplier effect within our organization and even outside of it is quite rewarding. I now want to see how we can use our learnings to have an impact in society and continue our multiplier effect at an even broader level."

Peter is a great example of someone who identified a clearly defined group of people he wanted to serve. And he was able to pursue his goal and deepen his alignment with his purpose within his organization. In a way, he created his own role, and even paved the way for other similar roles in other companies, with discipline, determination, structure, and a deep desire to leave a legacy and help others.

Your Future

Contemplating the future can provide profound insights related to your purpose. Specifically, thinking about who you want to become, the impact you want to have, and the kind of legacy you wish to leave behind.

Reflecting on your future contributions to society or your community, whether through a career, volunteering, or personal initiatives, and developing a clearer understanding of your desired impact, can provide helpful guidance to what actions to take today aiming toward that vision.

Roz Savage is an English ocean rower, environmental advocate, writer, and speaker. She holds four Guinness World Records for ocean rowing, including the first woman to row solo across three oceans: the Atlantic, Pacific, and Indian. She has rowed over 15,000 miles and spent cumulatively over 500 days of her life at sea in a 23-foot rowboat. Roz has authored two books: *Rowing the Atlantic: Lessons Learned on the Open Ocean* and *Stop Drifting, Start Rowing*. In 2010, she was named Adventurer of the Year by *National Geographic*. In 2012, she was a World Fellow at Yale. In 2017, she took up a position at Yale, lecturing on Courage in Theory and Practice.

But Roz wasn't always at sea or even in sports. As a matter of fact, she graduated from Oxford University with a law degree and spent the first 11 years of her career working as a management consultant. What changed? Envisioning two versions of her future.

In her early thirties, Roz's life appeared successful and happy on the surface, but something wasn't working for her at a deeper level. A turning point came when she decided to write two versions of her obituary—a "fantasy obituary" that captured the life she dreamed of living and one that captured her life if it continued on its current trajectory.

Realizing how different these two pictures of her life looked made her realize that she needed to make a dramatic change in order to live a life that she had "actually been born to live, free from fear, free to flourish." That's when Roz began her new journey as a rower and environmentalist.[3]

What seemed to be a simple envisioning exercise about her future helped Roz discover her deepest values and motivation and, at the same time, allowed her to imagine her desired future and consolidate that future in her mind. The *why* behind her obituary, and the *who* she wanted to become in the second version, evidently energized her significantly more than her current lifestyle and became what made her take the leap and completely transform herself.

While the ways in which Roz altered her life are quite acute, and coming from a privileged situation, we share it as a poignant way to illustrate the power of reflecting on the legacy one wants to leave behind and who we want to become. We don't expect most people to take such gigantic leaps and leave their homes behind to jump into something so adventurous, but we do encourage you to pause, reflect, and consider where you are heading now and what future you want to live. Whether it's spending more time with your children, signing up for the course that can help you switch functions at work, getting a promotion, devoting more time to your hobbies, signing up as a volunteer to support a cause you're passionate about, being more supportive to colleagues, becoming a mentor, or starting your own business, we invite you to begin your exploration of who you want to become and the legacy you want to leave behind. As Roz Savage says: *"If your comfort zone isn't growing, it's shrinking."*

MICRO-PRACTICE

Consider your long-term goals and aspirations for yourself.

- What do you see?
- Who would you like to be?
- How do you want to feel? What kind of qualities do you want to embody?
- Which values do you want to stand for? Notice if there's something you can visualize easily (without forcing yourself but more effortlessly) about your future life.
- Who do you envision?

Who Do You Admire?

Is there someone you admire so much, you may feel a little envious of them? Most people do (whether or not we like to admit it). Yes, the person you closely follow on Instagram or LinkedIn. The innovator you read frequently about. The leader you want to work for. The speaker you book front-row tickets to go see. The local community leader whose text messages bring a smile to your face. The volunteer you look up to.

Some people see admiration that edges into envy as negative, but we always say that emotions contain wisdom, and envy is no exception. Instead of feeling guilty about responding "yes" to that earlier question, explore what about that person makes you admire them.

When you recognize and appreciate something in someone else, it often signifies that there's resonance with the vision you hold for yourself in the future. For example, if you admire someone's dedication as a parent, it might indicate that playing a vital role in someone's upbringing is part of your own values and purpose. Similarly, if you appreciate someone's charismatic presence as a speaker, it could suggest that charisma and connection with others in a similar way hold significance in your own life. Reflecting on what you admire may be a source of guidance, like a mirror to your own aspirations, presenting something that matters to you.

MICRO-PRACTICE

Check in with yourself right now: Who are the people who have played or currently play a role in your purpose journey?

Clear as Water

Moving from autopilot to becoming aware of your what, why, and who can bring clarity about many different aspects related to your purpose. Reading this chapter may have helped develop a clearer vision around where you are and what's next on your purpose journey. Perhaps you had many aha moments, or noticed that something crystallized for you. You may feel clear as water. Or your water may still be a little muddied and you may need to wait until the sediments fall to the bottom to have greater clarity. These steps aren't insignificant and may require time. Either way, we appreciate that you've decided to dip your toes in or dive deeply into these topics. In chapter 5 we will use the clarity you have gained to move into action.

CHAPTER 5

Aligned Action

A ship in harbor is safe, but that is not what ships are built for.

—John A. Shedd

With greater clarity and awareness about your what, why, and who, it's time to move into action by cultivating daily moments of purpose alignment. In this chapter, we consolidate everything we've explored thus far on how to deepen your connection to your purpose, at a personal level, with an action orientation. We start by identifying what's at the intersection of the elements you uncovered in chapter 4 and share methodologies to build habits, envision a desired outcome, and take action.

You can go through this process to increase your sense of purpose where you are (i.e., without making big job, career, or life changes), or you might be looking for a bigger reset. In either case, we encourage you to give the exercises a try. This will help you see where you already have clarity and might not need more awareness or action right now, and where you might want to focus and dive deeper in your Purpose Reset.

Remember that a Purpose Reset is a continuous practice of building awareness and putting it into action:

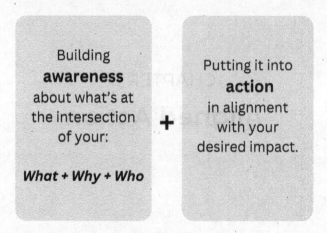

Building
awareness
about what's at
the intersection
of your:

What + Why + Who

+

Putting it into
action
in alignment
with your
desired impact.

AT THE INTERSECTION OF YOUR THREE ELEMENTS

The exercises outlined in chapter 4 were meant to help you build awareness and greater clarity around your what (skills and strengths), why (values and intentions), and who (the impact on your community and world beyond the self). Now, it's time to put it all together and explore what's at the intersection of those three elements, for you, today:

- **Step 1:** Consider drawing on a piece of paper the image that follows and fill it out with all the insights you've gained so far for the following questions:

WHAT	WHY	WHO
• What are my top strengths and skills? • What interests me the most? • When do I find myself in a state of flow? • What activities bring me into my fulfillment zone?	• What are the values I want to stand up for? • What gives me a sense of meaning and fulfillment? • Which life events have shaped my intentions, pursuits, or the causes I want to work toward? • What legacy would I like to leave behind?	• Who do I admire? Whose steps would I want to follow? • Who do I want to serve, work with, support, or partner with? • Who do I want to become? • Who do I envision as I think of myself in the future?

What's at the intersection
of these 3 elements?

- **Step 2:** Observe what you wrote and answer these questions:
  - What words resonate the most with you under each category?
  - What can you find at the intersection of these three elements?
  - Out of everything you see, what's one area that generates curiosity, interest, and enthusiasm in your life today?
- **Step 3:**
  - What insights can you draw about any action you could take in the short term?
  - What does this exercise tell you about your longer-term vision?

Once you have a clearer sense of what actions to take following the steps above, it's time to crystallize your personal intention and desired impact into a purposeful statement for yourself. What do you envision as your long-term purpose-aligned life (let's say 5–10 years into the future)? What might be a needed version of that vision in the mid or short term? What might be possible for you to start this year?

COURAGE TO TAKE ACTION

Action starts with the development of a greater sense of purpose exactly where we are, in our current jobs, family, community, and roles. From that starting point, we can begin making mental shifts, changing limiting beliefs, and courageously taking small steps.

Courage comes from the Latin root *cor* (from which the French *cœur* or Italian *cuore* evolved), translating to "heart," the quintessential symbol of love. If you recall, we started this book by referencing the shift from ladder to love that is part of a Purpose Reset. It's a reminder to take action that is fully authentic and aligned with your true essence, to gather inner strength to have the heart to act, and . . . yes, to follow your heart.

Now, we know this may sound nice and all, but moving into action isn't always easy. Especially when in our heart of hearts we know a big change is needed. Trust us, we've been there. Fears and questions of all kinds can come up, making us go back to what's familiar and avoiding change.

We may have fears about our reputation (*What will others think of me?*), financial stability (*How can I make this change happen when I have so many bills or financial responsibilities or people who depend on me?*), credibility (*Who am I to believe I can make this change happen?*), skills (*I'll never develop the skills needed for this change or be as good as so and so*), or failure (*What if it all fails? What if I become a failure?*).

Many fears can be valid in your situation. Many of them may be unnecessary obstacles preventing you from taking action. Only you know your own circumstances and what's feasible for you. Just remember that there will never be a perfect moment to act, fully absent from fears or risks. There will always be a little voice in our heads that will be afraid of something. The trick is to discern between a true concern and a distraction.

MICRO-PRACTICE

Set aside some time to journal following this prompt: "If everything in my life, starting today, meets or exceeds my most optimistic expectations, what will my life be like in five years?" We recommend writing in the present tense (as if it were happening right now) and including as many details, emotions, and descriptions as possible.

Check in with yourself right now: What are the top fears that come up when you consider making a change toward greater purpose alignment?

CULTIVATING CHANGE

When it comes to creating habits and taking steps (large or small!) that bring us closer to purpose alignment, we like to think about three layers of change:

1. **Outcomes.** When we focus on outcomes, we're looking at the desired end goal or result, such as: changing jobs, switching careers, finishing a degree, sitting on a board, landing a volunteering role, getting a promotion, launching a business, and so on. We have an opportunity to envision our purposeful life without needing to know the details of how to get there.

2. **Process.** When we focus on the process, we're looking at *what we're doing* in support of reaching the desired goal or testing ideas of where we want to go before we fully commit to them. For example, implementing a new routine or practice, taking a class, building your professional network, reaching out to certain people or groups, cultivating a new skill, and so on.

3. **Identity.** The third layer of behavior change to create a habit is identity, which focuses on our beliefs and how we see ourselves in the world. Behind every system of action is a system of beliefs. It's hard to change a habit if we never change the underlying beliefs that led

to our past behavior. And the truth is that deep behavior change is related to identity change. For example, if you believe that success means a high-status title and big salary, but you discover that your purpose is more aligned with working independently, then you'll need to update your belief around success to be free to make the changes you want to make.

Outcomes are about what you get.

Processes are about what you do.

Identity is about what you believe.

To take action toward change, all of these layers are useful. It's quite common for many people to begin the process by focusing on what they want to achieve, leading to outcome-based goals. An alternative is to generate identity-based goals. With this approach, we start by focusing on *who we wish to become.* Or we can focus on the process and take step-by-step action, asking, "What can I do to figure this out?" All three are important; it's worth getting a sense of which of these layers might be most energizing to you, which feels most stuck or fuzzy.

Let's say that Jackie wants to get promoted to a leadership position and create a culture of well-being within her team. Instead of aiming for the specific outcome (promotion), she may consider, "Who is the type of leader that prioritizes well-being at work?" Perhaps someone who focuses on creating a healthy space for collaboration, trust, balance, and wellness. Her focus shifts from getting promoted to a leadership position (outcome-based) to being someone who values and prioritizes well-being for their team (identity based). The identity-based change may end up being more long-lasting (you don't really *end* the process of building a particular type of culture), while outcome-based can be very specific with an end result, which is the promotion in this case. The process is important here too; Jackie will need to work with her manager and/or the HR team to understand the steps necessary for a successful promotion case, leading to her purpose-driven outcome becoming a reality.

Let's put these three pieces together. Reflect on and answer the following questions:

- **Outcome:** What is your vision for the destination/outcome?
- **Identity:** Who would you become in this vision? What qualities do you need more of?
- **Process:** What experiments can you run to test the vision or small ways you can work toward the vision?

CREATE AN EXPERIMENTAL PROCESS

As you take action to align with your purpose, we encourage you to engage an attitude of experimentation. Actions give you more data points to reflect on, building awareness of your who, what, and why that then allow you to take more actions. Consider what hypotheses you want to test. For each one, focus on collecting important information about what matters to you, what it feels like to engage in this way, and what you want and don't want more of.

When we think of the many actions we've taken over the years, we can see the wide range of activities we've tried, almost as if by using our lives as testing labs. For instance, to bridge her marketing career and desire to facilitate workshops (described in chapter 3), Carolina started teaching workshops on marketing at a coworking space in her city. Though it was an activity she did on evenings and weekends, it confirmed her love of being in the facilitator role and gave her valuable experience in designing workshops. She also experimented with learning computer programming and soon realized that wasn't a good fit for her. In her twenties, Steph tested out a desire to work in graphic design by taking design and web development classes, designing websites for friends, and taking on marketing and design work at her job. These experiments helped her see that though design was an interest, it wasn't really her purpose. Yet, other actions she's taken, such as volunteering at a crisis hotline, trying out a short coaching training, and testing coaching sessions for free on friends, gave Steph insights into her desire to work closely with people.

Early in his career, Rich worked as a rehabilitation therapist in a community mental health clinic, which helped him realize how much he loved that type of work. Later in graduate school, Rich combined this interest in counseling and coaching others with an interest in helping teams and organizations achieve their goals. He volunteered as a facilitator for team development workshops, served as an intern at a college career counseling center, and worked as a research assistant for a professor who specialized in leadership assessment and executive coaching. Rich drew on these lessons, and once he got his graduate degree, worked for many years as a learning and development director in large companies.

In *Working Identity,* professor of organizational behavior Herminia Ibarra suggests that you "identify projects that can help you get a feel for a new line of work or style of working. Try to do these as extracurricular activities or parallel paths so that you can experiment seriously without making a commitment." Consider side projects, temporary assignments, volunteering, a class you can take, a book to read and learn more. As you go through these experiments, reflect on what you found engaging. Ibarra also suggests that you "stop trying to find your one true self. Focus your attention on which of your many possible selves you want to test and learn more about."[1] Especially if you feel unsure or drawn in many directions, consider running many experiments—perhaps several small ones at once or a few in sequence—to learn more about which direction feels most compelling.

PURPOSE RESET PRACTICE

- What hypotheses do you have about what would bring more purpose into your life? Write out as many theories or ideas as you have. Then you might pick a few to prioritize testing out.
- Brainstorm experiments you could run to test your hypotheses. (Brainstorming rules apply: no bad ideas and you aren't making

any commitments yet! You might also ask a friend to brainstorm with you for a more expansive set of ideas.) What are some small actions you could take to learn more?

- Are there any actions that feel exciting to you? That feel easy to try? Which actions feel scary or intimidating (but might be a very valuable experiment)?

(RE)DEFINING YOUR ROLE: ARE YOU A CLEANER OR AN AMBASSADOR?

As we've mentioned, the third layer of behavior change is a shift in identity. Are there deeper beliefs about yourself, who you want to be, and what work means to you that might need to be updated as you align with your purpose? Updates in identity might shift how you see the role of work in your life, might help you make a bigger transition, or might just give you a greater sense of purpose exactly where you are.

It turns out, how you identify and define your job matters. A practice first described by Yale School of Management professor Amy Wrzesniewski, job crafting or "cognitive crafting" is a process of shifting your perspective to create more meaning. Wrzesniewski surveyed hospital cleaning staff and found that the staff who identified as *cleaners* found their work less meaningful than those in the same role, but thought of themselves as *ambassadors* supporting the patients. The ambassadors did extra, from chatting with lonely patients to making sure to clean the ceiling in view from the hospital beds. Changing how you think about the purpose of your work can make it more enjoyable and meaningful.[2]

In their book *No Hard Feelings*, Liz Fosslien and Mollie West Duffy share a perfect example. When a SpaceX employee who worked on the manufacturing floor was asked about his job, he said: "The mission of SpaceX is to colonize Mars. In order to colonize Mars, we need to build reusable rockets because it will otherwise be unaffordable for humans to travel to Mars and back. My job is to help design the steering system that enables our rockets to land back on Earth." He could have just said, "I'm an engineer."[3] By focusing on the greater purpose of his work, his daily tasks take on a greater sense of impact and importance. We love the idea of starting where you are to enhance an immediate sense of purpose if it's possible before diving into bigger changes. If nothing else, it can support you to feel prouder of your current work and set a higher standard for the level of purpose you want to move toward.

MICRO-PRACTICE

- Imagine meeting someone new. How would you describe your job to them?
- Imagine meeting someone who only wants to know about the impact that your work has (not your title or tasks). How would you describe your job to this person?
- Given these reflections, is there a new way you want to identify and define your work?

For larger and/or longer-term changes, there are many ways to think about identity. We encourage you to reflect broadly on what work and career means to your identity and sense of self. For some people, career is vital and we identify with our profession. It can become a lens through which we see the world and shape our mindset. For others, work will be more practical. We might identify as a good worker or good colleague without the role or specifics of our job becoming a significant part of how we see ourselves.

In either case, you might consider other aspects of identity that connect to your role at work or roles you play in your family or community. Do you see yourself as an expert? A leader? A teacher or a parent? Perhaps you are an activist, or maybe more of a diplomat? Are you more of a creative builder or an innovative disrupter? The identities you associate with will reflect the strengths and interests you illuminated in chapter 3.

Importantly, you might have a default or autopilot identity that you need to outgrow. Perhaps you still see yourself as the remedial math student even though you're now a successful engineer; or you may still think of yourself as someone who chokes on their words, even though you regularly and successfully give important presentations. As you engage in your Purpose Reset, it's an opportunity to update any old autopilot identities and align the identity you take on with the vision you are heading toward.

As we conclude the part of *The Purpose Reset* that focuses on you as an individual, and begin to transition into what a reset looks like for teams and organizations, consider the following reflections:

- Are there any insights you've uncovered thus far that you'd like to share with the people you work with or a manager?
- What about the intersection of your what, why, and who may have an impact on your team, partners, stakeholders, clients/customers, or broader communities in your day-to-day life?
- What are some opportunities to deepen the connection between your personal purpose and your work?

We hope the new insights you were able to gain in this section help you in your personal journey to start, deepen, or reignite your connection with your purpose. May it be an enriching and fulfilling process for you, and may all your talents, values, strengths, and personal experiences be of service to you and those around you.

PART III

THE TEAM
RESET

CHAPTER 6
Finding Purpose Together

The story goes that when architect Christopher Wren was rebuilding London's St. Paul's Cathedral after the Great Fire of 1666, he asked three bricklayers a simple question: "What are you doing?" All three had the same job—laying the bricks of the new cathedral walls—but each shared a different answer. The first bricklayer saw their role in a straightforward way, responsible for building a wall, brick by brick. The second bricklayer saw building the wall as contributing to the re-creation of the grand cathedral. The third bricklayer perceived the bigger purpose, that each brick laid was a tribute to God.[1]

This story is often told with the conclusion that the third bricklayer, who sees the greater purpose, is the most motivated, productive, and committed. However, this story also illustrates the nuance of developing a sense of purpose on a team level. Each person doesn't need to define their personal sense of purpose in the same way for the cathedral to be built.

Regardless of different interpretations, a shared sense of team purpose can engage employees, igniting a sense of meaning, collaboration, and contribution. Or, a sense of mismatch will leave people disengaged and dispirited. The team is the functional unit of purpose at work, and purpose either comes alive or falls apart at this level. It's within the team that individuals use their skills, pursue their interests, and get to see the direct impact of their work. Being part of a team can itself be a source of purpose.

A clear definition of a team's purpose is a vital bridge connecting individuals to the full organization's purpose and greater impact. Part III of *The Purpose Reset* lays out blueprints for building this bridge. This chapter describes what purpose means for teams and unpacks the importance of purpose at a team level, sharing details and research about how purpose leads to team performance. The following chapter explores how to build awareness of what a team's purpose is; and chapter 8 describes how to create a team purpose statement and put it into action.

WHAT IS PURPOSE FOR TEAMS?

Let's revisit our definition of purpose, centering the team as an entity:

Purpose is the ongoing process of understanding and connecting your team's strengths, values, and desired impact with aligned actions to unlock your team's full potential and enable them to be of service.

Purpose is an important fuel source for a team. It should answer the question "Why do we do what we do?," which functions in several important ways:

- A team's purpose directly **connects the dots between daily tasks and the bigger picture**. An organization's mission or purpose might feel abstract, idealistic, or future-focused, and it can be hard for individuals to see how their work contributes on a day-to-day basis. Team purpose creates a clear connection between the daily activities and outcomes of the team and the greater mission of the organization.
- Purpose aligns team members toward a **common goal**. This fosters clarity, effective decision-making, and collaboration. Team members should feel a sense of accountability toward the team's purpose.
- While working toward a common goal, individual team members may have different roles and contributions. At the team level,

individuals see how they can live out their individual purpose and contribute their skills and strengths to the team. Sometimes, this will be obvious and core to their role, or it might require some creativity—maybe redefining their role or job crafting, taking on new projects, or volunteering for an extra role, committee, or other opportunity.

- Importantly, **belonging to a team** can itself be a big source of purpose. Developing relationships, helping one another, mentoring newer teammates, and fostering connection and fun can all be meaningful. Being willing to do things for one another and seeing ourselves as part of something larger can be inherently purposeful.

Ideally, at the team level, there is a sense of resonance and alignment between top-down organizational purpose and the bottom-up purpose from teammates. However, aligning team members' individual purposes to a team purpose that also aligns to the whole organization's is challenging. Teams do not need to aim for an exact match, but instead a sense of general alignment.

Teams also need to see the impact of their work and feel recognized, and see that the organization's purpose is being put into action. Teammates become allies in a greater effort, serving as sources of strength, collaboration, and hopefully fun too.

What is a team? Put simply, a team is a group of individuals working together. Within an organization, there may be multiple levels of teams— divisions, functional teams, cross-functional teams. For *The Purpose Reset*, any of these levels can define their sense of purpose and likely should spend some time making it explicit.

1 + 1 = 3

Outstanding team performance requires a combination of motivation, engagement, alignment to goals, and team members that feel both a sense of belonging and that they are capable of peak performance. In this way, a high-performing team becomes *more* than the sum of its parts. By strengthening and building on each individual team member's strengths and purpose, and aligning that with the purpose of the team in service of the greater organization and world, the team structure amplifies individual purpose in service of the collective.

All of these factors blossom with a sense of purpose as we'll explain and unpack in this chapter, including these key performance benefits:

- Motivation and engagement
- Shared goals and vision
- Autonomy
- Contribution, belonging, and meaning
- Innovation

Of course, there are many additional factors that contribute to a high-performing team that are not specifically related to purpose, but having a strong, shared purpose drives high performance in several essential ways.

When we think of a high-performing team, we think of individuals with different, complementary talents, knowledge, and interests coming together for a shared purpose that is enacted over time. This diversity of skills and perspective allows team members to approach problems from different angles and come up with innovative solutions. It allows people to build on each other's ideas, divvy up work, and lean on each other's strengths. In this way, team performance defies usual math and becomes $1 + 1 = 3$.

Motivation and Engagement

As we saw in Part II, one key way that purpose leads to sustained high performance is by increasing motivation and engagement. Although traditional corporate ideas rely on carrots (like salary and bonuses) and sticks (such as negative performance reviews or the threat of being fired) to motivate employees, this is far from what research shows are effective motivation strategies.

For example, if you were completing a jigsaw puzzle, would you want to be paid? Research surprisingly shows the answer is no. In a foundational study, researcher Edward Deci offered one group of study participants money for each puzzle they completed, whereas the people in the control group weren't offered anything. When the research staff left the room, the people working for money stopped their puzzle work, whereas the ones working without pay continued for their own enjoyment.[2] The experience of the puzzle—a feeling of engagement and enjoyment—was more motivating than money. Described in their foundational book on intrinsic motivation, *Why We Do What We Do*, Edward Deci and Richard Flaste suggest that internal motivation can be far more effective and motivating than external rewards.[3]

When people are paid enough that money is no longer a source of stress (a reasonable goal for an employer that cares about both their employees' well-being and their longevity at the organization), motivation comes from three main sources: autonomy, mastery, and contribution. According to author Dan Pink, when these elements are in place, people feel intrinsically motivated.[4] In other words, when an organization creates a clear vision and goals, treats their staff well, and then gets out of their way to allow people to do their best work, they will!

Moreover, having passionate, motivated employees benefits the whole team. Research from Ning Li at the University of Iowa finds that people who are authentically motivated to contribute above and beyond (dubbed an "extra miler") help drive performance for the whole team. They tend to help more often (e.g., pitching in when others are sick or overloaded) and use their voice to speak up on behalf of the team. Indeed, Li's study shows that the motivation of an extra miler can drive greater performance more than all other members combined.[5]

Shared Goals and Vision

High-performing teams have a clear understanding of what they are working toward and why. When this is missing, team members will likely move in different directions. In contrast, when team members are aligned on their values and priorities, they feel a healthy accountability to the purpose and mission of the team.

On April 13, 2019, just before 7 AM, the world's largest plane, the Stratolaunch aircraft, took off from the Mojave Air & Space Port for its first flight. Our friend and Search Inside Yourself certified teacher Hanna Steplewska was working as Stratolaunch's VP of Business Development and was there for the big event. The plane flew above the Mojave Desert for approximately 150 minutes, achieving a maximum speed of 189 miles per hour at altitudes up to 17,000 feet, before landing safely back at the spaceport's main runway. This moment was years in the making, requiring a clear and shared vision for success. Hanna was part of the team that worked to see this day happen. Leading up to and during the eventful day, she described using the micro-practice of asking herself "What would be of service?" to center herself and reconnect with the goal and purpose of the project. It helped her focus and really take in the meaning of this important, yet chaotic, moment.[6]

Experts say that purpose streamlines the way decisions are made. "It's an inside-out strategy rather than outside-in: you don't just look at where the opportunities are and where you could make a lot of money as a way to decide where you ought to be. You decide where you want to be strategically, based on what you want to do," according to Michael Beer of Harvard Business School and a director of the Higher Ambition Leadership Alliance.[7]

Autonomy

This clarity around goals from a defined purpose enables autonomy, a key factor for high motivation and performance. Researchers Richard Ryan and Edward Deci in their groundbreaking "self-determination" theory posit that autonomy is essential for motivation and the foundation of success and fulfillment.[8] Autonomy refers to the degree of independence and control employees have over their work tasks and decision-making processes.

When employees are granted autonomy, they often experience higher levels of intrinsic motivation. They have a greater sense of ownership and pride in their work. The sense of autonomy also leads to more growth and mastery, which is meaningful in and of itself.

Clarity of goals and purpose is a prerequisite for autonomy to lead to performance that is aligned with the organization's direction. When an organization's management creates a clear enough vision and frame, and then gives employees freedom to pursue these ends in their own way, people tend to be more inspired, creative, and effective.

The Inherent Purpose of Team: Service and Belonging

About a year before I (Steph) joined the Search Inside Yourself team, I met a friend of a friend who was about to take a long vacation. "I'm actually going to miss my colleagues while I'm away," she told me. "I really love them." She said it with sincerity and emotion. I believed her, and yet felt skeptical. Truly loving your coworkers? This was unfathomable to me at the time. I'd worked for teams that were well-functioning, with enough connection and respect to get good work done. I'd worked in environments where I felt a special connection with one or two people in the midst of larger disconnection and dysfunction. But this woman was expressing a level of connection and belonging that I didn't think was possible at work.

Once I joined the SIY team, I understood. It was the first time I was part of a whole team that felt connected to one another and to a shared purpose. It was novel. I looked forward to seeing my colleagues, regularly greeted them with hugs, cared about what was happening in their lives, and felt a deep sense of belonging within the team and organization. I got to experience love and connection as a part of my regular workday. I thought of this woman's words often; she'd foreshadowed my own experience and expanded my understanding of what is possible when a team has a deep sense of meaning and belonging.

Feeling connected and a sense of belonging to a group, and contributing to your colleagues and the team, is inherently meaningful. A study from

Blake Allan at Purdue University found that when our tasks involve helping others, we tend to perceive our work as more meaningful.[9] Relatedly, studies by Sonja Lyubomirsky show that acts of kindness when done for ourselves are enjoyable while we're doing them, but only acts of kindness for others lead to longer-lasting happiness.[10]

Generally, often known as "helper's high," performing acts of kindness for others increases our own happiness, engagement, and purpose. In addition, a team member may get a specific sense of purpose from taking on a role on the team that uses their social intelligence and awareness to make sure everyone has space to contribute, or in following up with team members that seem upset. This is not just nice to have, but actually vital for team performance.

Compelling and counterintuitive research on what makes a team high performing comes out of Google. When I (Rich) worked as Google's Director of Executive Development (responsible for development of Google's senior leaders), my team had a chance to collaborate with the People Analytics team, responsible for a "data-driven understanding of human resources practices and programs." People Analytics had recently completed a study on the characteristics of the most effective managers at Google, very helpful for managers' skill building and performance. Next, they wanted to study not just individual performance, but also team effectiveness. They named it Project Aristotle for the philosopher's quote: "The whole is greater than the sum of the parts."

Project Aristotle analyzed the qualities of 180 of the most effective, high-performing teams at Google. At first, they were stumped. Features they expected to matter, such as individual intelligence, number of superstars on a team, and manager style, didn't. Instead, they discovered that the unwritten norms of *how* a team worked together was the most important factor that led to success and the sense of the team being stronger than its parts. Researcher and business school professor Amy Edmonson dubs this "psychological safety" and defines it as a "shared belief held by members of a team that the team is safe for interpersonal risk-taking."[11]

Psychologically safe teams actually reward risk-taking and vulnerability. Team members can experiment and try different approaches, share ideas, and overall be vulnerable without having to be concerned about rejection and ridicule. While psychological safety came out as the number one factor, other factors were found to be important as well, including team structure, role clarity, dependability, and feeling like your work makes an impact. All of these contribute elements to high-performing teams.

In particular, Google's team noted two behaviors that the high-performing teams shared: team members speak in roughly equal amounts (referred to as "equality in distribution of conversational turn-taking") and have an overall high social awareness. In other words, in these high-performing teams, team members each had space to contribute and they sensed when others were upset or felt left out. In Google's Project Aristotle, dependability ranked high as well. Google summarized this as: "When my teammates say they'll do something, they follow through with it."[12] The feeling of being part of a team where everyone is contributing their best, is reliable, and is doing meaningful work is a satisfying and fulfilling experience.

In contrast, teams with very low psychological safety display pervasive mistrust and a punitive culture, which results in lack of collaboration, high competitiveness (within the team and against other teams), and low engagement. Teams with low psychological safety operate from a place of fear and mistrust and therefore become risk-averse. Innovation and execution excellence can be limited in teams with low psychological safety, leaving them prone to underperforming or failing.

Our sense of connection also contributes to our overall well-being. Connection is characterized by a sense of care, kinship, and having positive interactions with others. Our capacity for and cultivation of caring relationships and positive social interactions figures prominently in scientific conceptions of well-being. In fact, positive relationships are better predictors of health than various biological and economic factors. Social connection also buffers against depression and anxiety.[13] Of course, we should all have many supportive and positive relationships outside of work, and our work should allow time to be with our friends and family. At the same time, we spend so much of our waking time at work that it is vital for our well-being to cultivate connection among our colleagues.

Innovation

According to a McKinsey report, while 84% of executives agree that innovation is critical for their business, only 6% are satisfied with their innovation performance.[14] With psychological safety and clear goals, a team will be aligned and high-performing, but how does it come up with new ideas? Purpose is a powerful driver of innovation. It can be an important bridge between the desire for innovation and successful execution. In many ways, innovation is an outcome of the benefits explored earlier. When people are experiencing meaning behind their work, they are more likely to generate novel ideas, explore unconventional solutions, and take risks to address challenges.

Innovation means exploring uncharted territory, which is inherently risky and therefore vulnerable. Brené Brown, author and research professor at the University of Houston, draws out this connection: "We have fallen victim to the idea that we're supposed to be comfortable all the time." But that's not where progress comes from. "Vulnerability is the absolute heartbeat of innovation and creativity. There can be zero innovation without vulnerability."[15] In order for employees to become vulnerable, they must both feel safe in the team and be motivated by an individual and/or shared sense of significance. Moreover, purpose-driven teams exhibit a greater degree of resilience in the face of setbacks. When purpose is the orientation, teams can learn from failures and have more motivation to innovate.

Teams are a crucial home for innovation. One person on their own might come up with new and innovative ideas, but they will likely lead to a small outcome when enacted individually. When a group of people aligns and works together, innovation translates into impact and the team fulfills the promise of 1 + 1 = 3.

WHERE IS YOUR TEAM?

As we explore the many benefits of purpose for high-performing teams, you might consider which aspects already reflect where your team is, and which ingredients your team could use more of. The following chapter explores ways to develop awareness of what your team's purpose is. We hope this chapter leaves you motivated to enhance your team's purpose with a sense of why this is so useful, even essential, for how we work together, and with the possibility that you can feel connection and love with your colleagues.

MICRO-PRACTICE

Take a moment to consider the key benefits of purpose for team performance:

- Motivation and engagement
- Shared goals and vision
- Autonomy
- Contribution, belonging, and meaning
- Innovation

In which aspects is your team already strong? Where could you use a bit more of these qualities to enhance your team's well-being and performance?

To what degree is your team operating as more than the sum of its parts (1 + 1 = 3)? What would it look (and feel) like if your team were even more connected, aligned, and innovative?

CHAPTER 7

Developing Awareness of Your Team's Purpose

It often doesn't occur to us to make a team's purpose explicit. An organization's purpose might be declared, or its mission or vision statement may be publicly available. As individuals, we often think about what is meaningful to us (and now after Part II, you should have more clarity about your personal purpose). Yet, how these two come together for a team is often a key missing piece.

The first step of the Purpose Reset for a team is to develop **awareness** of what purpose looks and feels like for the team. This includes two vital components: group awareness of individuals' purpose and strengths and a shared sense of the why of the team. Ideally, there is a cascading effect:

Individual team members contribute their
strengths and interests to the team (acting
out their unique purpose), and, in turn,
the team's activities and success (as the
team enacts their purpose) will contribute
to the greater organization's purpose.

For now, the goal is to enhance and sharpen your **awareness** of these aspects of your and your team's purpose, where it is strongest and most vivid, and where it's still vague or distant. This chapter focuses on reflection you can do on your own; the next chapter focuses on exercises to do as a team or group.

The Purpose Reset formula starts by building awareness of the what, why, and who of the team:

WHAT
Our strengths
and skills.

WHY
Our values and
intentions.

WHO
The impact on people,
community, and the
world around us.

- *What* does the team do? At the team level, purpose requires identifying the skills, strengths, interests, and gaps on a team, as well as the goals and responsibilities that the team has for the organization. This is a big opportunity to bring individuals' superpowers and sense of purpose alive.
- *Why* does the team exist? Teams should define a clear and shared understanding of how their efforts contribute meaningfully to the organization's short-term goals and longer-term mission. The team should be able to see their work acknowledged and recognized by others in the organization.

- *Who* does the team impact? Teams need an understanding of all of the stakeholders that are impacted by their work, including the team members themselves, cross-functional teams, and outside partners. There may be an inherent sense of meaning from being part of the team and opportunities to develop a stronger sense of purpose just in the team camaraderie.

As we build awareness around purpose at a team level, remember that awareness is built from both external and internal cues. External cues are the observable and tangible ones. They might include the outcome of a team's work, the team's impact on other teams and the overall business, and the team's impact on stakeholders, customers, and perhaps even the industry and world. With these tangible aspects of purpose, it would be easy to overlook the internal cues, which are vital as well. They include: How does a team feel about their work? What is the physical, embodied experience of working with (or without) a clear sense of meaning and purpose?

PURPOSE RESET PRACTICE

Exploring Internal Cues

Let's take some time to explore your internal cues. We recommend journaling your response to the prompts below, setting a timer for about two minutes per prompt. Try to keep writing for that whole time in a stream-of-consciousness style, without stopping to edit your response. Alternatively, you can just check in with yourself and contemplate the following questions:

- Over the last week, what did work feel like? What emotions and physical sensations dominated?
- Did you feel connected to your colleagues and team?
- In what moments did the team feel like it was most aligned and connected?
- When did the team's way of working feel the least meaningful or most disconnected from a sense of purpose?
- What big work challenge is your team facing that will require you to lead more effectively?

Becoming more aware of your team's purpose can be an important mindset shift from autopilot to aware. We often have a vague or fuzzy sense of a team's purpose, but when forced to articulate it, find that it's not crisp enough to be useful, or that different team members have different ideas about what exactly the purpose is. Depending on how clearly defined and understood your team's purpose is already, and considering your role on the team, you could start to build on either what, why, or who, or all three together.

WHAT DOES YOUR TEAM DO?

Is your team buried in spreadsheets? Or perhaps you spend all day meeting with customers or you're designing new products. The *what* part of the Purpose Reset formula focuses on how we spend our time. What your team does on an hourly, daily, and weekly basis forms the backbone of the experience of work for employees.

Our tasks and ways of engaging in work fill the workday and determine which strengths and skills we get to use. For teams, it's vital to understand what the team is doing and what strengths and talents each team member contributes to the group. The biggest contributor to the *what* of the team is understanding and leveraging the strengths of the individual team members, and then seeing how the strengths of individuals can complement and enhance one another.

A starting point to understand the *what* of your team is to reflect on your own contributions and the team as a whole:

- What tasks do you do in a given day (e.g., data analysis, emails, strategic thinking, supporting customers)?
- Which tasks do you like the best? Are there things you do beyond the scope of your role (or don't get to do) that you would like to contribute to the team?
- What are the top three to five skills that these tasks require?

- In which of your skills or tasks do you feel most confident? What gaps do you see?
- Thinking about the whole team, what activities is the team doing?
- Thinking back over the last 6–12 months, what has the team been most successful at? What skills and strengths made that happen?
- What, if any, are the skill gaps? Are there important tasks no one wants to do or that keep getting postponed?

One power of being part of a team is that you don't have to do this yourself! It can be hard to see your own strengths and skills. Team members can support one another by reflecting back the best parts of team members (more on this in the next chapter).

From the basic *what* of tasks and skills, consider how your team is working together and what the experience of being part of the team feels like:

- How does the team work together? Do team members tend to work more independently or collaboratively? What is the cadence of meetings? How much shared responsibility and feedback is there?
- When you work with other teammates, how does it feel? Do team meetings feel connecting and motivating, or isolating and dispiriting (or something else)?

The answers to these questions are key ingredients in building awareness of the team's purpose; keep building by considering:

- When work is going well and there is a sense of purpose or meaning, what does this feel like?
- What supports this feeling and sense of purpose?

Reflecting on these questions is the first step to build awareness of *what* your team does. In the next chapter, we'll share a way to dive in deeper by sharing strengths in a team through a reflected best self-exercise that you can do with your team members.

WHY DOES YOUR TEAM EXIST?

When I (Rich) was the head of learning and development at eBay, I visited one of our customer service teams to help their leaders recruit and retain team members. "It's a really hard job," I remember one customer service executive telling me. "People call in with a lot of emotion. They can be very upset. They are demanding solutions. And team members have to manage this all efficiently and at a high volume of calls. It can be hard for team members to deal with that day-in, day-out," the executive told me. "What keeps people at it?" I asked. They responded that, ultimately, team members felt that they were serving to support the small, usually family-run businesses that made up the majority of eBay's operational base. "We keep mom-and-pop operations that sell stuff out of their garages in business," was how one customer service team member described it to me. "That's why I care to show up every day . . . to help make their business be the best they can be." Clearly, having a sense of impact and the specific ways that their work would benefit others was a huge factor in motivating and engaging team members. They knew their *why*.

A team that is working with a strong sense of purpose will feel clear about how the team's activities benefit their stakeholders and contribute to the organization's larger purpose and vision. In Google's search to figure out what makes the best teams (Project Aristotle discussed in the previous chapter), they found that one of the top five attributes of a highly successful team is "impact." Google's report summarizes it as: "I understand how our team's work contributes to the organization's goals."[1] In contrast, if you've ever had the experience of being on a team working hard on a project that seems unrelated to the company's strategy, you've had a taste of missing the *why* behind a team.

Knowing why a team exists and how its contributions matter is vital for sustained motivation and performance. Based on their research, Google put together a "Team Effectiveness Guide" to help people identify where they could improve and provide questions for reflection.[2] The guide suggests the following signs that your team needs to improve meaning:

- Work assignments are based solely on ability, expertise, and workload, and there is little consideration for individual development needs and interests.
- There is a lack of regular recognition for achievements or milestones.

The guide also suggests to ask yourself: Does the work give team members a sense of personal and professional fulfillment?

Your team, whether composed of a handful or dozens of people, should have a clear and strong sense of how their efforts meaningfully build toward the organization's mission. As Google's guide suggests as well, the team's accomplishments should be recognized and the work should give people an opportunity to feel fulfilled.

MICRO-PRACTICE

Take a moment and reflect: Why does your team exist?

Does the answer come quickly, or do you need to think it through? How compelling is the answer?

This is a quick gauge of how much your team might need a stronger sense of purpose—the longer it takes to answer the question "Why does your team exist?" and the more murky or vague the answer, the greater the imperative for more clarity.

The first step is to build awareness of the clarity of your team's purpose and how this clarity is influencing day-to-day functioning of the team. In the next chapter, we'll share how to create a team purpose statement to really build the sense of *why* for your team.

WHO DOES YOUR TEAM IMPACT?

When the three of us—Rich, Steph, and Carolina—decided to kick off the process of writing this book, a writing coach recommended starting by writing a love letter to our reader. Yes, each one of us wrote a love letter to you, and we still have them in a Google Drive folder. The exercise authentically connected us with the person turning the pages of this book—your needs, desires, longings—and with our purpose as we began this meaningful project.

During the many months and long hours it took us to write this book, the letters served as inspiration. Bringing you to mind, our readers choosing to read our words among the many other available books, would immediately reconnect us to our purpose. We actually ended up including some of the paragraphs from those letters in the book itself, bringing forth our true voice and how we'd speak to someone we care about (now you see why we keep talking about love throughout the book).

In a similar way, considering *who* your team impacts can be a source of inspiration even when they are people you have yet to meet. Who your team impacts and connects with are people that your team gets to love.

To build awareness of who your team impacts, map out all of the stakeholders you can think of (and you might ask colleagues or consult your org chart for input too). Consider as many audiences as possible:

- The team members themselves (and their families and communities)
- Teams that your team collaborates with on projects or products
- Any teams that your team might feel at odds with (e.g., R&D vs. regulatory compliance), any people or teams that tend to complain about your team's work or vice versa
- The organization as a whole
- Customers, clients, and end users
- Other outside stakeholders
- The industry as a whole, or broader community that might be impacted

First, just brainstorm a list or draw out a map of stakeholders. Then reflect on the following questions:

- How does it feel to take in the whole picture of all of the stakeholders? Is it clarifying, overwhelming, something else?
- Who is the number one most important stakeholder?

- Are there stakeholders whose needs are often deprioritized or not consulted?
- For any teams that seem at odds with yours, what is the shared purpose?

While I (Carolina) was working in Silicon Valley, our marketing vice president led a training with her entire organization focused on people. I thought it was going to be yet another boring corporate virtual training, where I'd have to watch videos of actors presenting office scenarios, scroll through long texts the software wouldn't let me skip, click on colorful virtual flash cards with long definitions, and answer quizzes with obvious incorrect answers. But the experience surprised me: it was an in-person training to deepen our ability to see the people we worked with—customers, team members, and cross-functional partners—through a new lens. Literally. We were given virtual reality devices and were asked to walk in someone else's shoes. Each person was assigned another stakeholder to "embody" for the duration of the training.

As soon as I put on my headset, I noticed that my hands looked darker and seemed to belong to someone significantly older than me. If I remember correctly, I "became" a 65-year-old Black woman in the United States and had to go through various scenarios as her. As a Latin American woman who didn't grow up in the same country as this woman I was embodying, I was able to learn, not just intellectually, but in an experiential way, the types of events and situations she faced on a daily basis at work as well as some of her family's history.

The activity was meant to show us the real, raw human experiences behind the people our marketing team worked with, understand our biases, practice challenging conversations from someone else's perspective, and see the world based on another person's context and history.

Not only did we learn about the people assigned to us in a completely new and unforgettable way, but after we finished the activity, we walked to the cafeteria as a team, exchanging stories with a new, more empathetic tone toward one another, and feeling a deeper sense of connection among ourselves and with the people we served or worked with.

Even without VR headsets, having teams really consider and experience the perspective of who your work impacts is essential—and meaningful. These are people that you get to love and care for through your work. For many teams, seeing the clients and stakeholders that your team impacts may be straightforward and fairly easy to imagine. However, it's worth taking time to be exhaustive and consider if there might be people or processes that your team impacts, perhaps downstream, that you're not used to being aware of.

Start Bringing Awareness of Purpose Alive in Your Team

A simple starting point for managers and leaders is to start talking about purpose, meaning, and impact in meetings, internal emails, HR processes, and more.

It's important for this to feel grounded in honesty and realism for it to truly be motivating. You might start with yourself: What is your sense of purpose and meaning at work? Do you have an honest and compelling answer? What are moments when you feel it most strongly? Then, find opportunities to share about it with your team explicitly and authentically.

You can also start engaging teams and work groups around this topic. For example, starting a team meeting with a quick check-in round asking each person, if they're willing, to share a one- to two-minute response to prompts like "What has been meaningful to you this week?" or "What is a moment from the past week when your work felt most impactful?"

A prompt we've used at SIY is "If you really knew me, you'd know . . ." This can be a wonderfully connecting prompt as is, or you might sculpt it toward purpose with the variation: "If you really knew me, you'd know that what really lights me up is . . ."

Remember that purpose is about engaging your team, not squeezing more out of them. Google's Project Oxygen, which studies the behaviors of the most effective managers, found that top managers "express interest in and concern for team members' success and personal well-being." This is in addition to other attributes, including coaching, empowering the team, and having a clear vision.[3] It's important that bringing purpose to the team feels authentic and connecting, and that team members have chances to reflect on and share what is meaningful to them.

BUILDING AWARENESS OF ANY PURPOSE DISCONNECTS

As you build more and more awareness of your team's purpose, we believe in starting with and building on the strengths. Focusing on and enhancing what sense of purpose already exists builds momentum and engagement. However, it's also important to be honest about ways that purpose feels lacking for individual team members and for the team as a whole.

As the center layer in an organization, the team level is where the top-down and bottom-up needs meet. Middle managers are often the ones squeezed between the competing goals set from upper management and the on-the-ground reality, which can create tension and stress. Indeed, supervisors and managers tend to have higher rates of depression and anxiety than both owners and workers.[4] These middle managers also have a degree of influence as the place where these forces are coming together. Managers can help the team see and understand the larger system that is exerting influence on them.

In particular, there are many types of disconnect that can exist as teams try to align between individuals and the organization. A few common mismatches:

- **Individuals don't feel like their purpose fits within their role or what the team needs.** In the short term, truly understanding what the individual's purpose means to them, what skills or strengths they would like to be using, and what they care about is an important starting point. There may be ways they can recraft their role to enhance their sense of purpose. We remember an employee in our team who was responsible for program management really wanted to bring more connection and resilience to the team, so she organized a series of well-being workshops for the whole organization. In the longer term, this might mean that the team can take on new work, expanding or changing their scope. Or it might mean supporting the individual to shift roles or even find a new career path.

- **Too much purpose can feel like a "passion tax."** As we briefly shared in Part II, when employees feel passionate about their work, others around them are more willing to ask for extra unpaid and more demeaning work. According to research from Duke University, it's called "the legitimization of passion exploitation," or a passion tax.[5] Researchers found that people are more likely to ask passionate employees to work on weekends, work unpaid, and perform tasks beyond their job description. It can lead to exploitation, burnout, and losing your best team members.

- **The team doesn't have a shared sense of purpose.** Perhaps it hasn't been clearly defined, or team members hold different ideas of what the main function of the team is, or they are used to working so independently, there is no sense of commonality. Start by understanding why this dynamic exists, how it can hinder the work, and how it might benefit team members (e.g., avoiding conflict, allowing people to keep doing what they're used to). A team lacking a shared understanding is ripe for some focus on creating a team purpose statement together (more on this in the following chapter).

- **The team's work doesn't feel connected to the organization's mission.** If it's hard to see your team's work reflected in the mission and priorities of your larger division or full organization, it might be that your team could think more creatively about your purpose in a way that enables greater connection, or it might mean advocating for your team's voice in the larger system more. Perhaps your team is doing important work that deserves more recognition and/or more influence.

- **Lack of authentic organization and team purpose can cause moral distress.** A lack of attention to meaning can be actively demoralizing, especially when people are asked to do things that aren't values aligned. At its extreme, this is called moral distress or moral injury, a term developed primarily in the context of military and healthcare settings to describe the psychological distress that results from actions or experiences that violate one's moral or ethical beliefs and expectations. Experiencing moral distress often involves guilt, shame, and a sense of inner conflict due to participating in or witnessing events that transgress one's values. The concept of moral distress (at least in the academic world) dates back to research describing symptoms observed among Vietnam veterans. In the seminal paper by Brett Litz and his colleagues, they defined moral distress as resulting from "an act of transgression that creates dissonance and conflict because it violates assumptions and beliefs about right and wrong and personal goodness."[6] Though most research around moral injury has been conducted on military personnel and veterans and healthcare workers, many of the questions on the moral injury symptom scale apply to a workplace, such as "I feel betrayed by leaders I once trusted" or "I have a good sense of what makes my life meaningful."[7] Of course most organizations are not putting their employees in literal life and death situations that tend to lead to the greatest sense of moral distress; however, this concept highlights the importance of integrity and authenticity as vital qualities of purpose initiatives.

Acknowledging your team's current state and any existing points of disconnection is an important first step. We have to see things clearly and accept what is before we can create lasting change. There can often be a powerful feeling of relief from naming what's not working. When shared in a team, solving the problem can become a shared goal.

As Carl Jung is known for saying: "The right question is already half the solution to a problem." The more critical question for your team at this point in time might not just be "What is our team's purpose?" but something more specific, such as "What is getting in the way of us feeling more purposeful?" or "How can our team's purpose align more closely with the organization's five-year plan?" An honest assessment of these types of disconnects will support you in taking meaningful action to help your team build and enact a shared sense of purpose.

MICRO-PRACTICE

Take a moment to deepen your shift from a default or autopilot view to greater awareness:

- Why does the team exist?
- What is becoming clear about your team's purpose?
- What is still unclear?
- What disconnects exist that might need to be acknowledged or addressed?

CHAPTER 8
Acting on Purpose Together

When Niki Lustig worked at Twitter (now X) as a leader within the Learning and Organizational Development team, she realized that managers needed to enhance the sense of purpose within their teams. Lustig explained: "One of the things we get challenged with all the time is helping leaders and managers define the purpose of their team's existence. What does that look like in terms of anchoring teams' objectives to the work they're doing, and how does that tie to the broader vision of the company?" To answer this, she started an initiative to help managers define the unique purposes of their teams. It started with an internal "Purpose Pre-Work Survey," with nine prompts, designed to take 10 minutes to respond to in total. The first three prompts engaged people at an individual level, the middle three were about teams, and the last three were for the organization as a whole:

1. What excited you most about taking your job here?
2. What gets you out of bed every day to come to work?
3. What impact do you personally want to have on our company?
4. What do you want our team to be doing that we aren't?
5. Describe what our team does that no other team at the company does/can do.

6. In three words, what is the essence of our team's purpose for existence?
7. What is one thing you wish that everyone at the company knew about our team?
8. What would an ideal partnership look like with our clients?
9. What are some ways we can educate the company about how to partner with us and leverage our team more effectively than they are today?

After completing the survey, employees would read their colleagues' responses with an eye toward "What leaps off the page?" Lustig describes that this is such an inspiring exercise, it's worth doing on its own. However, she didn't stop there. She then invited teams to attend a Purpose Workshop, where they worked to meld the different responses into a cohesive statement for the team.[1]

At the time, tweets could contain a maximum of 140 characters, so Lustig made sure the purpose statements were only 140 characters, too, making a direct link from the purpose workshops to Twitter's core product. She also planned each purpose workshop to be 140 minutes.[2] The care Lustig took to weave together individual, team, and organizational purpose into a process that is reflective, collaborative, and meaningful is exactly the type of action that many teams need to bring their purpose alive and act together.

When it comes to acting on purpose at a team level, we want to underscore that the team is the bridge between the individual team members and the organization as a whole. Actions that promote a sense of purpose for the team should enhance and build on the team members' purpose and strengths, and should reflect the organization's intentions as well.

A team's sense of purpose can—and often should—be articulated differently from the organization's mission statement in order to more precisely reflect the team's contribution. At the same time, it should connect the

**dots between the team's daily tasks and the
organization's greater impact rather than
being totally different or disconnected.**

In this chapter, we share a number of actions a team can take to define its purpose, support individuals to share their sense of purpose and how it contributes to the team, and continue integrating purpose into team processes. We begin with some simple methods to get started; these are great ways to gauge interest in the topic and the need for a clearer definition of your team's purpose. We then explore a "bottom-up" approach, how to capitalize on team members' strengths to build a stronger team. We also share a "top-down" approach to help the team bring the organization's purpose down to meet the team's role by crafting a team purpose statement—the core of bringing purpose to a team and a main focus of this section. Finally, regardless of how a team's sense of purpose is defined or created, seeing the impact of the team's work is an essential part of building motivation and momentum. In the final section of this chapter we share ways to integrate purpose into how a team operates (e.g., a review process, team meetings, off-sites, and annual planning sessions), which is vital to continue to keep purpose alive and impactful.

**A team's purpose shouldn't just
be stated, but enacted.**

There is no one right way to engage with your team around purpose, so think of this section as a menu of different approaches that you might try out. Feel free to combine and augment them as needed to fit the needs of your team. Collaborating with your team for the group as a whole to crystallize a shared sense of purpose is key.

GETTING STARTED: INTRODUCING PURPOSE TO YOUR TEAM

There are a number of ways you might engage your team to reflect on purpose and meaning in their life and work. Depending on the existing dynamics of the team and your role, you might decide to start with a lighter touch, or you could dive into a big team effort or host an off-site focused on this topic.

To help you decide how to start, consider why it's important to enhance a sense of purpose on your team now: Are you looking for more motivation and engagement? Does your team feel motivated by their tasks, but unsure about how their work fits into the larger organizational picture? Or perhaps a greater connection to purpose and impact would help the team celebrate their achievements? Is there a change in the team's composition, in organizational strategy, or in the market that makes this ripe timing for a Purpose Reset?

If you want to start out with small touch points—perhaps to gauge interest, to bring the topic forward as a team member, or to start ramping up a larger process—consider one of these ideas:

- **Use a team meeting to have each person share about their sense of purpose.** If the team is small and/or has a high degree of trust, you might have everyone on the team share during one meeting, or you might have one person take five minutes or so at the beginning of the meeting, and rotate through the whole team over multiple meetings. For larger teams or for a safer, less vulnerable version of this exercise, divide the team into breakout groups of perhaps three to five people where team members share and discuss, and then aggregate themes from the subgroups to share back to the full team. You can use prompts such as:
  - What makes you feel alive? What at work gives you a sense of meaning?
  - How do you think of your sense of purpose in life (including ways that aren't engaged at work)?

- What do you have to achieve in your lifetime for your own sense of fulfillment?
- **Start with informal check-ins.** Via Slack, email, or another communications method, start occasional threads encouraging people to share using questions that enhance a sense of purpose, such as: When were you most engaged or in a flow state this week? What was a peak moment? Who did you make a difference to? Did you see someone on our team have a positive impact on someone else?
- **Engage the team in an exercise to connect the dots from the organization's purpose to the team's.** This could be a discussion around the prompt of "How does the organization's purpose and mission roll down to our team? How does our team contribute to this larger goal?" It could also be more creative. In his book *Cultivating Culture*, Brad Federman suggests engaging the team in an exercise where the group is broken up into smaller subgroups, and each one draws a picture of the connection between their work and the organization's success using pictures, symbols, and/or words. Then each team presents their picture to the full group.[3] An exercise like this might be connected to an annual planning process or goal review, or to a celebration of achieving some team or organization-wide goals.
- **Incorporate questions about purpose into an employee survey.** Especially if there is an existing organizational employee survey, include questions that get at a sense of purpose or meaning. As we mentioned in our introductory chapters, the Great Place to Work 2021 survey of over 330,000 millennial employees at US companies found the following questions useful for retention (which also make great prompts for discussion): Are you proud of where you work? Do you find meaning in your work? Do you have fun at work?[4]

From these simple starting points, to continue to enhance the team's sense of purpose, you can start with either the "bottom-up" or "top-down" approach. Either way, connecting the dots from individual team members to the team to the whole org is an essential through line to draw.

BUILDING FROM THE BOTTOM UP: RECOGNIZING THE STRENGTHS OF THE TEAM

> To build a strong team, you must see someone else's strength as a complement to your weakness and not a threat to your position or authority.
> —Christine Caine, Australian activist and author

As we explored in the previous chapter, high-performing teams bring out the best in each team member. Instead of competing with one another in cutthroat ways, strong teams use an intimate understanding of the strengths and skills of each teammate to collaborate and potentially differentiate roles. This section shares a few different ways a team can bring the strengths of each team member forward.

As you engage with your team around the topic of purpose, there might be colleagues for whom meaning and contribution are not top of mind. They might see their work as more transactional, serving to support their family financially or allowing them to pursue another purpose outside of work. Their sense of purpose doesn't need to come from their job as long as they are meeting the expectations for their role. Kim Scott, former leader at Apple and Google and author of *Radical Candor*, writes: "There's nothing wrong with working hard to earn a paycheck that supports the life you want. That has plenty of meaning."[5] Especially for people for whom work is more transactional, focusing on strengths is a very inclusive way to foreground what is best about each team member.

Team members that are less focused on work, perhaps because they are focused more on family, caregiving, or an outside hobby or project, might simply be on a slower growth path within this role. Scott makes an important distinction between "rock stars" and "superstars." To create a cohesive team, you need both. Rock stars are excellent performers on a gradual growth path. Superstars, on the other hand, demonstrate excellent performance and steep growth. Rock stars need to be recognized and rewarded for the important role that they play. Superstars need to be given new opportunities and challenges. Scott gives this important advice for managers: "In order to distinguish between the two, you must let go of your judgments and your own ambitions, forget for a while what you need from people, and focus on getting to know each person as a human being."[6] Focusing on strengths is a helpful way into purpose and performance for teams. It helps rock stars feel recognized and valued, and can engage everyone, including employees who see work as more transactional.

The following three team practices are designed to help teams recognize strengths. The first provides straightforward ways to have team members share about their strengths. The second uses team members' knowledge of one another to help reflect strengths back to each team member. And the third is a lighter, more fun way to identify strengths with creative job titles. You don't need to do them all; you might pick one to use now and come back to others in future years. Or this section might inspire you to create your own variation that will work even better for your team and organization.

Team Practice Exercise 1: Sharing Strengths & Purpose

Teams can (and should!) build a greater sense of purpose from the bottom up by bringing to light the strengths and purpose of each team member. At its most simple and straightforward, this can mean taking time for colleagues to share about themselves. At a team meeting or off-site, take time for team members to describe their strengths and sense of purpose using one or more of these prompts:

- When is work most meaningful to you?
- What parts of your day give you the most satisfaction and sense of flow?
- What do you consider your strengths? What positive feedback do you get most consistently from peers or clients/customers?
- What do you think of as your superpower?
- What strengths and interests do you have that don't get expressed at work?
- What are you most curious about? How do you want to grow?

Note if there are strengths and interests that team members aren't using, especially if you are a manager or leader. It can be powerful to notice patterns in the people on your team and to note opportunities to assign work in the future based on these underplayed skills. Even just recognizing the fullness of a person's talents can feel very connecting and motivating.

MICRO-PRACTICE

This practice is especially for managers: Take a moment and list the names of each person on your team and brainstorm one or two things that they are good at or that they seem to truly enjoy. Make sure to include yourself as part of the team! Then look to see where one team member might use their strengths and interests to help out another team member or the team as a whole.

You might choose to share some of your reflections, perhaps in your next one-on-one meetings, or this simply might create a more appreciative mindset in general or as you engage in the exercise below.

Team Practice Exercise 2: Reflecting Strengths & Purpose

Instead of having team members share directly about their strengths, team members can be a mirror for one another. Colleagues can take time to reflect the strengths, skills, and impact that they see in their teammates. This is valuable for a team because it helps team members see and bring out the best in their colleagues. Individuals might get to hear about strengths that others see in them, including ones that they might have a hard time seeing in themselves.

One powerful way to do this is through a version of the Reflected Best Self (RBS) exercise, which was developed based on research from the Center for Positive Organizations at the Ross School of Business, University of Michigan.[7] The goal of this exercise is to have a clear answer to the question "When am I at my best?" Understanding this is powerful for individuals, and even more so when each team member can be seen and understood by their colleagues. This supports a team to best see and leverage one another's strengths, and cultivates a culture of appreciation. This powerful approach can be used as a stand-alone exercise, or can be done after the above exercise to deepen and extend it.

The Center for Positive Organizations offers a full assessment for individuals and teams. Short of engaging with the full version, a way for your team to use the ideas of the Reflected Best Self exercise on your own is briefly summarized here.

When offering this exercise, you might introduce it by sharing that the premise of this exercise is that the best version of each individual emerges when they are using their strengths, and that the best version of a team will leverage and build on the strengths of one another. By soliciting feedback from peers, colleagues, and others, team members gather stories of specific instances where each member has excelled, providing a foundation for recognizing individual strengths. Then, after sharing individual strengths with the team, the team can also reflect on the group's strengths as a whole.

The specific steps to deploy this exercise are as follows:

Step 1: Create a Best Self Portrait of Individual Strengths—Each team member collects feedback from people who know them well answering the question "When have you seen me at my best?" with specific examples. Team members can request feedback from friends, family, former colleagues or those outside of the team, or any other significant people in their life. Alternatively, to keep it simple, this exercise can be done within the team, with team members providing feedback to one another.

Then, these stories are looked at together to find themes and patterns. This can be done individually by team members, or could be done in pairs where team members can talk through the themes together and reflect patterns for one another. The themes should reflect the strengths, talents, and positive qualities highlighted from the stories shared. Each team member creates a self-portrait that represents their "best self." The portrait could be written or visual; it could be simple and straightforward or creative and poetic. The portrait should be meaningful to the person and should clearly communicate who they are at their best to the team.

Step 2: Share Best Self Portraits—Each team member then presents their portrait to the team. After each team member shares their portrait, the rest of the team might simply applaud, share appreciations, or reflect on things they have learned about the person. This exercise can also be a chance to provide gentle challenges where a colleague's strengths can be enhanced. The intention of the exercise is to see a person's strengths (i.e., what they already do well!), not to provide criticism. However, especially if your team has a learning culture and a high degree of psychological safety, this can be an opportunity to share about how a team member might lean even more into their strengths.

Reflections might also distinguish between desired versus actual strengths. Desired strengths are areas we want to be good at, whereas actual strengths are what we're already good at (regardless of whether we enjoy using these strengths). Separating these is extremely helpful, especially within a team. There may be things that we think we are good at because we care about them and want these things to be strengths, when actually they are interests and we need more skill-building in these areas. On the flip side, team members might be using strengths that they would prefer not to keep using.

Step 3: Create a Team Portrait—As a team, look at the collection of individual strengths on the team to create a picture of the strengths of the team as a whole. This portrait depicts how the team leverages team members' combined strengths to achieve shared goals and purpose. This Team Portrait can be visual, graphic, or written out. Discuss how to apply strengths in various aspects of work, and if any key strengths are missing for what the team needs:

- How might team members apply their strengths in various aspects of their work that they aren't already?
- How do team members feel they can apply their strengths in service of other team members or the team as a whole?

- What are common strengths and themes from individual team members that show the strengths of the team as a unit?

From the Team Portrait, the team might develop an action plan to integrate these strengths into team processes, projects, and interactions with other teams or stakeholders, or the portrait might inform an existing annual goal-setting and planning process. In addition, the sense of "best self" that team members gain from this process can be applied in personal situations too.

Team Practice Exercise 3: Creative Job Titles

London Business School professor Dan Cable and Wharton Business School professors Adam Grant and Justin Berg studied a local chapter of the Make-A-Wish Foundation, where the chapter's CEO, Susan Lerch, invited employees to create fun titles to supplement (not replace) their official ones. The study found that the new, creative titles made employees' jobs more meaningful and helped people focus on the more purposeful aspects of their jobs.[8] So, when you enter the Michigan office of the Make-A-Wish Foundation, you might meet the Fairy Godmother of Wishes (the chapter's CEO) or the Sweetheart of Structure & Salutation (the office manager). At this office, they've found a fun way to engage a team around their unique purpose and strengths through creative job titles.

Cable describes: "The exercise causes job incumbents to ask themselves, 'What is the purpose of the work, and what is my unique connection to it?'"[9] He developed a simple method for how to encourage employees to retitle for a greater sense of purpose:

- **Step 1:** Employees reflect on their job's purpose and about what aspects of the job they do especially well (compared to their peers or competitors).
- **Step 2:** Employees brainstorm potential new titles on their own or crowdsource ideas from the team and manager, and decide on a new title to share with colleagues internally.

These titles can be used for internal purposes only; they never need to be public or shared with clients or stakeholders. The titles are just one part of a fun and playful internal culture, which helps dull tasks become more engaging, and makes it easier to deal with the tragedies and solemn events that are part of the Make-A-Wish Foundation's work supporting kids with life-threatening conditions.[10] Cable has also repeated the experiment with a hospital and a brewery to have groups of employees determine their own titles. In both cases, employees experienced an increase in job satisfaction.

I (Carolina) was inspired by this approach and gave myself the title of Chief Evolution Officer (CEO) when I founded my start-up, Plenari. It reminds me about my true, highest purpose: personal and collective evolution toward our fullest potential and flourishing. You'll see my title on my LinkedIn profile and website as I want this reminder to be explicit for myself and others (plus, I don't love the word *executive* in the traditional CEO concept).

• • •

Using one of these three exercises (or another one that you come up with) gives you a sense of the team's building blocks, a detailed view of your team members' strengths and sense of purpose. This enhances how the group comes together and how the team can become more than the sum of its parts. From here, continuing to build up, to understand how the team's work contributes to the company, and in turn, how the organization-wide mission cascades down to the team, is essential.

BUILDING FROM THE TOP DOWN: CASCADING ORGANIZATION TO TEAM

A company will have a mission, vision, or purpose statement, but for a team it's often just assumed that the team's purpose is clear. The main way to cascade purpose from the larger organizational purpose is to create a team purpose statement. A team's purpose should make a direct and vivid connection between the outcome of the team and the larger purpose of the full organization.

Most teams can benefit from having a clear and compelling statement of its purpose or mission. In his book *Cultivating Culture*, Brad Federman writes: "If employees do not see the bigger picture, they run the risk of feeling unimportant or as though their work is nothing more than an assignment. This has drastic impacts on motivation, happiness and productivity."[11] Because having a team purpose statement is so central to bringing purpose alive for teams, this section spends a bit of time exploring the process.

At its core, the statement should answer: "Why does this team exist?" It should include elements of the what, why, and who of the team. The purpose should resonate with team members (feeling meaningful and motivating) and be perceived as valuable (providing clarity and utility). A good (or good enough!) purpose statement will articulate shared goals, create focus, and allow prioritization for the team. The purpose statement becomes a touchstone that the team can return to when making decisions, navigating change, and planning for the future.

Who Writes the Team's Purpose Statement?

Since the most important audience for the team purpose statement is the team itself, the team should have some role in creating it, but this might vary. The whole team might be involved, a subset in a task group, or perhaps just a few people who take the lead. The team might help translate the straightforward version into something more meaningful, symbolic, or personal for them. Kim Scott, the former leader at Apple and Google we introduced earlier, gives a great example of this: "Insisting that people have passion for their job can place unnecessary pressure on both boss and employee. I struggled with this at Google, where we were hiring people right out of college to do dull customer-support work. I tried convincing them that we were 'funding creativity a nickel at a time.' One young woman who'd studied philosophy in college, called BS immediately. 'Look, the job is a little boring,' she said. 'Let's just admit that. It's OK. Plutarch laid bricks. Spinoza ground lenses. Tedium is part of life.' I loved her approach to finding meaning, but it was unique to her. A slogan like 'Spinoza ground lenses' would not have been inspiring for the broader team."[12]

Scott's story spells out the tension around team purpose. A manager cannot impose a sense of purpose or convince a team that work is more meaningful or fun than it is (this will come off as inauthentic and likely backfire). Yet what motivates one individual team member might not motivate another.

In other words, there is no one right way to do this. Your team's process will depend on a number of factors, including the size of the team, their level of engagement, how much time and attention is needed for this topic, and the culture of your team and organization. If the whole team is not involved in the creation of the team's purpose statement (i.e., if a leader or subgroup has been developing it), you can engage the full team and seek meaningful feedback to create buy-in after there is a strong draft of the purpose statement. This section spells out a general process and considerations, which you can use to help design a process to try out with your team.

What Does a Team Purpose Statement Look Like?

Depending on the culture of your team and organization, a team purpose statement might be short and to the point or more poetic or symbolic. On their blog, the leadership and performance management software company Saberr shares a few examples. A more formal statement for an HR team might be: "As an HR team, we strive to create an environment that stimulates creativity and empowerment, so that we keep our employees motivated, productive, and happy." Whereas a simpler example could be: "Empower our people's creativity." Or a less formal, more playful example would be: "Make <<Company Name>> a place where our employees actually look forward to Monday."[13]

A simple and straightforward starting point to create a team purpose statement is to articulate the what, why, and who of the team using the Purpose Reset framework:

- What does your team do? Describe it in a simple and factual way.
- Why? What is the outcome?
- Who do you do it for, and what is the impact on others?

Then, these components can be brought together in a short statement:

"We _____ {what your team does}
in order to _____ {the outcomes or why your team does this}
so that _____ {the impact on the organization and stakeholder}.

To take SIY Global as an example, the organization's mission is to "humanize work."

- For the marketing team, this means creating and amplifying helpful ideas, programs, and resources to as many people as possible. A statement might look like: **We** create and promote resources and programs **in order to** build awareness and interest of SIY Global's solutions **so that** people in organizations have the tools and skills to humanize their work.
- For the corporate sales team, there is a sense of purpose in connecting with organizations to bring our programs to people who wouldn't necessarily engage with emotional intelligence and personal development tools, but will when those tools are brought to their workplace. A statement might look like: **We** partner with client organizations and sell SIY programs **in order to** bring these programs to more people and into more companies **so that** SIY Global can bring emotional intelligence to many people and support more human-centered workplaces.
- For the finance team, it's about making sure that the organization can carry out its mission in a sustainable way and caring for the team. A statement might look like: **We** pay people, keep the books, and provide vital financial information **in order to** care for employees and ensure the financial sustainability of the company **so that** SIY Global continues to be a leader in the movement to humanize work.

How a purpose statement is worded reflects differences in the orientation of a team or organization. As Mark Bonchek, founder and CEO of Shift Thinking, points out, some companies frame their purpose as being *for* their customers whereas some see themselves as enacting the purpose *with* their customers. The difference between Dunkin' Donuts and Starbucks highlights this:

> Dunkin Donuts: make and serve the freshest, most delicious coffee and donuts quickly and courteously in modern, well-merchandised stores.

> Starbucks: to inspire and nurture the human spirit—one person, one cup and one neighborhood at a time.[14]

Both are clear statements that capture the mission of the respective organizations; however, Dunkin' Donuts is simpler, more straightforward, and has less emphasis on the why and who; it might be the perfect statement for a team that likes simple clarity. The Starbucks mission statement, on the other hand, emphasizes a greater meaning to the work and will better inspire a team that connects to this language.

MICRO-PRACTICE

Creating a Simple Team Purpose Statement
Start by creating a short purpose statement as illustrated above. Do this just off the cuff—no need to overthink it! Fill in the blanks:
    "We do _____ in order to _____, so that _____."
    Thinking about this as a rough starting point, to what degree does your team need more clarity around purpose? Would other team members agree with this statement? Does it feel compelling?

From this short team purpose exercise, consider if there is a need for a deeper process to flesh out a purpose statement for your team. The clarity that an explicit team purpose statement creates supports the important shift from *autopilot* to *aware*. Many of us have a vague or squishy sense of why our team exists, but actually thinking through how the what, why, and who come together creates a greater sense of alignment. As you develop your team purpose statement, considering the unique qualities of your team and the company can be inspiring. In their advice on this subject, recruiting company Indeed encourages teams and organizations to determine what sets the company apart from competitors, considering the following:

- Are we providing a different product or service?
- Do we have a different target audience?
- Are we solving a particular pain point that no other company is solving?
- How do we enhance our customers' lives?[15]

We suggest also considering:

- What values does our team or organization have that set us apart?
- How does our team work together and treat others in ways that are unique?
- What unique experience, product, message, or way of relating does our team want to bring to our stakeholders and the world?

It's okay if some of this sense of uniqueness is aspirational! You can think of this unique quality of purpose as a guiding principle that your team wants to grow into. Once you have a purpose statement articulated, it's important to continue to grow into it and keep it alive by seeing how your purpose actually plays out.

Considering All Stakeholders

For some teams, really fleshing out the answer to "Who do you do it for?" and looking at the team's impact on others will need extra thought and attention. As you and your team build your purpose statement, make sure that you're identifying and including all stakeholders, with a focus on your most important ones (and including the team members themselves!). For some teams, this will be relatively simple and straightforward. For teams operating in heavily complex or cross-functional ways, or whose work impacts many downstream stakeholders, taking time to build a detailed list of all stakeholders will be useful. Building on the awareness exercise in the previous chapter, your team can consider both the team's overall stakeholders, as well as which ones each team member serves, and then explore differences, what tensions these differences might create, and what ideal outcomes look like.

Creating Buy-In

If the whole team has not been involved in the creation of the team's purpose statement, it's essential to share it with the full team for feedback, leading with the following discussion questions:

- How does this statement feel? What comes to mind? What emotions come up?
- What is motivating or inspiring about this purpose statement? What falls flat or feels inauthentic?
- Do you see yourself/your role reflected in this?
- Does this articulation of purpose feel useful? Would it help guide you in hard decisions or conflicts with teammates?
- What would make this purpose statement more meaningful to you?

You might also share your team's purpose statement with key stakeholders outside of the team for their feedback and buy-in, and to let them know how much you have them in mind as your team goes through their day-to-day workflow. Mark Bonchek wrote about the importance of a shared sense of purpose in the *Harvard Business Review*. He explains that customers "want it to be their purpose too. They don't want to be at the other end of your **for**. They want to be right there **with** you. Purpose needs to be shared."[16] As you share with customers and clients, listen for what is meaningful to them both in terms of outcomes and in how you and your organization are supporting them.

When you can't directly check in with stakeholders, you can still find creative ways to take their perspective into account. For example, when planning a recent summit our team led in Europe for our group of certified teachers and clients in the region, we wanted to make sure everything we planned centered around our audience and their needs. In particular, as a team based in the United States, we made an extra effort to design an experience that would be relevant to the multicultural audience in attendance. As we planned the event, I (Carolina) brought a handful of colorful balloons into our conference room, blew them into different sizes, and drew faces on them. Each balloon was meant to represent a different audience group. Before finalizing a decision, we made sure to "check" with each one of them, to make sure their perspective was included and their needs were being met. It seemed silly at first—and a couple of team members had puzzled looks on their faces when they first arrived in the room. Yet having the balloons "sitting at the table" with us ensured our decisions took into account various perspectives, cultural norms, and needs. Even though this symbolic act was imperfect compared to having actual people in the room, it actually expedited our decision-making and allowed us to include many different stakeholders' input through the power of our perspective taking.

MICRO-PRACTICE

Even without a big process around purpose or engaging with your stakeholders, ask yourself: What is the shared purpose that you can work on *with* your customers and stakeholders? Whose voices are often missing?

When Is a Purpose Statement Complete?

Remember that the goal of a purpose statement process is to find an articulation of your team's purpose that is useful, clear, and motivating. Your team's purpose statement is meant to connect your team members' work and what motivates them and what the organization is aiming at. Instead of seeing it as a bridge that needs to be perfectly engineered, think of it as a tin-can telephone. It's an imperfect, useful way of making a simple and important connection.

Alignment at the team level doesn't mean including everything; many aspects of an individual team member's purpose might not fully fit. There may be other ways that they can live out their purpose, perhaps outside of work, or in taking on other tasks at work that are not their main role. For example, if someone really likes to network and introduce people to one another, they might have an informal role of making connections for the team. There might be elements of a team member's purpose that they can grow into over time, or ways the team might try to expand their scope to better utilize the skills and interests of their employees. It can be a work in progress.

SEEING THE IMPACT

Every year, the SIY team holds an end-of-year celebration—a shared meal, a time for recognition, and a chance to take stock of the year and our accomplishments. For a team that cares a lot about empathy and compassion, we also have a surprisingly cutthroat white elephant gift exchange!

One year, we all piled into our conference room to find an odd pile of books on the conference table, arranged into a circle like a kiddie pool. Peter Bonanno, who was the director of product at the time, joined with a mysterious bag. He shared about the impact that our team had had that year, recounting all of the thousands of people we'd reached with our core Search Inside Yourself program. Numbers are abstract and hard to visualize, though. From his bag, he poured thousands of M&M's into the center of the table one at a time with each color representing a different way we'd reached people. Blue M&M's were all of the Google employees, yellow were people who had attended open enrollment programs, red were participants from other companies, green represented the global certified teacher community, and brown were people our teachers had taught the program to. M&M's kept pouring onto the table, held in by the stack of SIY books! It was a delightful sight.

To really feel the impact of all of the work, we often need to see it more tangibly (or literally savor it!). Peter had translated a vague sense of impact into a joyful and memorable experience. It also lasted—we had M&M's in our kitchen for months! Peter helped us see and feel the impact of our efforts, which is essential for sustaining purpose and motivation as individuals and team members comprising an organization.

You don't need to sort M&M's into single colors like Peter did to really bring a strong sense of purpose alive. Teams can do a lot to recognize each team member's contributions, make sure that the team's efforts as a whole are seen and recognized, and demonstrate how the organization's overall mission is translated into action and outcomes.

Seeing the impact of our work is especially meaningful and motivating when we hear directly from people who were helped. Imagine you were making cold calls to fundraise for scholarships for your alma mater. Would you be more motivated if you first heard a personal story from a scholarship recipient who shared poignantly about how the money funded them through college before you start making calls? A study from Wharton School's Adam Grant found that you might raise almost 400% more after hearing such a personal and impactful story directly from the person who benefited.[17]

Though everyone's sense of what is meaningful will vary, research on meaningful work shows that people tend to find their work more worthwhile when they have a sense of helping others (called "task significance"). In the first longitudinal study on this, Blake Allan at Purdue University conducted a survey of over 600 university alumni to ask them about the significance of their work. The survey asked how much they agreed with statements like: "My job provides opportunities to substantially improve the welfare of others." The study found that the more people believed in the significance of their work, the greater the sense of meaning they had later on.[18] In other words, significant tasks lead to an ongoing sense of purpose. Allan himself suggests that employers might help workers to find more meaning by helping them make contact with the people who benefit from their work.[19]

You might consider who your team could hear from that can share about the positive impact of their work and help enhance this sense of meaning. Which stakeholders, clients, or customers (internal or external to your organization) might be excited to share their story?

One reason we need to see the positive impact of our efforts is that negative emotions weigh more heavily than positive ones.[20] Though we thrive on feeling valued, appreciated, and positive, it takes effort to create and reinforce the positive. Team dynamics are a critical place to enhance positive meaning. In a connected and well-functioning team, individual teammates will be motivated to support one another and contribute to the overall performance of the team and organization. Team practices can increase the awareness and motivational drive of this sense of helpfulness.

MICRO-PRACTICE

Your **team meeting** can start with a short check-in round where each person shares one way their work has helped others or each person might share something helpful another teammate did for them.

At a **team off-site, or as a quarterly check-in**, your team can spend time reflecting on how your work has helped others, including stakeholders or customers, other teams, the organization as a whole, and perhaps the industry or world as a whole. You might break your team into smaller groups to brainstorm and have each come back and share.

Recognition Versus Appreciation

You can probably think of times when your achievements have been recognized—when you made your sales goal, a project launched on time, or you gave a brilliant presentation. But can you remember being appreciated just for who you are? Mike Robbins, author of *Bring Your Whole Self to Work*, highlights the importance of both recognition and appreciation at work. It's important to understand the difference and include both recognition and appreciation for your team.

Robbins describes: "Recognition is about giving positive feedback based on results or performance . . . Appreciation, on the other hand, is about acknowledging a person's inherent value. The point isn't their accomplishments. It's their worth as a colleague and a human being."[21]

Recognition can be formal (a bonus, promotion, or award), or informal (an email or note, verbal thank-you, or public recognition in a meeting). This is meaningful and motivating; we want to feel like our achievements are recognized, both as individuals and as a team. However, recognition is for past performance and is outcome oriented.

Appreciation, on the other hand, doesn't depend on accomplishment. As people inevitably hit challenges, it will be their character, resilience, and sense of purpose that help them continue forward. Appreciation might look like reflecting on a team member's positive qualities, such as if they have been really creative in coming up with new ideas, even if they haven't worked out in the anticipated ways. The point is not to diminish recognition (or let employers off the hook from paying people well), but that appreciation about who your colleagues are is an undervalued form of feedback. Taking time to appreciate the virtues our colleagues bring to the team and ways that they support us is very meaningful and helps create a culture of collaboration.

Some of our favorite (and cost-effective) ways to show appreciation include taking time in team meetings for appreciation, writing timely messages of appreciation (by email, Slack, or even by hand!), and just saying a simple "thank-you" in the course of a meeting or conversation that speaks to someone's positive qualities and character.

MICRO-PRACTICE

Reflect on how you might be more proactive about recognizing and appreciating people you work closely with. As you consider seeing the impact of your team members and the team's work, how can you both recognize their efforts *and* appreciate them for the positive qualities they bring to the team?

WEAVING PURPOSE INTO THE
RHYTHM OF THE BUSINESS

Once a statement of purpose is clear for your team, how do you keep it alive? Inevitably the excitement and momentum of going through a purpose-based process will fade as day-to-day work moves forward and new challenges arise. A team needs rituals to weave purpose into how it works; this could involve incorporating the purpose into discussions, meetings, or other team activities. There should be a way that new team members are introduced to the team's purpose in a meaningful way.

Here are a number of suggestions to consider for how you can weave purpose into a team's operations. We offer these as ideas that might resonate with you, or—better yet—that you might adopt and make your own in conjunction with your team.

Onboarding New Team Members—One essential ritual involves introducing new team members to the team's purpose in a meaningful way. The team purpose might be shared during the interview process to see how the candidates align with the group's purpose. Then, when the new team member joins, it's essential to find meaningful ways to engage them around the team's shared purpose. This ensures that every member, regardless of when they join, understands and embraces the overarching goals and values guiding the team's efforts. This could be a straightforward process, such as walking through the team's purpose statement together during onboarding, or something creative, like the existing team sharing a skit that shows their purpose and impact and the new hire sharing about their personal sense of meaning and purpose.

Make It Visible—The purpose statement should be visible, whether that's as a poster in the office, a statement at the top of key team documents, a symbol on team member's desks, M&M's, or something else that fits with your way of working.

Annual Goal Setting and Planning—Revisit the team's purpose during annual goal-setting and planning sessions. Aligning objectives with the overarching purpose ensures that the team's long-term vision remains at the forefront of decision-making processes. This is also a time when the team's purpose statement might need to be updated as some goals are achieved and new ones are added, and as the organization shifts strategy.

Purpose in Performance Reviews and Incentives—Integrate the team's purpose into performance reviews and factor it into how raises and bonuses are determined. Assessing individual and collective contributions against the backdrop of the team's purpose reinforces the connection between daily tasks and the broader organizational mission. Make sure that team members are recognized for ways that they contribute to one another's success and to the team functioning well as a whole. Reviews are also a chance to make invisible work visible.

Corning is a great example. Known for their innovative products, like the bespoke gorilla glass made for the iPhone and iPad, in their Corning Fellows Program they evaluate and reward fellows not just for being the lead author on an innovative patent, but also for when they are a supporting author on other people's patents. Corning recognizes and values people who spend time helping and supporting each other.[22] In this way, Corning makes sure that employees' evaluation and financial incentives are aligned with the whole team's success. If an employee's performance—and in turn salary, bonuses, and promotions—is evaluated on individual achievements only, then employees receive the message that their contributions to the greater team aren't as important.

Reconnection in Team Off-Sites and Meetings—Regularly reconnect to the team's purpose during off-site retreats and routine team meetings. This can be done in simple ways, such as opening a meeting by asking the team to share the most meaningful highlights of their work. These occasions can provide longer dedicated time for reflection, sharing, and realignment, fostering a collective commitment to the shared mission. Giving team members quiet time to reflect or journal on their own, or share in smaller groups of two or three, and then rejoin the whole can be a powerful way to deepen understanding.

Assign Tasks with Purpose and Strengths in Mind—If you're a manager, when assigning tasks, consider the purpose and the strengths of individual members. As a team member, advocate for taking on work that aligns with your sense of purpose, as we saw in chapter 4's Fulfillment Zone exercise. This not only ensures that responsibilities are distributed effectively but also allows team members to contribute in ways that allow greater resonance between their skills and the team's overarching goals.

Learn Together—Help purpose be contagious by encouraging people to share strengths and interests. This also helps to establish a culture of continuous learning by encouraging people to teach and mentor one another. Encouraging team members to share anything from new useful tools to specific skills to areas of knowledge that are related to the team's work fosters a collaborative environment. You might encourage people to share, but don't force them to or it will become a chore rather than a meaningful activity.

Share Purpose and Impact with Other Teams—Promote cross-functional collaboration by sharing your team's purpose and its impact with other teams in the organization. This enhances transparency and also facilitates a broader understanding and appreciation of the collective goals. Sharing can be straightforward (e.g., an email bulletin) or more connecting (perhaps a joint team meeting) or creative and fun (a video montage or collage!).

Inform Decisions with Purpose—Infuse purpose into decision-making processes, whether it involves hiring new team members or selecting projects. Considering the alignment of decisions with the team's purpose ensures that every action contributes to the larger mission. Your team might already have some decision-making framework that purpose can be woven into, or you might create a new, simple practice. For example, there can be a team practice before making a big decision, or when there are differences of opinion, to pause and ask: How does this support our team's mission? Just stopping to consider this question helps to realign the team and depersonalizes the conversation, allowing for broader perspectives.

Weaving Purpose into Your Team

Consider the list above in light of how your team operates, including the cadence and content of team meetings and off-sites, your planning and review process, how you work with other teams, and how you currently celebrate successes.

- Which ideas might be easiest to implement?
- Which ideas might be most meaningful and impactful?
- Do any of these ideas align with things that your team has already been asking for more of?
- Where do you feel the most personal excitement to try something with your team?

Consider these ideas as a starting point to be customized and integrated organically into your team's culture. There might be a process of experimentation, testing out a few of these ideas to see which work well for your team; continue those that work and adjust or let go of those that don't. The goal is not just to follow a set of practices but to make them uniquely yours, reflecting the collective identity and purpose that drive your team forward.

LETTING THE PROCESS BE IMPERFECT

As you engage your team around the topic of purpose, remember that purpose is a process, an evolving journey of alignment. The more awareness you and your team members build, the more aligned action you'll be able to take. More action, in turn, creates more awareness, and might require adjustments in your understanding of purpose and actions that enhance it.

For example, the team's purpose statement likely won't capture everything in the organization's purpose statement. The team's statement should contribute to the full organization, but it will define the more specific role the team is playing. As the goals or organization of the whole organization change, the team's contribution will likely need to shift, too, which might require team members to use different strengths, take on new roles, or create meaning in new ways.

Evoking purpose with your team might also bring up challenges to address. Perhaps the team doesn't feel like their work is recognized by another team or the organization as a whole and believes new ways of sharing impact more publicly are needed. Or perhaps team members don't feel like their work is very meaningful, maybe projects are canceled, or they can't see the big picture. The process might need to be an ongoing one to figure out why there isn't a greater sense of meaning, what can be cultivated, and what the team might need for greater alignment and motivation.

As you finish this section on creating purpose for your team, we suggest you think of all of the exercises and ways of engaging we've shared as a menu. You don't need to eat every item! You might start where you had the most excitement and energy, or where you think the team could benefit most, or you might find a way to gather some input from the team. Importantly, don't let perfection be the enemy of creating and sharing something useful. The best you can do is to start, to let people know that finding purpose is a process, and engage them in an ongoing and deepening ripening of purpose, meaning, and collaboration as a team.

Of course, your team purpose relies on connecting to a strong organizational purpose. If your organization's purpose is unclear or the organization is not fully enacting it, the whole company might be due for its own Purpose Reset, which is the focus of the next section.

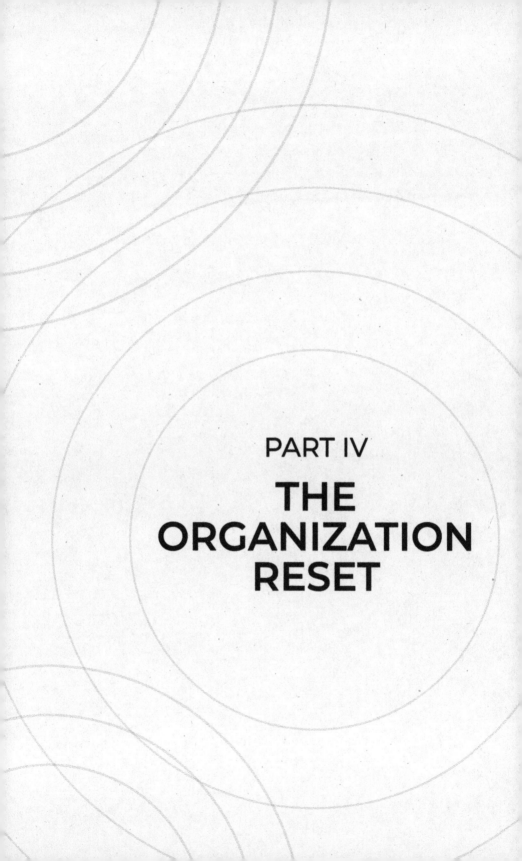

PART IV

THE ORGANIZATION RESET

CHAPTER 9

The Importance of an Organization's Purpose

U p until this point we have addressed aspects of purpose that we would call "experience near"—your personal purpose and the purpose of a team you might work on. In transitioning now to consider the purpose of an organization you work for, we acknowledge that we may be moving into a more "experience distant" or abstract idea of purpose. Try this thought experiment: When you think about the company you work for or some of the everyday companies whose products and services you use, what comes to mind? How often do you ask the question, "How does this company define its purpose?" Yet the purpose of the organizations that we put our effort toward, that employ us and take up so much of our waking hours, matters greatly for both our experience of work and for the success of the organization itself.

In this chapter we will explore why the purpose of an organization matters to both the people within the organization and also its external stakeholders. We will also discuss how purpose is critical for long-term success, and explore what makes up an organization's purpose. Let's begin with why purpose is important in organizational life.

ORGANIZATIONS GET ORGANIZED
AROUND PURPOSE

An organization's purpose is especially important for the stakeholders that arguably fuel its success: its employees. A company's purpose can offer a sense of meaning, structure, and direction for its employees. When employees understand how their roles and personal sense of purpose contribute to the broader purpose and mission of the organization, they are more likely to feel that their work is important and impactful. Research indicates that purpose-driven companies outperform their peers in terms of employee satisfaction and loyalty.[1] Employees who feel aligned with their company's purpose are 79% more motivated to work and 33% less likely to leave their jobs. They are more engaged and committed, and report higher levels of productivity and job satisfaction. [2]

Purpose also provides a framework that guides decision-making and prioritization within an organization. This sense of direction is critical for employees as it helps them understand what is expected of them and how they can contribute to the organization's success. Employees who believe in their company's purpose are more likely to trust their leaders and feel confident in the strategic direction of the company.[3]

When employees infuse internal processes—from product development to research and development to sales and marketing—with a strong sense of purpose, it shows. It's then translated into products, services, and operations in service of that cause. Customers may not explicitly think about the company's purpose, but they can see it in their products, communications, interactions, and beyond. Customers can feel purpose alignment and they can also feel it when a company isn't aligned with a purpose they care about. In the next few chapters, we'll see the profound impact this purpose alignment has across the organization (this chapter), how to build more awareness of whether your organization is aligned with its stated purpose (chapter 10), and how to take action for a Purpose Reset (chapter 11).

PURPOSE RESET IN ORGANIZATIONS: AWARENESS + ALIGNED ACTION

The journey to a Purpose Reset for an organization begins with two fundamental components of purpose that we've previously described: awareness and aligned action.

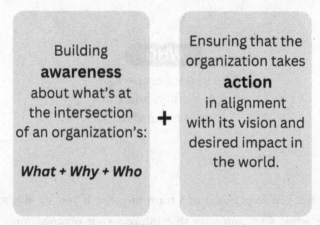

Building **awareness** about what's at the intersection of an organization's:

What + Why + Who

+

Ensuring that the organization takes **action** in alignment with its vision and desired impact in the world.

Awareness

Awareness involves being able to recognize and articulate the organization's core purpose—the reason it exists beyond making a profit or providing a service. Some interesting examples of organizational purpose include IKEA's purpose, "To create a better everyday life for the many people"; Spotify's, "Unlock the potential of human creativity"; and Unilever's, "To make sustainable living commonplace." Beyond grand statements, however, for an organization's purpose to be effectively enacted in the world, awareness and integration of purpose must permeate every level, from the executive suite to the frontline employees. Purpose then can inform every aspect of the organization's culture and operations. But in order for people, culture, and operations all to align on and integrate purpose, a deep awareness of the organization's strengths, values, and desired impact in the world (its what, why, and who) that inform the organization's purpose is necessary.

WHAT
Our strengths and skills.

WHY
Our values and intentions.

WHO
The impact on people, community, and the world around us.

Whether you are a leader or a team member, if you are able to understand the what, why, and who that informs your organization's purpose you can take the next step and integrate purpose into the actions and decisions you undertake in your everyday work in the organization. Sometimes building awareness can also highlight the ways an organization might not be staying true to its what, why, and who—what we call "purpose drift" (something we will explore in greater detail in the next chapter). Even then, the awareness of the gap between purpose and its practice in an organization can highlight the need for a Purpose Reset.

Aligned Action

"Aligned action" is the process of translating awareness into your day-to-day actions and decisions that align with and deliver on the organization's purpose. Aligned action is possible to varying degrees for everyone in an organization—not just its leaders. Ideally, every action and decision, from hiring practices to product development to customer service, should be made with the organization's purpose in mind. The actions of everyone in the organization will demonstrate how clearly aligned or misaligned it is with its core purpose.

PURPOSE AS "FIRST PRINCIPLE" OF ORGANIZATIONAL LIFE

Given the primary role that purpose plays in every aspect of an organization's success, purpose is nothing less than a "first principle" in organizational life. In the fields of science and philosophy dating all the way back to Aristotle's first book on physics,[4]

A first principle represents the base, primary, or foundational concept upon which all other ideas and concepts are built.

Purpose functions as a first principle for building a high-level road map for how the organization will make good on its strengths, values, and intended impact in the world. Purpose as a first principle can guide an organization from its founding through growth and scaling. Airbnb, for example, has successfully harnessed its purpose to scale itself into a global company.

Airbnb is now a household brand in most parts of the world, but in 2008 it was just an idea dreamed up by two friends and roommates who could not make their rent. In order to make some supplemental income, the two friends, Brian Chesky and Joe Gebbia, decided to put an air mattress in an empty room in their apartment and make it a kind of bed-and-breakfast to earn some extra cash during the weekend a very large conference was scheduled to take place in their hometown of San Francisco.

It also wasn't any old conference coming to town; it was the International Council of Societies of Industrial Design / Industrial Designers Society of America (ICSID/IDSA) World Congress, an international design conference, and Chesky and Gebbia were recent art school graduates and designers themselves. So the IDSA conference was meaningful to them, they knew it would be big and draw in people from all over the world, and they knew the creative types who would be attending.

The two friends then deliberately set about publicizing their offbeat but economical idea of an "airbed & breakfast." They created a clever website they knew would appeal to the creative crowd at the conference. In fact, Chesky and Gebbia went a step further and touted the hyper-local aspect of their airbed & breakfast offering, describing it (truthfully) as "two designers create a new way to connect at this year's IDSA conference."[5] They put the word out on design blogs and the website of the conference organizers, who thought it was a fun and novel idea.

Immediately Chesky and Gebbia had takers and their "airbed & breakfast" was booked for the full weekend. Their very first guest, Amol Surve, was an international student from Mumbai who had recently graduated and was on a tight budget. He described the "airbed & breakfast" offering this way: "I was trying to hack and go to the conference, and they were trying to hack and make rent. It was, like, a perfect match." Two other guests also booked to stay on air mattresses in Chesky and Gebbia's apartment, and a business was born.

A year later, in 2009, Chesky and Gebbia formalized and pitched their business to investors, with the guiding purpose that "AirBed & Breakfast" allowed customers to "book rooms with locals, rather than hotels." Today, as of the writing of this book, Airbnb (they changed the name of the business later in 2009) is a global company operating across 220+ countries and regions with 7.7+ million annual listings and 1.5+ million guest visits booked.

In many ways, the first principle of "booking rooms with locals, rather than hotels" is still the operating ethos, though they have refined that purpose into the mission statement, "to create a world where anyone can belong anywhere." The first principle still informs Airbnb's culture and how its people work together today, with a focus on how "our creativity allows us to imagine new possibilities, our responsibility to all of our stakeholders, our community based on connection and belonging."[6] Airbnb also allows its employees to live and work anywhere. The ethos of creating a sense of authentic connection and belonging anywhere in the world remains a part of Airbnb's culture. The origin story of Airbnb—and the original purpose—is clearly very much a part of their operating ethos and business model today, only at a much grander scale.

The benefits of a clearly defined and commonly understood purpose are far-reaching for organizations. When looking through the research, we see that purpose-driven organizations have a positive impact on:

1. The people and culture inside of the organization
2. The customers and other stakeholders—any individual, group, or organization that has an interest or concern in an organization
3. The overall performance/success of the organization

Let's look at some examples for each of these categories.

DO EPIC SH*T

When Carolina and Rich worked at Google, its mission statement, "to organize the world's information and make it universally accessible and useful,"[7] felt inspiring to us and to many people who worked there. Google's mission at times did feel "epic" and meaningful at the same time. We found the mission to be simultaneously audacious, daunting, a bit grandiose but nonetheless cool.

In fact, I (Rich) remember walking into work one morning soon after joining Google and seeing a poster on a wall that read, "Do Epic Sh*t." I felt inspired and a little intimidated, but admittedly it was also exciting. What if I showed up every day and worked on epic ways to enable Google's purpose of "organizing the world's information and making it universally accessible and useful"? That orientation was definitely energizing and engaging to me. My role at the time was to lead executive development across the company, which meant that my team and I were responsible for leadership development activities for the senior-most leaders at Google. I saw my role as helping to build and expand the capability of those senior leaders so that they were as well equipped as possible in terms of leadership skills to deliver Google's audacious purpose. My personal sense of purpose centered on enabling wise, skillful, and emotionally intelligent leaders, so my personal purpose and Google's purpose aligned in a wonderful way. I saw that my personal purpose could serve Google's purpose well by helping a generation of their leaders uplevel their leadership with much needed capabilities. In many ways, the experience I had with connecting to Google's purpose is the very way that purpose can serve as a guiding principle or North Star for people in an organization: it can serve simultaneously as an anchor point, an aspiration, a source of meaning, and motivation.

The experience we had at Google of how a highly aspirational purpose can motivate its employees isn't that unusual. Studies show that the alignment of an organization's purpose with those of its employees has emerged as a crucial factor in fostering motivation, engagement, and, ultimately, sustainable growth. A clear and well-defined organization purpose attracts and motivates employees and creates a strong organizational culture. A *Harvard Business Review* Employee Engagement Survey[8] found that organizations with a high level of alignment between their purpose and that of their employees had, on average:

- 37% higher employee retention rates
- 42% lower absenteeism
- 26% higher profitability

These results indicate that aligning organizational and individual purpose leads to tangible benefits that positively impact organizations.

Purpose Enhances Motivation and Employee Engagement

As we've mentioned, employees are more likely to feel a sense of meaning and fulfillment in their work when they understand how their efforts contribute to a larger purpose. Research[9] also clearly shows that when employees are engaged, satisfied, and have a clear sense of the organization's purpose, they generally are more motivated and productive. Why does engagement matter? Engaged individuals are not just passively fulfilling tasks; they are actively invested in their work and its end result. It matters for organizations because if employees aren't engaged, the business suffers. Badly.

Organizational studies present evidence that employee engagement has an impact on key business outcomes that include absenteeism, turnover, safety (at-work accidents), product quality, cross-functional collaboration, employee commitment, resilience, and productivity. What's more, a Gallup report found that when comparing employee engagement levels between top- and bottom-quartile business units and teams within organizations, there was a 23% increase in profitability, the ultimate desired financial outcome.[10] The same report identifies purpose as one of the five drivers of employee engagement. Without question, purpose matters in terms of our engagement and motivation as employees, with direct repercussions on the business.

Purpose Fuels Innovation

Purpose-driven organizations are also more likely to foster a culture of innovation. Employees who understand and connect with the company's purpose are more motivated to contribute ideas and take initiative. Think about some of the big innovations that you've encountered and chances are they were fueled by an organization with a distinct purpose. We've already mentioned Google's "organize the world's information and make it universally accessible and useful." Another example is Merck Pharmaceuticals' purpose, "To use science to save and improve lives around the world,"[11] which it drew on to develop the world's #1 top-selling drug, Keytruda (widely used to fight an array of cancers, it has generated over $200 billion in revenue over its lifetime).[12] Similarly, Procter & Gamble's purpose is to "provide branded products and services of superior value and quality to improve the lives of the world's consumers,"[13] and it has given those consumers innovations such as Tide laundry detergent (the first heavy-duty laundry detergent available to consumers), Pampers diapers (the first highly absorbent, disposable diapers), Head & Shoulders (the first two-in-one shampoo and conditioner), and the Swiffer WetJet (creating a simpler, more efficient way to clean). These clear purpose statements support innovation. Research by McKinsey & Company[14] suggests that organizations with a strong sense of purpose are more likely to encourage risk-taking and experimentation, key components of an innovation culture. Additionally, a report by Deloitte highlights that purpose-driven companies are better at leveraging diverse perspectives and creative problem-solving, leading to more innovative outcomes.[15]

A great example of a purpose-driven culture of innovation that resulted in one of the great turnarounds in history is the story of Lego. Many of us may have memories of Lego, and it's no wonder—Lego has been one of the world's most recognizable toy brands since its founding in 1928. That being the case, it underwent a significant turnaround in the early 2000s when it almost went bankrupt after investing in products and services like clothing, theme parks, television shows, and video games that did not powerfully deliver against its core purpose, "to inspire and develop the builders of tomorrow."[16] In order to create a turnaround, Lego divested from its poorly performing businesses and refocused on its core purpose and values to create a transformation that brought it from a company on the brink of bankruptcy to a thriving global powerhouse, at times showing more growth than companies like Apple and eclipsing other global toy brands such as Mattel and Hasbro.

Lego, as part of its turnaround strategy in the early 2000s through today, draws on its purpose to drive continuous innovation in product development and educational initiatives. Lego has consistently introduced new and innovative product lines that engage children in creative play while also incorporating educational elements. For instance, Lego Education offers products designed to teach science, technology, engineering, and math (STEM) concepts through hands-on learning. Lego has also committed to sustainable practices by aiming to produce all core products and packaging from sustainable materials by 2030. This includes developing new bio-based plastics and investing in renewable energy. These efforts have reinforced Lego's reputation as a forward-thinking and responsible company, driving customer loyalty and opening new markets in education, entertainment (Lego movies), and sustainability.

Lego's turnaround is a testament to the power of strategic focus, purpose-driven innovation, and a deep understanding of core brand values.[17] By returning to its purpose and its roots and engaging with its loyal customer base, Lego not only avoided bankruptcy but also reestablished itself as a leading global brand.

Purpose Supports Organizational Resilience

When an organization faces challenging circumstances, having a well-defined purpose can also serve as a guiding force to help employees navigate difficult times. Microsoft is an example of an organization that harnessed its mission to create a Purpose Reset, exercise resilience, and emerge from a difficult period with success.

In the early 2010s, Microsoft faced significant challenges. The company was struggling to stay relevant in the rapidly evolving technology industry, particularly with the rise of mobile and cloud computing. Competitors like Apple and Google were dominating the mobile market, and Microsoft's traditional software business model was under threat. The company also had to navigate internal cultural challenges and innovate to remain competitive.[18]

Under the leadership of CEO Satya Nadella, who took the helm in 2014, Microsoft embarked on a transformative journey by coming back to its purpose during that critical period. According to Nadella, speaking of that time, "Every person, organization, and even society reaches a point at which they owe it to themselves to hit refresh—to re-energize, renew, reframe, and rethink their purpose."[19] Harnessing this purpose, Nadella and team shifted the company's focus toward cloud computing and productivity solutions, aligning with its purpose of empowerment. Then and now, Microsoft describes its purpose, "to empower every person and every organization on the planet to achieve more."[20] Microsoft made a strategic pivot to cloud computing with its Azure platform as well as its Office 365 suite, which created a cloud-based subscription model but also offered users continuous updates and seamless collaboration tools, empowering them to work more efficiently and effectively. Microsoft also embraced open-source software development for the first time and acquired GitHub, all of which aligned with its purpose of empowering developers and fostering innovation. Microsoft's latest moves also include major investments in artificial intelligence, including its 49% investment stake in OpenAI and build-out of Microsoft AI across its product sets.

Microsoft's purpose-driven approach under Nadella's leadership led to exemplary organizational resilience and a remarkable turnaround. The shift to cloud computing and a subscription-based model significantly boosted Microsoft's financial performance. Microsoft regained its relevance in the tech industry, becoming a leader in cloud computing, AI, and productivity solutions. The company's stock price soared, reflecting investor confidence in its long-term strategy. Microsoft's turnaround helps illustrate how purpose helps leaders and team members make strategic decisions, prioritize, and maintain a sense of stability during challenging times.[21]

> **Innovation and resilience often go hand in hand as innovation requires that an organization navigate its failures and keep focused on improvement *not despite but because of* the setbacks that it experienced.**

During the pandemic, the three of us were working as part of the leadership team at the Search Inside Yourself Leadership Institute (SIYLI). Like many organizations, we faced unprecedented challenges as the lockdowns caused us to lose most of our customers and revenue. Our strength has always been delivering live, in-person training focused on developing professional and personal skills centered on mental and emotional well-being, emotional intelligence, resilience, and thriving. However, within a span of less than three months, we experienced an 80% revenue loss for the year due to widespread cancellations.

Despite these setbacks, the core purpose of SIYLI—to enable the practices of science-based mindfulness and emotional intelligence—remained clear and deeply felt by our team. We recognized that the skills we taught were precisely what the world needed during the crisis.

It would not be an exaggeration to say that everyone on the team felt deeply aligned with the organization's purpose because it also aligned with their personal sense of purpose as dedicated practitioners of mindfulness and emotional intelligence in their own lives. The main work of the team was to connect this powerful sense of alignment with the work that lay ahead to reinvent the business. Driven by this sense of deep alignment, we were all able to tap into the personal and collective sense of motivation to reinvent the business for all-digital delivery, adapt to the new needs in the world, and rethink everything we had done previously to ensure survivability.

In a span of a few weeks, we successfully reformatted our content and launched our newly designed virtual offerings. Initially, the response was slow, but as our customers adapted to the new normal, we saw a steady increase in demand for our virtual training sessions. By the end of the year, a significant portion of our business had returned, and we were able to support our community with brand-new resilience and mindfulness-based programming, key skills during such a difficult and uncertain time.

In retrospect, it's clear to us that our compelling purpose provided the motivation and direction needed to navigate the crisis. The collective commitment of our team to our shared purpose was a driving force behind our successful transformation. By staying true to our purpose and adapting quickly to new circumstances, we were able to not only survive but also continue to make a positive impact in the lives of our clients and program participants.

WHEN PURPOSE INSPIRES TRUST IN THE BRAND

Up until this point, we have discussed the importance of purpose within an organization and its power and impact as an organizing principle for those who work within it. However, the way stakeholders outside of the organization understand and perceive its purpose is equally crucial. External stakeholders—encompassing the public at large, customers, investors, regulators, and anyone else who can influence the success or failure of an organization—play a pivotal role in shaping the organization's ability to achieve its goals.

Understanding and engaging with these external stakeholders is essential because while internal teams are responsible for creating the products and services that embody the organization's purpose, it is the external stakeholders who ultimately support or hinder the realization of this purpose. The public's perception, customer loyalty, investor confidence, and regulatory approval are all factors that can significantly impact an organization's journey toward fulfilling its mission. By understanding the perspectives and needs of external stakeholders, organizations can create a harmonious relationship that not only supports their purpose but also drives sustainable success and positive impact in the broader community.

Customers today often seek more than just products or services; they look for brands with a purpose that aligns with their own values. A well-defined purpose can create a strong emotional connection between a company and its customers, fostering loyalty and trust. Having a clear and powerfully articulated purpose enhances an organization's brand reputation, customer satisfaction, and loyalty, all of which contribute to not only profitability but also sustainability.[22] In fact, 65% of consumers prefer to buy from purpose-driven brands, according to Accenture's Global Consumer Pulse Research from 2018.[23] Additionally, according to the same survey, 62% of customers want companies to take a stand on current and broadly relevant issues.

Some customers may even take a stand themselves and actively boycott companies when they perceive a company's purpose and values are not in alignment with their own. Examples of companies consumers have boycotted for a range of social and political reasons include Amazon (for its anti-union practices), McDonald's (for their perceived support for Israel during the war in Gaza), and Nestlé (for its aggressive sales and marketing of infant formula to new mothers). Clearly, as these examples illustrate, an organization's purpose and values can have a powerful impact on customer behavior, including buy/no-buy and boycott decisions that can significantly affect company success and the brand reputation.

According to the World Economic Forum,[24] 70% of consumers across the globe buy products and services from organizations that they feel are aligned in terms of purpose and values. Similarly, brand purpose and Environmental, Social, and Governance (ESG) considerations account for purchasing criteria for more than half of consumers globally, according to a Bain & Company report.[25] Purpose-driven companies, many with ESG-forward business practices, include Patagonia, BlackRock, Procter & Gamble, Caterpillar, Siemens AG, Salesforce, and Unilever.[26, 27]

A strong sense of purpose extends beyond aligning a company's internal operations; it is a powerful tool for building trust with a diverse range of external stakeholders, including investors, partners, and the broader community. An organization's commitment to a clear and meaningful purpose signals a dedication to a set of clear values, business practices, and social responsibility, fostering confidence and loyalty across various stakeholder groups.

Many investors, for example, are looking for companies that are not only financially sound but also align with their values, whether they are based on social, environmental, and/or ethical business practices and governance. One global survey[28] of individual investors found that 77% of them are interested in investing in companies or funds that aim to achieve market-rate financial returns while at the same time accounting for positive social or environmental impact. Of these same investors, 57% also indicated that their interest in these impact investments has increased in the last two years, and 54% say that they anticipate increasing their investments in sustainable investments in the next year. Similarly, 69% of European institutional investors and 50% of North American institutional investors say that consideration of ESG criteria is a part of their investment decisions, and 63% of all respondents say that they consider ESG because it offers a more "holistic" view of risk than standard investment frameworks.[29] So, for a large and potentially increasing number of investors, purpose-driven practices, many linked to ESG approaches, are important criteria.

Business partners seek reliability and shared values in their collaborations. A company with a well-defined purpose can attract and maintain strong partnerships by demonstrating a commitment to ethical practices and mutual goals. Companies like Adobe, which emphasize creativity and innovation, foster strong partnerships with other businesses and organizations that share these values, enhancing mutual trust and long-term collaboration.[30]

Finally, a company's engagement with the broader community significantly influences its reputation and social license to operate. Purpose-driven organizations that actively contribute to social and environmental causes earn (or lose!) trust and goodwill from the communities they serve. For example, Starbucks engages with communities through various initiatives aimed at social impact and sustainability. The company's commitment to ethically sourced coffee, reducing environmental footprints, and community service projects such as the Starbucks Foundation's support for youth, refugees, and veterans demonstrates its focus on social responsibility. These efforts are consistent with Starbucks's mission to "inspire and nurture the human spirit, one person, one cup, and one neighborhood at a time."[31] On the other hand, Starbucks has also been the target of public criticism, especially over the past decade, ranging from topics related to fair trade, marketing campaigns, and political positions. There's even a Wikipedia entry focusing solely on criticism of Starbucks, and numerous news articles discussing the economic impact of public criticism and boycotts on its stock price. The public notices when companies commit to or move away from their stated mission, which has significant repercussions for the organization.

A clear and compelling purpose serves to build trust with a wide array of external stakeholders, including investors, customers, partners, and the broader community. This trust is essential for long-term success and sustainability, as it fosters loyalty, enhances reputation, and attracts ethical and responsible partnerships, as we'll see in the next section.

MICRO-PRACTICE

- As a consumer, have you ever changed your position or attitude toward a company due to its actions with employees, in the community, or the world? How much does that matter to you when you make a purchase?
- As a leader, have you noticed any positive or negative responses from the public as a result of your organization-wide actions or statements?

ORGANIZATIONAL PERFORMANCE AND SUCCESS

One key distinguishing attribute of an organization with a clear purpose is that it goes hand in hand with long-term value. Companies focused on long-term value creation, driven by a purpose that is well integrated into their culture and operations, outperform their counterparts.[32] Deloitte's Global Human Capital Trends Report 2023,[33] which polled 10,000 business and HR leaders across every industry in 105 participating countries, found that organizations with a strong sense of purpose are not only more likely to have engaged and motivated employees but also 2.2 times more likely to outperform others in terms of financial performance. This data underscores the connection between purpose-driven organizations and their ability to achieve sustainable success.

CASE STUDY: WHY CUSTOMERS LOVE WARBY PARKER

Warby Parker's purpose is to "inspire and impact the world with vision, purpose, and style" and "demonstrate that a business can scale, be profitable, and do good in the world—without charging a premium for it."[34] The company has delivered on every aspect of its purpose statement, creating disruption in the eyewear industry by aligning its business model with its purpose of offering affordable, high-quality, and stylish eyewear while committing to social responsibility.

Warby Parker's mission to "do good in the world—without charging a premium for it" addresses a significant pain point in the eyewear market: the high cost of glasses. Warby Parker disrupted the usual way that glasses are designed, distributed, and bought: by bypassing traditional third-party manufacturing and supply chains and designing their glasses in-house, Warby Parker can offer high-quality eyewear at a fraction of the typical price. This direct-to-consumer model disrupts the market by making stylish, high-quality eyewear accessible to a broader audience.[35] This combination of affordability, convenience, social impact, trendy designs, and excellent customer service has created a popular brand that resonates deeply with customers.

Warby Parker's commitment to social responsibility is also a significant factor in its appeal. The company's "Buy a Pair, Give a Pair" program ensures that for every pair of glasses sold, a pair is distributed to someone in need. This initiative has distributed over 15 million pairs of glasses worldwide, making a substantial impact on global vision health.

Additionally, Warby Parker's focus on sustainability is evident in their use of environmentally friendly materials and practices. Their efforts to minimize their carbon footprint resonate with eco-conscious consumers who prioritize sustainability in their purchasing decisions.

Warby Parker has successfully disrupted the eyewear industry by aligning its business model with its purpose of offering affordable, high-quality, and stylish eyewear while committing to social responsibility.

This chapter's case studies and research are all meant to shed light on the idea that a clear and inspiring purpose benefits all stakeholders in an organization's ecosystem. The organization itself benefits from a clear purpose in that it provides direction, enhances performance, and helps team members deliver impact. For individuals, an organization's purpose can lead to higher levels of motivation, engagement, commitment, well-being, and satisfaction. By taking deliberate steps to define and communicate their purpose, organizations can unlock these benefits and make a positive impact on society and the world while achieving sustainable growth. In the next chapter, we will explore how organizations can bring awareness of purpose forward and what differentiates purpose from vision, mission, strategy, and other guiding principles in organizations.

PURPOSE RESET PRACTICE

Name the Purpose

Try this micro-practice to assess your understanding of your organization's purpose. After you complete the reflection you can compare it to the stated purpose, vision, mission, and/or values of the organization:

Pause and reflect. In one sentence, describe what your organization's purpose is:

- What are its strengths?
- Values?
- Desired impact in the world?

How well does your understanding compare with the stated purpose of the organization?

CHAPTER 10

Developing Awareness of Purpose in Organizations

Unlike individuals and teams who might be building their sense of purpose from scratch, we assume that most organizations already have some sense of purpose in place. However, having a purpose defined on paper is not the same as living it out in everyday operations and decisions. It is fairly common that there is a gap between the aspirations stated in a purpose and the day-to-day operational realities in organizations. Think about your own organization or some of the organizations you might have worked for. How often can you say that they have stayed true to their purpose? Such questions and any gaps they reveal are exactly why we think it is important to build awareness of how purpose operates within an organization. We can begin by looking at how well an organization operates from foundational elements, such as understanding its values, mission, and vision. These elements serve as the bedrock of an organization's identity and guiding principles that together contribute to the fulfillment of its purpose.

**Developing an understanding and
awareness of how well an organization
is fulfilling its purpose requires a shift
from being in autopilot mode—in which
routines and inertia may lead the way—
to a more conscious, intentional state.**

Moving from autopilot to awareness as an organization requires a candid assessment of whether the organization is still aligned with its declared purpose or if a recalibration is necessary. Being honest about the current state of purpose alignment means acknowledging when a small reset might be needed to fine-tune and realign with core values and mission. It also involves recognizing when the organization has significantly drifted from its purpose, necessitating more substantial changes.

This chapter will explore how to build and maintain this awareness, ensuring that the organization's purpose remains a living, breathing part of its culture and operations. We will also explore what happens when, in that honest self-assessment, an organization is no longer operating from its core purpose, what we call the experience of a "purpose drift." As a corrective to purpose drift, we will explore how organizations can create a Purpose Reset. Finally, we will delve into strategies for honest self-assessment, engaging stakeholders in meaningful dialogue, and making the necessary adjustments to realign with the true north of the organization's purpose. By doing so, organizations can navigate a return to being purpose-driven, with integrity, coherence, and a renewed sense of direction.

PURPOSE, VISION, MISSION, AND VALUES

We have described purpose as a "first principle" that is defined by the "what, why, and who" of the organization—its strengths, values, intentions, and impact. Fortunately, there are also other principles that organizations can draw on to help create awareness and clarity: vision, mission, and values.

Let's look more closely at these organizing principles, how they relate to and differ from purpose, and then look at some real-world examples.

Purpose, vision, mission, and values are distinct yet very connected elements that can work dynamically together to structure, define, and guide organizations. According to the Values Institute, "The mission, purpose, vision, and values statements guide a company. Taken together, the statements give the company strategic direction, informing business strategies."[1]

In the context of the Purpose Reset that we discuss in this book, we would like to clearly define the terms in the context of an organization, as follows:

Purpose *is the ongoing process of understanding and connecting strengths, values, and desired impact with aligned actions to unlock your (organization's) full potential and be of service.* The purpose of an organization answers the question about *what* the organization's strengths are, *why* the organization was created (values and intentions), and *who* the organization serves (its impact on people and the world).

Vision *describes how the world would be different if the organization were to achieve its highest aspirations.* For example, the vision of the Search Inside Yourself Leadership Institute from its founding is to "create the conditions for world peace." Vision usually describes an ideal state. As you can see from SIYLI's vision, it is aiming for nothing less than a world where suffering due to deep conflict is eliminated, one in which we all might like to inhabit!

Mission *is a description of how an organization will deliver on its strengths to fulfill its purpose and/or vision.* The mission outlines the specific activities and strategies used to fulfill that purpose. The mission serves as the practical road map to achieve the purpose, and something all internal and external stakeholders can understand and connect with the purpose/vision.

Values *are the principles and ethics that an organization will prioritize while fulfilling its mission.* Values influence decision-making within the mission by helping to define the ethical framework and behaviors expected from employees while executing the mission. Values also tie an organization back to its purpose; in fact, per our previous discussion of the "what, why, who," values are a foundational component that informs intent and impact in an organization.

It is helpful to understand how clarity of purpose combined with a clear vision, mission, and set of values are strong guiding principles for an organization's aspirations and focus and can be highly engaging for its employees as well as customers. Apple, Inc. is a good example of how a compelling brand has been created with a clear purpose, vision, and mission.

Everyone is familiar with Apple products and even its very famous marketing slogans, such as "Think Different." Few people are probably able to clearly articulate Apple's purpose. Apple states that its purpose is to "change the world through technology."[2] It reflects the company's commitment to innovation and improving people's lives through its products. Today, few would deny the fact that Apple is indeed transforming the world through its technology.

Apple's vision is to "create the best products on Earth and to leave the world better than we found it."[3] You can see how this vision is aligned with its purpose, emphasizing the company's aspiration to deliver groundbreaking technology that changes the world for the better. The vision speaks to some elements of its purpose, particularly the impact it hopes to have in fulfilling its purpose.

Next, Apple's mission describes how Apple will fulfill its purpose and vision. Apple's mission is "to bring the best user experience to customers through innovative hardware, software, and services."[4] The mission speaks to the capabilities and strengths of the organization and how those will help inform the fulfillment of its purpose. From early on but especially with the launch of its beautifully designed, simple, and yet robust products such as the iPod, iPhone, MacBook, iPad, and AirPods, Apple has established itself as a design and innovation leader, consistent with its mission.

Finally, Apple's stated values are: Privacy, Environment, Inclusion and Diversity, Racial Equity and Justice, and Supplier Responsibility.[5] These values guide their product development, design, and sustainability efforts, as well as their workplace culture and organizational development.

Apple is a good example of the interlocking but distinct differences between purpose, vision, mission, and values. If operating in an ideal way, the values help guide how the mission and purpose are fulfilled and what the vision of a better world would look like. That being said, there are also clear examples where Apple does not live up to these ideals. Reports of horrible working conditions in its supplier factories such as Foxxcon and the suicides that resulted as a consequence of the despair of its workers are a major issue for Apple.[6] What can be described as monopolistic or exploitative practices in its App Store also suggest that Apple is not aligning well with its stated values around innovation and inclusion.[7] And there may be open questions for many as to whether building beautifully designed, innovative, and compelling smartphones justifies some of the social ills that result from the misuse of such compelling technology.[8]

The complexity of Apple's business and vision, contrasted with the reality of the impact that the company can have on its stakeholders and customers, is a powerful demonstration of the importance of checking an organization's impact against its stated purpose and values. Whatever view you may take on Apple's purpose and related vision, mission, and values and how the company delivers on them, these organizing concepts are enduring for Apple and have informed—to greater and lesser degrees, depending on your perspective—the company's operating model.

It may seem from our definitions and the discussion above that an organization's purpose would be very clear for everyone in the organization. That isn't always the case. In fact, it's quite common to *not* hear leaders and members of an organization speak about the purpose that an organization serves in the world. Often they will instead describe new strategies and products or discuss the organization's financial performance or impact. Why is that? In these cases, it's likely the organization is experiencing purpose drift.

When people aren't talking about purpose in an organization very much at all, it is often a sign that the organization has "drifted" from its original purpose and that the reality inside the organization is far different from its original purpose.

When an organization experiences purpose drift, it means it is operating in a way that is not in accordance with its strengths, values, and desired impact in the world.

THE PURPOSE DRIFT VERSUS THE PURPOSE RESET

Purpose-aligned organizations commit every aspect of the organization's operations, from strategic decision-making to everyday interactions with employees, customers, and stakeholders, to deliver on their purpose. In such organizations, the purpose acts as a North Star, guiding actions and decisions, and ensuring that all efforts align with the overarching mission. Over time, this alignment between purpose and action builds trust, loyalty, and a strong reputation in the marketplace.[9]

In contrast, an organization that has experienced purpose drift has deviated from its original purpose, mission, and values. This can happen for various reasons, such as shifting market dynamics, leadership changes, or short-term pressures overshadowing long-term goals. When purpose drift occurs, it can erode trust, disengage employees, and confuse stakeholders about the organization's true values. This drift often occurs gradually, as the organization responds to external pressures, market demands, or leadership changes without maintaining a clear focus on its core purpose.

Customers and partners may become disillusioned if they perceive the organization as insincere or opportunistic. According to a Pew Research Center survey,[10] for example, public perception of technology companies has become increasingly negative over the past few years. The percentage of people who view tech companies positively dropped from 71% to 50% between

2017 and 2021. This decline is attributed to various factors, including perceived overreach, inadequate handling of data privacy, and failure to address social responsibilities effectively. This erosion of trust highlights the critical impact of purpose drift on public perception and stakeholder trust. Similarly, a report by Accenture[11] emphasizes that younger generations, particularly millennials and Gen Z, are highly attuned to corporate purpose. These consumers are quick to shift their loyalty away from brands that do not consistently demonstrate their stated values through their actions. The research indicates that companies failing to authentically live out their purpose risk losing market share and consumer loyalty, with purpose-driven brands being more likely to retain customers and command higher spending.

If there is purpose drift in the organization, take it as an opportunity to create a Purpose Reset.

What is critically important during a purpose drift is for the organization's leaders, employees, and all other stakeholders (board members, customers, shareholders) to be open, honest, and authentic about the drift, and then take action to rectify it by recommitting themselves to being a purpose-aligned organization.

To correct purpose drift and realign with their core mission and values, organizations need to undergo a Purpose Reset that includes regular self-assessment, transparent communications, leadership commitment, cultural integration of purpose, and purpose-driven strategies and decision-making. By taking these steps, organizations can correct course when they stray and ensure they remain true to their foundational purpose.

Ultimately, purpose drift can undermine the organization's long-term success and stability, as the foundational purpose and principles that once drove its achievements become obscured or neglected. Let's look at recent examples of successful Purpose Resets (CVS Health and Pixar) and one example of a company that has experienced purpose drift (Boeing).

CASE STUDY: CVS HEALTH

In 2014, news headlines in the United States announced that CVS Pharmacy would become the nation's first drugstore chain to stop selling tobacco products. Leaders at CVS, a public company with more than 300,000 employees and a market capitalization of more than $130 billion as of the writing of this book, realized that selling tobacco didn't align with its purpose statement of "helping people on their path to better health," among other reasons. CVS didn't just remove tobacco from its retail stores; it urged other retailers to follow suit, and kicked off a variety of smoking cessation campaigns to help people quit smoking. The company also rebranded as CVS Health to reflect its broader commitment to healthcare.[12]

As expected, CVS lost $2 billion in annual cigarette sales in the first year of its new policy. This initially created a huge concern for stockholders. Yet, pharmacy sales jumped. According to a Salesforce .org analysis, "These changes resulted in a 10% increase in revenue, notably via growth in pharmacy benefits management—a business play that might not have been possible without its renewed focus on purpose. Living its purpose also led CVS to a $69 billion merger with Aetna and significant stock gains."[13]

Eliminating tobacco products from its retail stores was a key step for CVS Health to align its operations with its larger purpose and to reflect consumer demands. At the time the decision was made, CVS found that 62% of adults agreed that retailers had an obligation to limit access to tobacco products.

Most recently, given the rise in teen e-cigarette use, CVS started to create multimillion-dollar initiatives to prevent youth smoking, including a pledge not to work with advertising or public relations agencies who work with tobacco and e-cigarette companies.[14] "This hasn't been just a nice-to-do strategy or a PR initiative, this is a fundamental way we go about our business," stated Eileen Howard Boone, former SVP of Corporate Social Responsibility & Philanthropy at CVS.[15]

And while CVS Health still sells many other products that can be harmful to people's health, such as food with high sugar content and alcoholic beverages, they continue to take action toward increasingly greater alignment with their mission. CVS Health shows us how the Purpose Reset is a dynamic and ongoing journey, one that needs to adapt to the zeitgeist.

Admitting When You're Off Purpose

CVS Health admirably recognized that selling tobacco products was misaligned with its purpose—that it had experienced a purpose drift—and was willing to risk revenue to correct it. It can be challenging to admit that your organization has drifted away from its core purpose, but a drift is not unusual.

> **To admit that you have experienced purpose drift, you need a culture (in your own mind, team, and organization) where it is safe to make mistakes.**

A great example of an organizational culture that has consistently promoted openness, vulnerability, and psychological safety is Pixar Animation Studios. Pixar's culture of psychological safety allows team members to share ideas freely, take risks, and learn from failures without fear of retribution.[16] The company's unique culture has been pivotal in its success, allowing team members across the organization to openly share input, experiment, and cocreate iconic and beloved movies, including *Toy Story*, *Finding Nemo*, *Up*, and *Inside Out*, among others. This type of culture of psychological safety is helpful to draw on not only when creating innovative products and services but also when needing to address critical aspects of the culture, including the capacity to admit that you've drifted away from your declared sense of mission and purpose.[17]

It's also helpful to recognize that we humans will do a lot to justify our actions! Social psychologist Elliot Aronson describes this as "cognitive dissonance reduction." When we experience dissonance—a mismatch between our intentions or identity and our actual impact—it gets uncomfortable. The mismatch can lead to rumination, keep us up at night, and challenge beliefs we have about ourselves as good people. We naturally want to reduce this sense of dissonance and discomfort by creating justifications for our behaviors or by opting to actually change our behaviors. In an interview with Aronson, Adam Grant discusses the example of a prosecutor who refused to recognize DNA evidence that would exonerate people they had put in prison.[18] Because the idea that they put away innocent people was so against the prosecutor's self-concept, they were not able to take in and act on the new DNA evidence.

To really admit when we've gotten away from our purpose, we have to be willing to look at things anew and not just rationalize our past decisions. It's helpful to remember that purpose is a process, and feedback about where you're off target is needed to help you realign. When employees are experiencing high levels of stress and/or burnout, that can be a cue that a purpose reset is needed. Other signals that a purpose reset may be needed include high attrition, divisive and highly political work cultures, poor performance across multiple teams, diminishing quality of products and services, and exceedingly low trust in leadership.

MICRO-PRACTICE

Ask yourself these questions as you think about your organization's purpose and potential purpose drift, and notice what comes up:

- What am I (are we) justifying in my/our work or on behalf of my/our organization that I'm actually a little uncomfortable with?
- Where am I resisting taking in feedback about the organization?
- Are there stakeholders in this organization that are unwilling to care about the feedback about the organization that is shared with them?

Notice any tension that arises as you answer these questions for yourself. It could be a sign that there is purpose drift in your organization.

If a purpose drift is left unaddressed in an organization, it may fundamentally change the culture and operating models of the organization—often for the worse.

It is one thing to change the purpose of an organization intentionally to optimize the impact of its original purpose or update it. It is entirely another thing to allow a purpose drift to occur and not address it, or worse, to fundamentally change the purpose of an organization such that it moves away from its values and a sense of integrity. As of the writing of this book, the plight of the storied aerospace engineering company Boeing presents us with a cautionary tale about what happens when a purpose drift permeates the culture of an organization and has disastrous effects both within the organization and, perhaps even more tragically, for the millions of customers it affects.

PURPOSE DRIFT CASE STUDY: BOEING

Boeing, once a symbol of engineering excellence and corporate integrity, has seen a dramatic decline in its reputation and financial performance over recent years due to purpose drift. The company, previously known for its commitment to safety, quality, integrity, and sustainability, faced significant challenges that highlighted a deviation from its core purpose, mission, and values. These challenges, which began decades ago when the company started to institute aggressive cost-cutting in order to prioritize returns (over quality), culminated in the chain of tragedies and crises involving Boeing's 737 MAX plane. The purpose drift that Boeing has experienced has had profound and far-reaching implications for its reputation, stock price, and overall financial performance.[19]

The Purpose Drift Begins

The beginning of Boeing's decline can be traced back to some of the leadership and strategic changes that went into effect in the late 1990s.[20] In 1997, Boeing's former CEO Philip Condit made the decision to acquire its key competitor, McDonnell Douglas. Compared to Boeing, McDonnell Douglas prioritized cost-cutting and upgrading older airplane models rather than designing and building new planes. Boeing's headquarters were also moved from its original home in Seattle to Chicago to obtain tax benefits. The move effectively separated leadership from the company's main operations and engineers, who remained based in Seattle. The purpose drift had begun: Boeing, which describes its purpose then and now as, "Lead on safety, quality, integrity, and sustainability,"[21] had effectively separated important decision-making, notably including production and quality control, from its operational base.

Next, Boeing transitioned out Philip Condit as CEO and brought in former McDonnell Douglas executive Harry Stonecipher, who reinstituted the cost-cutting focus that was a part of the McDonnell Douglas culture. Stonecipher is on the record stating, "I changed the culture of Boeing, that was the intent, so that it is run like a business rather than a great engineering firm."[22] Stonecipher resigned abruptly two years later after violating the company's code of conduct concerning a conflict of interest in an extramarital affair he had with another Boeing executive.[23]

Unfortunately, the next CEO, Jim McNerney, had only three years of tenure at the company and no background in aviation, and he continued the campaign of cost-cutting and using savings to buy back company stock in order to increase its market value. Boeing at the time (2011) was also facing increasingly stiff competition from Airbus. Manufacturing issues persisted, however, and in 2015 McNerney was replaced as CEO by Dennis Muilenburg, a longtime Boeing employee who started there as in intern in 1985.

Unfortunately, Boeing continued with the approach of upgrading existing planes rather than designing and building new ones (in the interest of speed and cost savings) and opted to undertake a five-year program to upgrade its 737 MAX planes. The aircraft was designed to be a more fuel-efficient version of the popular 737 model. However, it was later discovered that Boeing had implemented a new software system, the Maneuvering Characteristics Augmentation System (MCAS), without adequately informing pilots or providing sufficient training.

This cascade of cost-cutting measures and purpose drift started to translate into fatalities. In October 2018, Lion Air Flight 610 crashed into the Java Sea shortly after takeoff, killing all 189 passengers and crew. Five months later, in March 2019, Ethiopian Airlines Flight 302 crashed under similar circumstances, resulting in 157 fatalities. Both crashes were attributed to the malfunctioning of the MCAS system, which forced the aircraft into a nosedive despite the pilots' attempts to regain control.

Investigations revealed that Boeing had prioritized speed to market and cost-cutting measures over safety and quality. Internal documents showed that some employees had expressed concerns about the safety of the MCAS system but were overridden by management pressures to expedite the aircraft's certification and delivery. This focus on financial performance and market competition over core safety values marked a significant deviation from Boeing's long-standing commitment to engineering excellence and safety.

Impact on Reputation

The fallout from the 737 MAX crashes was severe. The aircraft was grounded worldwide, and Boeing faced intense scrutiny from regulatory bodies, airlines, and the public. The company's reputation for safety and reliability was severely tarnished. In late 2019, Boeing CEO Dennis Muilenburg resigned, and the company underwent leadership changes in an effort to restore trust and realign with its core values. There are even websites and apps that inform passengers if their upcoming flight uses a Boeing plane or not and how to find alternatives.

Financial Consequences

The financial impact of the crisis was profound. Boeing's stock price plummeted as confidence in the company eroded. In the immediate aftermath of the crashes and the subsequent grounding of the 737 MAX, Boeing's market value declined by tens of billions of dollars. The company's stock, which traded at around $440 in early 2019, fell below $100 at the height of the COVID-19 pandemic in March 2020. Undoubtedly, Boeing's poor safety and quality record combined with the massively disruptive effects of the COVID-19 pandemic all contributed to Boeing's decline in value.

Despite efforts to regain certification and bring the 737 MAX back into service, during the early 2020s the financial performance of

Boeing continued to struggle. The company reported significant losses, with billions of dollars spent on compensation to airlines, legal settlements, and additional safety measures.

Long-Term Effects

By 2024, while the 737 MAX had returned to service and Boeing had made some strides in improving its safety protocols and corporate governance, the long-term effects of the crisis were still evident. The company's stock price, while recovering, remained volatile and below its pre-crisis highs.

The erosion of trust among airlines, regulators, and passengers continues to pose challenges for Boeing. Rebuilding its reputation will require a Purpose Reset of its own, with a consistent demonstration of its renewed commitment to safety, transparency, and integrity.

Boeing's deviation from its purpose, mission, and values in favor of financial expediency led to catastrophic consequences for its reputation and financial health. As Boeing navigates its path forward, the lessons from this period serve as a stark reminder of the cost of a purpose drift.

FROM AUTOPILOT TO AWARE OF PURPOSE

The case studies of CVS Health and Boeing are powerful illustrations of why it is important to understand when an organization is in "autopilot mode" and loses awareness of its core purpose and/or prioritizes the wrong things and then experiences purpose drift. In the case of CVS Health, the organization was able to harness its awareness of purpose drift to create a successful Purpose Reset that realigned the organization with its purpose and values. It is unclear as of the writing of this book if Boeing will be able to sustain and integrate the awareness of their purpose drift and right the organization.

We can see from this example that the ingredients for a Purpose Reset begin with awareness and (hopefully) lead to aligned action, so we'd like to return in this next section to the idea of how you might develop awareness of the what, why, and who of purpose in your organization.

MICRO-PRACTICE

Take a moment to shift from autopilot to more awareness of your organization's purpose. Reflect on these questions:

- Why does the organization exist?
- What is clear about your organization' s purpose? What is still unclear?
- What disconnects exist that might need to be acknowledged or addressed?

THE THREE DOMAINS OF PURPOSE IN ORGANIZATIONS: THE WHAT, WHY, AND WHO

Let's return to our definition of purpose and see how it includes elements that can move an organization from autopilot to awareness of purpose: **Purpose is the ongoing process of understanding and connecting strengths, values, and desired impact with aligned actions to unlock your (organization's) full potential and be of service.**

We described earlier how our definition of purpose above maps to the domains of the *what* (strengths and capabilities), the *why* (values and intentions), and the *who* (the people or environments impacted by purpose). We described how this three-domain model of purpose could be harnessed by individuals and teams. Applying a model of purpose to an entire organization involves a holistic examination of the core strengths, values, intentions, and impact that the organization aims to deliver for people and the planet. This integrated approach ensures that all facets of the organization are aligned and working toward a common goal, creating a cohesive and purpose-driven entity.

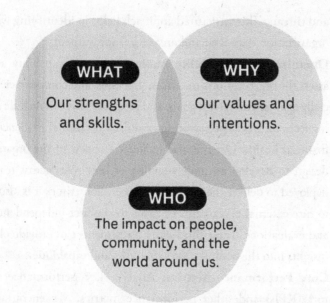

Our proposition here is that *all* of these foundational attributes of an organization matter for its purpose—what we have described as the *what* (strengths and capabilities), the *why* (values and intentions), and the *who* (those impacted by the organization). In many ways, the work for organizations is to ensure that there is a balanced approach to these different domains of purpose.

BECOMING AWARE OF THE *WHAT*: HOW STRENGTHS INFORM PURPOSE IN ORGANIZATIONS

There are a number of ways that organizations identify and become aware of their strengths and capabilities, and set about harnessing them. Here are a few suggestions of what organizations can do to assess their strengths (and areas for development):

1. **SWOT Analysis:** A SWOT (Strengths, Weaknesses, Opportunities, Threats) analysis is a classic way to systematically evaluate internal strengths and weaknesses as well as external opportunities

and threats. This structured approach helps in identifying what the organization does well and areas for improvement.

2. **Organizational Capability Audit:** Conduct a capability audit to assess the organization's resources, processes, and competencies, especially against its strategy, goals, and purpose. This can include reviewing technological assets, workforce skills, operational efficiencies, and financial health. Often it also includes a review of the organization design to develop an understanding of how roles across teams are deployed to deliver the desired outcomes. Sometimes it is also useful to hire external consultants or firms to conduct independent audits and evaluations. These third-party assessments can provide objective insights into the organization's strengths and capabilities.

3. **Core Performance Metrics:** Analyze key performance indicators (KPIs) and other performance metrics. We encourage you to include metrics around employee engagement and psychological safety (enablers of purpose) as well as direct business metrics. By examining areas where the organization consistently meets or exceeds goals, leadership can pinpoint specific strengths.

4. **Employee Feedback:** Regularly conducting employee surveys and questionnaires can help an organization gather insights on what employees believe are the organization's strengths. This can include questions about internal processes, company culture, operational efficiencies, and overall alignment with the organization's purpose. In addition, for deeper qualitative data, organize focus groups and workshops with employees from different departments and levels. These sessions can provide qualitative insights into the organization's strengths from the perspective of those who are deeply involved in day-to-day operations.

5. **Customer Feedback:** Conduct surveys to gather feedback from customers about their experiences with the organization's products or services. Positive feedback often highlights areas where the organization excels, and critical feedback can indicate purpose drift; both are important to build awareness.

6. **Market Analysis:** Perform market research to understand the organization's position relative to competitors. Identifying areas where the organization has a competitive advantage can help highlight core strengths and reveal areas where the organization is performing better than others.

Developing awareness of its own strengths and capabilities enables an organization to leverage its advantages, address weaknesses, and create a Purpose Reset that strategically positions itself for future growth. This organizational self-awareness is crucial for making informed decisions, fostering a positive organizational culture, and sustaining long-term, purpose-driven success.

BECOMING AWARE OF THE *WHY*: STAYING TRUE TO INTENTIONS, VALUES, AND ASPIRATIONS

In 2005, one of the founders of Etsy, Robert Kalin, who was a craftsperson himself, wondered what it would be like if artists and craftspeople could "be the protagonists of their own lives" and make a decent and sustainable income. At the time Kalin was a painter, carpenter, furniture maker, and amateur coder struggling to make ends meet. He shared his frustrations with his friends Haim Schoppik and Chris Maguire, who also had an interest in supporting independent artists. The three determined that they would team up to create a platform whose purpose was to provide a space for artists to connect directly with buyers who appreciated the value of craftsmanship and would be willing to pay for it.

What began as a series of conversations above a pizzeria in Brooklyn about how hard it was to make a living as an artist eventually led to the creation of a global e-commerce platform for artisans. Today, Etsy hosts over 7.5 million sellers and 95 million active buyers around the world, and is valued at over $10.94 billion.[24] Etsy is also routinely rated as a fun place to work, where employee well-being as well as learning marketing and business knowledge for small business is widely a part of the employee experience.[25]

The story of Etsy is a great illustration of how an organization's *why*—the intentions, values, and aspirations of not only its founders but all of its current employees—defines the everyday work inside the company. Whether it is software engineers, designers, marketers, or finance professionals, all focus on bolstering the strengths and capabilities of the artisan and craftsperson marketplace and by extension the creators themselves, thereby contributing to the fulfillment of Etsy's purpose. It's a great story of staying true to *why* Etsy exists as a company and what it aspires to do in the world. So, what about your organization? How can you understand your own organization's fidelity to its *why*? There are three dimensions that can clearly demonstrate how well an organization has aligned with its purpose: how leaders demonstrate the values and purpose of the organization, how its culture enables its purpose, and what the lived and felt experience is for employees. Let's explore each area of purpose alignment.

Leadership, Culture, and the Lived Experience

Internally, an organization's alignment with its *why* is often most clearly demonstrated by the organization's leadership, its culture, and the lived experience of employees working inside the organization.

> **You can learn a lot about how true an organization is to its deepest intentions, values, and aspirations by examining the decisions that get made as well as who and what gets recognized, rewarded, and promoted.**

Leaders play a crucial role in modeling and communicating organizational intentions, values, and aspirations. What leaders say and how they say it can significantly influence the organizational culture. You can observe how often leaders either articulate or fail to address the company's core values and aspirations in their communications, whether through formal speeches, internal memos, or casual interactions with employees.

Leaders also have to "walk the talk." When there is a clear alignment between what leaders communicate and their actions, it suggests that the organization is living true to its purpose. We've heard this referred to as a good "say-do ratio" for leaders. They do what they say they are going to do, all in ways consistent with the organization's values. On the other hand, if leaders say one thing but do another, and especially if this type of discordant behavior is more the norm than the exception, their organization may be operating out of alignment with their values.

One of the most telling indicators of an organization's commitment to its intentions, values, and aspirations is who and what gets recognized and rewarded. This includes who is promoted, which projects are highlighted, and what achievements are celebrated. To build awareness around this, noticing which employees get recognized and rewarded in an organization is one way to understand the values. For example, if an organization places a high value on innovation, then recognizing employees who introduce groundbreaking ideas or develop new processes reflects this commitment. Such recognition encourages a culture where creativity and forward thinking are not just encouraged but are essential components of success. On the other hand, if the organization consistently rewards achievements that seem to prioritize short-term gains over long-term value or ethical considerations, it may inadvertently signal that its professed values are not truly integral to the way that it operates. This misalignment can lead to confusion and disengagement among employees who are committed to the stated values but see little evidence of them being upheld.

Fulfilling the Why Out in the World

Another way to come to understand how well your organization is staying true to its *why* is to look at how the organization is interacting with and impacting the world around it. Even more telling is having a long-term plan in place to ensure it stays true to its *why* for the foreseeable future.

Patagonia provides a strong example of that organization's intentions, values, and aspirations that have created a positive global impact and created an enduring and beloved brand.

CASE STUDY: PATAGONIA
A Values-Based Approach to Business and Environmental Stewardship

Patagonia, a US-based outdoor clothing and gear company, has long been celebrated as a model of environmental responsibility. Patagonia's mission statement, "We're in business to save our home planet,"[26] reflects its values-based dedication to environmental sustainability. The company's commitment is evident in its product design, supply chain practices, and advocacy for environmental causes. Patagonia's business model also integrates sustainability at every stage of the product life cycle. As a final, definitive action toward its deep and lasting commitment to environmental protection and sustainability, in 2022 the privately owned company converted its ownership model into a set of trusts and nonprofit steward organizations that prioritize climate action and environmental protection. Under this new structure, all the profits from the company currently go to protect the environment and work to reverse harms resulting from human-induced climate change.

The structures, processes, and business model itself at Patagonia are therefore driven by a values-first approach.[27] Patagonia's values-based business practices include:

- **Responsible Manufacturing:** Patagonia was one of the first major outdoor clothing brands to use organically grown cotton, eliminating the use of cotton grown with synthetic pesticides and fertilizers.

- **Recycled Materials and Upcycling:** The company continually expands its use of recycled polyester and nylon. Notably, its iconic fleece jackets are made from recycled plastic soda bottles, and it encourages customers to recycle their products through its Worn Wear program. Patagonia also provides repair services, used gear stores, and trade-in options, emphasizing a consumer model that reduces waste.

- **Environmental Advocacy:** Patagonia actively engages in environmental activism. For instance, it has taken legal action against policies threatening national monuments.

- **Support of Grassroots Movements:** Through its "1% for the Planet" initiative, Patagonia pledges 1% of its sales to support environmental nonprofits, fostering a community of like-minded activists and organizations.

- **Transparency and Accountability:** Patagonia offers a detailed view of the supply chain and environmental impact of each of its products through the Footprint Chronicles, enabling consumers to make informed decisions.

- **Certifications:** Patagonia ensures its products meet rigorous environmental and social standards by obtaining certifications such as Fair Trade and bluesign.

Patagonia's approach to business demonstrates that profitability and environmental stewardship can go hand in hand. The company's success is not just measured by sales and revenue, but also by its profound impact on the planet. And, in many cases, Patagonia chooses to prioritize impact on the planet over short-term profit, for example in their switch to organic cotton. Patagonia not only practices what it preaches but also leads the way in corporate responsibility and environmental activism, and inspires other companies to follow suit. It has set in place a long-range plan to make good on its *why*, drawing directly from its intentions, aspirations, and values.

BECOMING AWARE OF THE *WHO*: HOW IMPACT INFORMS PURPOSE IN ORGANIZATIONS

A company's purpose is its reason for being, beyond profit. It articulates the broader impact the organization aims to make in the world. Up until now we have described how values (the organization's *why*) form part of the organization's purpose and how they operate in tandem with the organization's core strengths (the *what*) to harness the organization's capabilities and deliver impact in the world. The third and last component of an organization's purpose is the *who*—the actual impact that an organization has on people and the planet. So how do you become aware of your organization's impact? A clear and authentic sense of impact is critical for creating a purpose-driven organization, and it definitely inspires employees, attracts customers, and builds trust with stakeholders.

The World Central Kitchen (WCK) is a prime example of an impact-driven organization. Founded by chef José Andrés in 2010, their purpose statement says, "WCK's work is guided by our belief that food is a universal human right. Both in the communities we serve and in our daily workspace, we uphold and rely on our values to direct us toward fulfilling our shared purpose."[28] This purpose has steered its mission to provide meals in the aftermath of natural disasters and other crises, delivering immediate relief and fostering long-term resilience.[29] To date, WCK has served over 350 million meals to communities in need, those affected by natural and/or human-created disasters. WCK's impact is evident in its numerous relief efforts, such as providing millions of meals to Puerto Ricans after Hurricane Maria in 2017, aiding Ukrainian refugees since 2022, and (as of the writing of this book) serving as the primary aid agency operating in Gaza.

WCK stands as a testament to how a clear, impact-driven purpose can guide an organization's values, actions, and overall strategy. By focusing on the belief that food is a universal human right, WCK has made a substantial positive impact on countless lives, demonstrating the powerful role that purpose can play in driving meaningful, real-world change.

Often, it is the "line of sight" between an individual's purpose and the broader organization's impact that inspires and motivates. When I (Rich) worked at eBay as a Director of Learning & Development, for example, I remember being very positively impacted by the impact of my organization on our stakeholders, as I came to learn about it by attending what was called an eBay Seller Conference. The name of the conference pretty much describes it: if you had a business (small, medium, or large) that was utilizing eBay as a selling platform, this conference was (and is) a great information-sharing, resource-gathering, and community-building experience. I was moved to learn that most of the sellers were small business-people, often family-run businesses or "solopreneurs," who saw the eBay platform as a way to launch and grow their own retail businesses to a larger audience around the country and/or world. I could tangibly see eBay's values, which aspired to "connect people and build communities to create economic opportunity for all,"[30] in action at the Seller Conference.

Additionally, as an HR leader at eBay, I found that the company's purpose significantly informed and inspired my work. The palpable sense that we were offering a valuable service to our users and to the world at large fostered a deep sense of pride among employees. This pride translated into a strong organizational culture where everyone was committed to the company's purpose and mission. Drawing on eBay's purpose, I was able to implement HR practices that aligned with the company's values and goals. This included developing programs that supported employee engagement, professional development, and community involvement. By embedding the company's purpose and values into HR initiatives, we were able to cultivate a work environment that not only motivated employees but also aligned their personal goals with the organizational mission.

It was no surprise, then, that for a number of years, I went to work focused, motivated, and willing to give the very best of my mind and heart to the work. It would not be an exaggeration to say that I *loved* aspects of the organization and my role because I knew it was in support of a much larger community and enabling them to thrive. My role at eBay was one job in which I felt I had a positive impact on the organization and was able to perform at my highest level, because I felt that my values and personal sense of purpose were aligned with the values and purpose of the company. And because there was an element of love for the organization. One of the proudest moments in my working life was when I was recognized and promoted by my boss, who shared that my enthusiasm was highly engaging and infectious for others. I still consider my experience at eBay as one of the "peak career" time periods. It is also a good example of how both individual and organization purpose, when aligned, have powerful effects for all.

PURPOSE RESET PRACTICE

Assessing the Impact of Your Organization

Reflect on the following questions and acknowledge the reality of the organization's impact, evaluating its positive and negative effects on customers, society, and the environment.

- Is your organization fulfilling its purpose in terms of the impact it aspires to have in the world? Why or why not?
- What are some of the positive and negative impacts that the organization actually has for its customers? Society at large? The environment?
- What stakeholders do the leaders of the organization need to hear more from? What would be required to capture their voices?
- What needs to change internally in the organization for it to deliver its desired impact externally?

Based on your responses to the above questions, is your organization staying true to its aspirations and purpose?

In the long term, as many of our case studies from organizations including Patagonia and eBay illustrate, significant benefits result from purpose-driven impact. These companies demonstrate that when an organization commits to a clear and compelling purpose, and aligns its actions and decision-making processes with that purpose, it fosters a strong, positive impact on both internal and external stakeholders. This commitment not only drives financial success but also builds trust, loyalty, and a lasting reputation in the marketplace. We believe that a truly purpose-driven company doesn't tend to just follow industry standards—it seeks to set new ones.

PUTTING IT TOGETHER AROUND PURPOSE

Staying true to a purpose and an organization's desired impact can be challenging, especially in the face of pressure from shareholders, market competition, and/or financial targets.

It is always important to consider the conditions in which most people and organizations operate in today—a context in which high demands, constant change, complexity, and disruption are features and not bugs of organizational life.

However, aligning impact with purpose far outweighs the short-term challenges. When organizations buckle under such pressures, leaders and other people in the organization can lose sight of the organization's core purpose, mission, and values, and purpose drift occurs.

As we close this chapter, we invite you to ask yourself: How is my organization doing in terms of its alignment with its purpose?

MICRO-PRACTICE

Is Your Organization Aware and Aligned on Purpose?

Using some of the organization awareness-building from the previous chapter, try this micro-practice to get an understanding of the awareness and alignment with purpose in your organization:

- Pause and reflect. In one sentence, describe your organization's:
  - *What*—its core strengths
  - *Why*—its core values
  - *Who*—the impact the organization aspires to have in the world
- Compare:
  - Is your organization operating in a way that is aligned and consistent with its what, why, and who?
  - Is there purpose drift? Is a Purpose Reset needed?

We've shared numerous examples in this book about effective Purpose Resets—from our own reset at SIY Global to larger and more well-known Purpose Resets at companies such as Lego and CVS. Next, let's dive more fully into how your organization can undertake a Purpose Reset of its own.

CHAPTER 11
Making Good on a
Purpose Reset

When I (Carolina) decided to start my own business in 2023, I remembered the exercise Rich, Steph, and I had done a few months earlier, writing a letter to you (our intended reader for this book), and decided to follow a similar approach. It was meant as a fun, grounding, and visualization exercise, but ended up becoming a lot more than that.

One fall day, I sat down and wrote a letter addressed to my new business, Plenari (which is a learning academy for human flourishing and purpose). I closed my eyes and imagined that this entity was sitting next to me. I know it sounds strange, but stay with me. I started visualizing many aspects of this new organization. As soon as I wrote "Dear Plenari," words began to flow onto my yellow paper pad: "Your name and logo mark are symbols of the legacy we will leave behind, together: a world where humans can flourish."

The letter explained the types of services we'd offer, the impact those programs would have, the people who would feel inspired to be part of our community, the wisdom shared by our first employees, the laughter and hugs we'd exchange at our retreats, and how we'd all stand with conviction for our key values. It described not just what we'd offer, but how we'd bring our services to the world. It outlined some of the characteristics of the type of organization I wanted to see in the world: wholehearted leadership, compassion for all stakeholders, integrity, whole-human interactions, purposeful impact, and excellence in execution. The letter also included what Plenari wouldn't be: a few descriptors of my nonnegotiables and the type of actions it will never allow or stand for.

After completing the exercise, I reviewed what I had written, took a bright blue marker, and circled the words that stood out to me the most. Those became the backbone of my organization's purpose statement and, importantly, of our initial product development and marketing activities. I noticed how that crystallization of our awareness of our what, who, and why became the catalyst of our aligned actions. A Purpose Reset.

This example reminds us that aligning an organization's stated purpose with its actual impact requires radical honesty, transparency, and a steadfast commitment to living out that purpose in every action and decision. By genuinely assessing its impact and continuously striving to improve by understanding any purpose drift and endeavoring to create a Purpose Reset, an organization can not only achieve its business goals but also make a meaningful difference in the world. Remember, being a purpose-driven organization is an ongoing process as we have emphasized all along, which primarily requires the movement from autopilot (and the resulting purpose drift) to awareness and aligned action (a Purpose Reset).

EVERYONE IS INVOLVED IN A PURPOSE RESET

It may not seem obvious, but everybody in an organization has a role to play in creating a Purpose Reset. You may be asking yourself the question "Isn't a purpose set by the leaders or founders of an organization? And what influence do I have on an organization's purpose?" The answer is that everybody in an organization in one way or another touches the organization's purpose through their actions, decisions, and engagement on a day-to-day basis. Here is a map of the people (stakeholders) and activities that move an organization toward the activation of its purpose:

Stakeholder	Purpose Reset Questions	Purpose Reset Actions	Impact
Leaders and/or Founders	Is this organization aligned with our core purpose? How do I know? Are our goals aligned with our purpose? Is the culture we are creating consistent with the purpose we wish to embody? Are there any specific areas where the organization is currently experiencing purpose drift? Do we need a Purpose Reset?	Be honest about purpose drift. Articulate a clear and compelling need for a Purpose Reset. Integrate the purpose in strategic decision-making and organizational culture at all levels. Align incentives with purpose. Define success metrics.	Demonstrated commitment to accountability measures. A clear vision and buffer against competing demands/ pressures that subvert purpose.
HR/L&D or People and Culture Teams	How can we as an organization best get a read on how well we are delivering against our purpose? What initiatives/ levers are available to further align on purpose? How can we help leaders initiate or support a Purpose Reset?	Initiate purpose-focused assessments, through either existing platforms (e.g., employee surveys) or other tools. Design and maintain core metrics/ dashboard for purpose alignment. Recruit leadership participation and support for Purpose Reset initiatives.	Validation of the need for a Purpose Reset. Accountability mechanisms for progress against the Purpose Reset.

Stakeholder	Purpose Reset Questions	Purpose Reset Actions	Impact
Employees	How can I better align my personal values and goals with the organization's purpose? My role? How does the company's culture support or hinder our purpose? What opportunities exist for employees to get involved in purpose-driven projects or initiatives? How are purpose-driven behaviors and achievements recognized and rewarded within the organization? What mechanisms are in place for employees to provide feedback on how well the organization is living up to its purpose? What is the long-term vision for the company in terms of its purpose?	Ensure a personal connection or "line of sight" to purpose and translate it into day-to-day work activities. Have a way to be involved in creating and staying connected with the Purpose Reset, including: • Sharing feedback on employee surveys • Having discussions with team and managers • Sharing feedback in open company forums • Sharing stories of purpose (or lack thereof) from customers and stakeholders	Act as job-specific representative of the purpose for the organization.

Stakeholder	Purpose Reset Questions	Purpose Reset Actions	Impact
Customers	Is the organization that they are supporting making good on its promise of its purpose?	Become brand champions. Provide an outside perspective and feedback when the organization feels misaligned with their purpose.	Validation of the direction of the organization in the marketplace.

Of course, this map could be expanded even further; managers play an essential role (largely covered in Part III), marketing or PR teams might ensure alignment between purpose and external messaging, R&D teams ensure that areas of innovation connect to purpose, and so on. But to keep things as broadly applicable as possible, we'll dive a little deeper and focus the remainder of this chapter on:

1. What leaders can do to create a Purpose Reset for their organizations
2. What employees can do to contribute to a Purpose Reset

We want to focus on these two groups because they both operationalize the purpose of their organizations on a daily basis and also because they both have enormous influence in calling out purpose drift and enabling a Purpose Reset. So let's look more closely at the strategies and practical actions that leaders and employees can take to create a Purpose Reset in their organizations.

ESSENTIAL STRATEGIES FOR LEADERS TO CREATE A PURPOSE RESET

The commitment to a purpose-driven organization starts at the top. Leaders have an especially large role to play in a Purpose Reset as they directly impact the priorities and decision-making that align with the purpose of the organization. Leaders also have "positional power" and authority, based on their roles. In a 2023 *Harvard Business Review* article titled "How Leaders Can Create a Purpose-Driven Culture,"[1] authors Rodolphe Durand and Ioannis Ioannou note, "Overall, leaders shoulder the responsibility not just of directing their organizations towards purpose but of enacting it daily. Their actions, decisions, and communications set the example for the broader organization, accentuating the importance of purpose in everyday reality."

In essence, leaders articulate, authorize, and embody the principles of a Purpose Reset through the decisions and actions that they take on behalf of the company. In the context of a Purpose Reset, leaders can enroll stakeholders such as an organization's employees, board, shareholders, and key customers toward a Purpose Reset when they feel that the organization has strayed from its purpose or needs to rethink the purpose entirely.

Marvel Entertainment provides an example of how a company used a Purpose Reset to profoundly reinvent itself. The change took place when a pair of new leaders began to lay out a more expansive vision of the organization and moved Marvel Comics from being a beloved but bankrupt comic book publisher to the world-leading multimedia entertainment company Marvel Entertainment.

CASE STUDY: MARVEL'S PURPOSE RESET
The Transformation from Bankruptcy to an Entertainment Powerhouse

In the mid-1990s, Marvel Comics Group, a company synonymous with iconic comic book characters like Spider-Man, X-Men, and the Avengers, was experiencing severe financial distress. The entire comic book industry faced dwindling sales and was in danger of collapse. Marvel, which had been a dominant force in the industry, filed for bankruptcy in 1996. However, through strategic leadership, innovative business decisions, and a bold, purpose-driven vision for the future, Marvel transformed itself into a multi-platform entertainment juggernaut.[2]

The first major step in Marvel's turnaround was a leadership change. In 1998, Toy Biz, led by Ike Perlmutter and Avi Arad, took control of Marvel. They were later joined by David Maisel, a visionary chief operating officer.[3] They focused on stabilizing the company financially and laid the groundwork for a new strategic direction. Marvel at the time had a smaller catalog of characters than its larger rival, DC, and these characters were largely accessible only through its comic books.[4] The leaders at Marvel made the decision to simultaneously reinvest in its characters while also reinventing the way their stories interacted with one another and the mediums (now including film and licensable products) in which they appeared. "Marvel . . . went back to its other foundational principle: that characters could be intertwined and cross over into one another's storylines, and that by doing this you create a universe rich and complex enough that fans are drawn in and never want to leave," according to Adam B. Vary, reporting on Marvel's reinvention for *Variety*.[5] In effect, Marvel's new leadership took the organization through a Purpose Reset and refocused it on Marvel's *why*, *what*, and *who*.

The *Why*—Creating Resonant Stories Across Generations

Marvel's Purpose Reset in the 1990s–early 2000s harnessed its values of presenting its much-loved characters to have broad, multigenerational appeal.[6] When we talk about a Purpose Reset, we also talk about bringing the love of the work, and Marvel certainly focused on elements of its characters that made them beloved by their audiences, including having the superheroes face innately human struggles and triumphs, such as losing loved ones or falling in love.

Marvel's reinvention move was further solidified in 2005 when Marvel secured a $525 million loan from Merrill Lynch, using the film rights to 10 characters as collateral. This bold step allowed Marvel to self-finance its movies, reducing dependence on external studios. Marvel Studios was now able to create a connected universe where characters could cross over between films, creating a cohesive and expansive narrative. Marvel had returned to its *why*—connecting generations of fans across new, multi-platform formats to have access to their universe of beloved superheroes who now also interacted with one another. The Marvel Cinematic Universe (MCU) was born, and it represented both a return to Marvel's core strengths and a leap toward a new strategic playbook that broadened Marvel's appeals and entirely changed its fortunes.

The *What*—Leveraging Strengths Across Multiple Platforms

Marvel's innovative business model extended beyond movies. They leveraged their intellectual property (already their key strength) across multiple platforms (a critical expansion of their *what*), creating a synergistic approach to entertainment, including merchandising and licensing, television and streaming, and digital and interactive media.

Marvel's Purpose Reset further took shape in its merger with Disney in 2009, which centered on Marvel's *what*—its strengths and broad appeal to many different generations across a range of product offerings including not only comic books but now films, branded products, content licenses, and media production capabilities. Marvel doubled down on its strengths and amplified them in its merger with Disney.

Marvel continued to expand the MCU with ambitious projects and new phases. Films like *Black Panther* (2018), *Avengers: Infinity War* (2018), and *Avengers: Endgame* (2019) broke box office records and garnered critical acclaim. The MCU's success redefined the superhero genre and set new standards for blockbuster filmmaking, and all of it was built from Marvel's Purpose Reset centering on its *what* and *why*—its core strengths and values.

The *Who*—Marvel's Cultural Impact

Marvel's transformation had a profound cultural impact. The MCU's diverse characters and inclusive storytelling resonated with audiences worldwide. Films like *Black Panther* became cultural milestones, celebrating representation and breaking new ground in Hollywood. Marvel also shifted culture by helping us rethink the idea of a superhero by highlighting teams of heroes working together rather than individual superheroes saving the world solo. Marvel's superheroes were also now cast as highly relatable, grappling with core questions of identity, meaning, morality, and human connection. Even the villains in the MCU were represented with deeply human struggles—often they were conflicted figures dealing with past suffering, which led them to create an alternative (albeit misguided and often monstrous) vision for a world that they believed would be devoid of such suffering. Marvel effectively reignited love for their superheroes and villains![7]

• • •

Marvel's journey from bankruptcy to a multi-platform entertainment powerhouse that influences global popular culture is a testament to strategic vision, innovative business practices, and bold leadership—and a Purpose Reset put into play by those leaders. Today, Marvel stands as a symbol of resilience and creativity, continuing to captivate audiences and shape the future of entertainment. All of this success came from a Purpose Reset that was brought on during a low point in the organization's history, but that led to its reinvention and ascension to the top of its category.

As the example of Marvel illustrates, a Purpose Reset is built on the underlying strengths, values, and desired impact already existing in the organization. We should note that a Purpose Reset does not always have to be as dramatic as Marvel's.

> **Purpose Resets vary by degrees and magnitude. Sometimes a Purpose Reset is simply a matter of reconnecting to the purpose and inspiring stakeholders with that same purpose. Sometimes it may require wholesale reinvention of the company.**

Regardless of the type of reset being enacted, a leader's role is to play that essential bridging function that connects purpose to people. When a leader becomes aware of a gap between a company's purpose and its practices, they may seek to create a Purpose Reset. Leaders then play a key role in articulating the need for, vision for, and road map for a Purpose Reset. We'd like to offer a few practical strategies for how leaders can go about enacting a Purpose Reset.

Strategy #1: Be Honest and Authentic About the Need

Usually, most people in and around an organization have a lived experience of whether or not the company is operating in a way that is consistent with its history, culture, values, and purpose. Leaders in particular have a unique responsibility to "tell it like they see it" and admit if the organization has drifted from its purpose.

If you are uncertain as a leader as to whether your company has drifted from its purpose, there are many sources of data to help you gain awareness. Employees often express their thoughts and perspectives through feedback forums such as Pulse or engagement surveys, company meetings, chat groups, Slack channels, and so on. Shareholders have an annual meeting to hear from leaders and express their perspectives. Customers, board members, analysts, and the jury of public opinion all provide leaders with copious information on an organization's alignment with values and purpose. The onus is on leaders to listen and integrate the inputs about purpose.

PURPOSE RESET PRACTICE

Questions for Leaders

Here are some questions leaders can ask themselves *and* their employees to determine how well their organization is connected with its purpose:

- Is the culture we are creating in the organization consistent with our purpose?
- Are we aligned with *what* we are best at, our strengths?
- Are we aligned with our *why* as a business, our values?
- Are we aligned with *who* we aspire to serve, our impact?
- Are our decisions informed by our purpose?
- Are our business strategies and models informed by our purpose?
- Are we taking in all feedback from stakeholders and customers?

If you answer "no" to any of the seven questions above, you as a leader may want to consider if it is time for a reset. And to get an understanding of where to focus for the reset, consider the following questions:

- What are our employees and other stakeholders saying about our alignment with our purpose?
- Where is the gap between our intention and actual practice the largest?
- How can I best influence a Purpose Reset, given my role?

When you as a leader are able to engage in this type of inquiry, and also to compare your self-assessment with feedback from employees, it can provide needed information to take stock of how well the organization is living its purpose and how much it may have strayed. Equipped with this understanding of the need for a Purpose Reset and some of the areas to focus on, leaders can then communicate, integrate, and embody a Purpose Reset for the organization.

Strategy #2: Create Clarity

An organization's purpose should be as clear, simple, and understandable as possible, so much so that any employee or stakeholder of the organization should be able to repeat it easily. While at Google, for example, it was always easy for Rich to say that the purpose of the organization was to "organize the world's information and make it accessible." Similarly, when Steph worked for StopWaste, a local government agency in California, their mission was clear: to help Alameda County businesses and residents make better decisions about the products they buy, the resources they use, and the stuff they throw away. It felt clear and actionable, and enabled the organization to focus on different strategies, stakeholders, and forms of waste to achieve this clear purpose. When Carolina first joined American Express as an MBA intern, she was surprised to see that their mission, vision, and purpose were related to "customer service" versus the financial products it offered. But indeed, having clarity about the focus on "providing the world's best customer experience every day" was what informed product development, communications, and operations at the company, every day.

Having a clearly articulated purpose makes it easy to effectively communicate that purpose to all stakeholders, both internally and externally. When leaders can clearly define and convey the organization's purpose, it enhances alignment, engagement, and trust. Here are some principles for a clear and well-defined purpose:

1. **Make the purpose a reflection of the what, why, and who.**
   Example: Interface (a large-scale manufacturer of commercial flooring that transitioned a significant part of its operations to carbon-neutral and sustainable processes and materials) has a purpose that states, "We want to restore our planet and leave a positive impact."

2. **Make the purpose inspirational and achievable.**
   Example: Starbucks's purpose is to "inspire and nurture the human spirit, one person, one cup, and one neighborhood at a time."
3. **Make the purpose direct and simple.**
   Example: IKEA's vision is to "create a better everyday life for the many people."

By tapping into a simple, clear, and direct purpose for the organization, leaders can help ensure that employees and other stakeholders are aligned and inspired by the purpose, as well as the mission and values represented in it.

Strategy #3: Inspire People with Purpose

Here are some actions leaders can take to spark inspiration about the organization's purpose and embed it in the organization's culture:

- **Share a vision.** Clearly articulate the organization's purpose, ensuring it is communicated effectively across the organization. Share the purpose-driven vision (the ideal future state) in a way that is relatable and compelling, highlighting how each employee's role contributes to the broader mission.
- **Lead by example.** Demonstrate the values, work ethic, and behaviors you expect from others. Employees are more likely to trust leaders who both lead and follow.
- **Be visible and accessible.** Create opportunities for employees to engage with you around purpose. Show up for teams on the ground level to understand their challenges and show genuine interest in their contributions. This visibility reinforces the importance of every employee's role in achieving the organization's purpose.
- **Tell stories.** Share stories of how the organization's work impacts customers, communities, and the world positively. These stories can illustrate the tangible benefits of the organization's purpose and make it more personal and inspiring for employees.

- **Give regular updates.** Use regular updates, meetings, and storytelling to keep the purpose alive.
- **Embed purpose in daily operations.** Integrate the organization's purpose into daily operations and decision-making processes. Create performance metrics that prioritize purpose. Ensure that policies, practices, and strategies reflect the organization's purpose, values, and mission.
- **Recognize and reward alignment.** Recognize and reward employees who exemplify the organization's purpose through their work. Highlighting purpose-driven achievements in performance reviews, awards, and public acknowledgments reinforces the importance of aligning with the organizational mission.
- **Create dialogue forums.** Establish platforms for open communication where employees can share ideas, feedback, and concerns related to the organization's purpose. This could include town hall meetings, suggestion boxes, or regular team check-ins.
- **Act on feedback.** Show that feedback is valued by taking actionable steps based on employees' and other stakeholders' suggestions and concerns.
- **Champion purpose-driven social initiatives.** Encourage participation in social impact initiatives (example: days of service) that align with the organization's purpose. This not only strengthens the organization's impact but also reinforces the importance of the purpose to employees and other stakeholders.

All of these strategies are available for leaders to utilize so that they can build awareness and align their organizations around purpose. Leaders are in a unique position to influence a Purpose Reset because they are able to pull all of the levers that are mentioned above. Is it really possible for leaders to do so? Can leaders truly engender behaviors that span from painting a vision of an aspirational future state all the way through to engaging in social impact initiatives? Can leaders really do all of that and run a successful and sustainable enterprise? We believe so.

**It is the work of leaders to demonstrate
for everyone inside and outside of the
organization how a Purpose Reset informs
the work of the organization and allows
it to achieve its desired future state.**

LEADERSHIP CASE STUDY: INTERFACE, INC.
When a Founder Created a Purpose
Reset for a Sustainable Future

When Ray Anderson founded Interface, Inc., in 1973, it operated as a traditional manufacturing company, focused on producing high-quality carpet tiles and generating profits. All of its products at the time were manufactured using petroleum-based and nonrenewable materials. Interface quickly grew to become the largest carpet maker on the planet and set the standard for flooring in corporate and commercial spaces. Interface's flexible, durable, and easy-to-install-and-remove flooring solutions replaced huge rolls of broadloom carpet and allowed organizations to reconfigure their workspaces, create open floor plans, and more. Interface experienced hyperbolic growth and within a decade was a Fortune 500 company, employing many thousands of employees.

In 1994, at the apex of its market valuation and stock price, Anderson had nothing short of an epiphany while reading Paul Hawken's book *The Ecology of Commerce*. The book's stark depiction of the environmental degradation caused by industry struck a chord with Anderson, prompting a deep personal reflection on Interface's environmental impact. Anderson realized that his company was part of the problem and decided it needed to become part of the solution.[8]

Inspired by his newfound environmental consciousness, Anderson set a bold new vision for Interface: to become the first environmentally sustainable and, ultimately, restorative company in the world. This vision was for Interface to have zero negative impact on the environment by 2020, and actually restore resources to the earth by 2030.

Transforming Interface into a sustainable business required a comprehensive overhaul of its operations, business model, and corporate culture. The key strategies that Interface implemented included reducing environmental impacts by using renewable energy, sustainable product design, closed loop recycling, and transparency and accountability measures. From a leadership and culture perspective, Interface emphasized the following:[9]

1. **Selling the vision.** They invested in turning the sales department, who engaged their customers, into sustainability, circularity, and regeneration experts.

2. **Telling stories and being vulnerable.** Leaders and team members shared about the personal insights on sustainability of its leaders from the founder on down (sharing about not just the what, but the why—internally within the company as well as in the media), including some of the mistakes as well as triumphs along the way, and the lessons learned.

3. **Sharing and celebrating moments of success.** They brought the team together to share progress as well as renewed commitment to the vision.

4. **Standing their ground.** Interface emphasized perseverance and navigating resistance.

5. **Believing.** Leaders displayed true passion and commitment to the vision and drew on that in the day-to-day work of reinventing the company.

With these elements of a Purpose Reset woven into the company culture, strategy, and operations, the transformation of Interface into a purpose-driven, sustainable business yielded remarkable results. By

2020, the company had achieved significant milestones toward its Mission Zero goals, including reducing its greenhouse gas emissions by 96% since the mid-1990s and creating sustainable carpeting using recycled materials.

Ray Anderson's vision and leadership left a lasting legacy at Interface and beyond. Even after his passing in 2011, the company has continued to innovate and push the boundaries of sustainability. Interface's ongoing initiatives include striving for carbon negativity and exploring new ways to restore the environment.

The case of Interface, Inc., illustrates how a profound shift in organizational purpose can drive transformative change. By aligning its business model with environmental sustainability, Interface not only mitigated its negative impact on the planet but also carved out a unique competitive advantage while leading the way in creating a more sustainable future.[10]

Interface shows that leaders are essential to purpose. Perhaps the key lesson is this: the more the leaders embrace, champion, and paint a vision for a Purpose Reset, the more likely it will succeed and help the organization reinvent—or simply stay true to—itself.

Strategy # 4: Demonstrate Deep Commitment

There are certain critical moments in the evolution of organizations in which their leaders are called to demonstrate deep commitment to the organization's purpose. There are times—"crucible moments"—when such commitment will be questioned, and it's even more important for leaders to double down on their commitment to an organization's purpose, mission, values, and vision.

Crucible moments are times of intense challenge in organizations, the metaphor of a "crucible" being used because the "heat is turned high" (as with a crucible when heated) on the organization to perform, reform, or otherwise justify itself. If you are a leader, crucible moments are usually pretty obvious by the amount of stress you feel, but you can recognize a crucible moment when some or all of these conditions are present:

- **Intense external pressure**—market downturns, competitive threats, regulatory changes, public scrutiny, etc.
- **Major internal crisis or conflict**—ethical breaches, cultural clashes, leadership disputes, etc.
- **A major, organization-defining strategic shift is required**—due to a need to change its business model, a merger or acquisition, entering a new market, the emergence of disruptive technology, etc.
- **Financial turmoil**—whether due to economic downturns, declining revenues, unexpected costs, or flawed business models
- **Societal and environmental challenges**—major social or environmental upheaval such as global pandemics, wars, social unrest, and changing expectations of companies

Here is a short playbook on some actions leaders can take to effectively navigate a crucible moment in a purpose-aligned way:

Purpose Reset Responses to Crucible Moments—A Leader's Playbook	
What	**How**
Be Real and Act with Immediacy	Communicate openly about the challenges faced, the decisions being made, and the reasons behind those decisions. People want to know "why." Act quickly while also being thoughtful about action. People appreciate leaders with a bias toward action in a time of crisis. Demonstrate the urgency by communicating frequently and consistently.

Purpose Reset Responses to Crucible Moments—A Leader's Playbook	
What	**How**
Demonstrate Visible Leadership	Everyone looks to their leaders in difficult times, so be present and visible during the crucible moments. Engage with teams, show solidarity, and provide a steadying influence. Visible leadership reassures employees and other stakeholders of the organization's direction and stability.
Rally the Team	If ever there was a need to motivate and inspire the team around purpose, a crucible moment is it. Be proactive about sending inspirational and motivational messages, especially ones that call out the inherent strengths of the organization and recognize the hard work, small steps, and victories that are met along the way.
Encourage Creative Solutions and Collaboration	Empower teams to think creatively and propose innovative solutions to the challenges faced. An environment that encourages experimentation can lead to breakthrough ideas and new opportunities, especially in tough times. Example: Apollo 13 returned to Earth due to the creative power of a small, cross-functional "tiger team" that hit upon a novel solution (i.e., using the moon's gravity to slingshot the space capsule back to Earth when it had lost all propulsion). Encourage the creation of your own tiger teams.
Enact Purpose-Aligned Prioritization	Prioritize actions and initiatives that reflect the organization's purpose. For instance, if sustainability is a core value, focus on solutions that minimize environmental impact even during tough times.

Purpose Reset Responses to Crucible Moments—A Leader's Playbook	
What	**How**
Find Quick Wins	Identify and implement short-term actions that can provide immediate relief or improvement. These quick wins can build momentum and show progress, while still aligning with long-term goals.
Celebrate Successes	Acknowledge and celebrate the efforts and successes achieved during the crisis. Recognizing contributions reinforces a culture of appreciation and commitment to the organization's purpose.
Conduct Post-Crisis Analysis	Conduct a thorough analysis after the crisis to understand what worked well and what didn't. Use these insights to improve future responses and reinforce purpose-driven strategies.

Strategy #5: Create Transparency and Accountability

Leaders can work with their teams to establish metrics to measure the impact of the organization's purpose. This could include social or environmental metrics, employee engagement surveys, and other indicators of how well the company is living up to its purpose and whether people are motivated by the work they do and the organization's culture. Regularly reporting on these metrics to stakeholders such as employees, investors, and the general public demonstrates commitment to purpose-focused outcomes, transparency, and accountability.

The Salesforce 1-1-1 model is based on a simple yet powerful idea: dedicating 1% of the company's equity, 1% of product, and 1% of employee time to philanthropic efforts. This model ensures that giving back is ingrained in the company's DNA and is measurable.[11] Salesforce's commitment to the 1-1-1 model is reinforced through dedicated structures, transparent reporting, active employee involvement, strategic product donations, sustained equity funding, and continuous stakeholder engagement. For example, Salesforce demonstrates public accountability on its 1-1-1 metrics by publishing detailed reports on its philanthropic activities, offering transparency about the company's contributions, and highlighting key metrics, success stories, and areas for improvement. By publicly sharing this information, Salesforce holds itself accountable to stakeholders and the broader community.

IKEA offers another good example of purpose-driven transparency and accountability. IKEA's purpose, as previously mentioned, is, "To create a better everyday life for the many people." Other than the products and services they provide, a key aspect of how IKEA fulfills its purpose is its commitment to sustainability and social responsibility. The company has set targets to become climate positive by 2030, meaning it will reduce more greenhouse gas emissions than it emits. IKEA invests in renewable energy, aims to use only renewable and recycled materials in its products, and works to promote fair labor practices throughout its supply chain. The company's annual Sustainability Report provides detailed updates on its progress, ensuring transparency and accountability.[12] The report provides quantitative data on various aspects of sustainability, such as energy consumption, carbon emissions, water usage, and waste management. This data-driven approach enhances the report's credibility and allows for objective assessment of IKEA's progress.

Additionally, IKEA's Sustainability Report tracks progress over time by comparing current performance against previous years. This allows stakeholders to see trends, improvements, and areas where further efforts are needed. IKEA's Sustainability Report does not shy away from discussing challenges and setbacks. By openly addressing difficulties encountered and areas where targets have not been met, IKEA demonstrates a commitment to transparency and continuous improvement. When discussing challenges, for example, the report often outlines the steps IKEA is taking to address these issues. This proactive approach reassures stakeholders that the company is committed to overcoming obstacles and achieving its sustainability goals. IKEA details how it has responded to stakeholder feedback in the report. By showing how input has influenced its sustainability strategies and initiatives, IKEA reinforces its accountability to stakeholders. Finally, to enhance credibility, IKEA's Sustainability Report often includes third-party verification of its data and claims. External audits provide an independent assessment of IKEA's sustainability performance, ensuring accuracy and reliability. IKEA's reporting also aligns with recognized global sustainability standards and frameworks, such as the Global Reporting Initiative (GRI) and the United Nations Sustainable Development Goals (SDGs). This alignment demonstrates IKEA's commitment to internationally accepted best practices in sustainability reporting. Finally, to illustrate its achievements, IKEA includes case studies and examples of successful sustainability initiatives. These real-world examples show how theoretical goals are being translated into metrics that measure practical actions and tangible results.

Strategy #6: Embed Purpose in the Organization's Culture

In order to make purpose a resonant and lived experience in an organization, it should be woven into the fabric of the organization's culture. Leaders can be champions for how purpose is used in decision-making, how employees are recognized, and how the company interacts with its stakeholders. Leaders can also regularly communicate the purpose to employees as well as recognize and celebrate instances where the organization or its employees exemplify the purpose. All of these social-cultural behaviors that a leader can enact reinforce the importance of purpose-driven behavior. These behaviors may include ethical business practices, environmentally friendly initiatives, and efforts to positively impact local communities.

At SIY Global we anchored ourselves with our purpose-driven culture when we made a very significant organizational restructuring to go from being a nonprofit to a for-profit benefit corporation. It was a "crucible moment" and a critical time in our organization's history, and it is no exaggeration to say that it was our culture that helped us successfully navigate our restructuring. Here's our story:

BALANCING PURPOSE WITH PROFIT: OUR PURPOSE RESET AT SIY GLOBAL

by Rich

In early 2021, as CEO of the nonprofit Search Inside Yourself Leadership Institute (SIYLI), I began exploring with the board of directors some ways we could restructure the company so that we could have access to significant capital investment to reinvent and grow the business. Collectively, we landed on a solution that enabled SIYLI to undergo a strategic transformation by creating a related for-profit entity, called SIY Global. This decision was driven by the desire to achieve greater financial independence, scalability, and long-term sustainability while staying true to the core purpose of enabling the practice of science-based mindfulness and emotional intelligence everywhere in the world.

Leveraging its reputation and track record in social impact, SIY Global positioned itself as a socially responsible education technology platform and we were able to attract investors who had a strong interest in social impact. In April of 2022, 10 years after the founding of SIYLI as a nonprofit, we launched SIY Global as a for-profit subsidiary of SIYLI.

One of the keys to our success in restructuring, attracting investment, and significantly scaling up our business has been our unwavering commitment to a purpose-driven culture. This culture has acted as a foundational pillar, guiding our decisions, shaping our strategies, and fostering an environment where both our employees and stakeholders feel deeply connected to the company's purpose.

Restructuring with Purpose

When we faced the need to restructure, it was our purpose-driven culture that provided a clear direction. Instead of viewing restructuring merely as a cost-cutting exercise, we approached it as an opportunity to realign our operations with our core values and mission. This perspective allowed us to make difficult decisions with a clear understanding of their long-term implications. We prioritized areas that directly contributed to our purpose, ensuring that every change brought us closer to fulfilling our mission. By doing so, we were able to maintain morale and engagement among our employees, who understood that the restructuring was a step toward a more focused and impactful organization.

Our orientation toward amplifying our purpose and a culture that would enable such a purpose also helped us with investors because it created a strong value proposition. Investors today are increasingly looking for companies that not only promise financial returns but also demonstrate a strong commitment to social and environmental responsibility. By clearly articulating our purpose and showcasing our commitment to making a positive impact, we were able to attract investment from those who share our values. Our purpose has not only differentiated us in the market but also built trust with our investors, who see their investment as a contribution to a greater good. This alignment with investor values has provided us with the financial support needed to scale our operations sustainably.

As we've embarked on the journey to scale up our business, our purpose-driven culture has continued to play a crucial role. Scaling up often brings challenges such as maintaining quality, managing a new team and helping to reengage legacy team members, and reinventing the culture to pivot from a nonprofit to a for-profit mindset (while still making good on our purpose). Our clear sense of purpose has acted as a compass, helping us navigate these challenges effectively. By embedding our purpose into every aspect of our operations—from product development to customer success—we have ensured that growth does not come at the expense of our purpose and values. This consistency has strengthened our brand, enhanced customer loyalty, and attracted top talent who are passionate about our mission.

A purpose-driven culture fosters a unified vision within the organization. Our commitment to purpose has also strengthened our relationships with external stakeholders. Customers, partners, and the community at large are more inclined to support and advocate for a company that aligns with their values. This support has been critical in expanding our market reach and establishing a loyal customer base. Our transparent communication about our purpose and the impact of our initiatives has built a strong reputation and trust, which are invaluable assets in today's competitive landscape. As we continue to grow, our commitment to our purpose remains unwavering, ensuring that we not only achieve financial success but also make a meaningful impact on the world.

Strategy #7: Actively Engage External Stakeholders

Leaders serve as ambassadors for the purpose of their organizations. They already serve as the public face of the organization and can actively engage with stakeholders, including customers, suppliers, and the community, to understand their expectations and concerns and align those stakeholders around the organization's purpose. Actively engaging with external stakeholders is crucial for organizations to ensure their strategies align with stakeholder needs and expectations. Here are several effective ways leaders can receive input from and collaborate with external stakeholders:

- **Surveys, Questionnaires, and Feedback Forms**—These provide quantitative data and qualitative insights from a broad range of stakeholders.
- **Stakeholder Meetings and Forums**—These include town hall–style meetings, focus groups, advisory panels, and industry expert committees.

- **Digital Engagement Platforms**—These include online forums and communities and social media.
- **Public Disclosures**—Leaders can embrace public disclosures about company performance, challenges, and future plans and make it a part of their leadership routines. Inviting stakeholder feedback on these disclosures ensures ongoing dialogue and accountability.

Receiving input from and collaborating with external stakeholders is essential for leaders to ensure their organization remains responsive and aligned with stakeholder needs. This collaborative approach not only enhances decision-making but also contributes to the long-term success and sustainability of the organization.

INVOLVING EVERYONE TO CREATE A PURPOSE RESET

An organizational purpose reset isn't solely the responsibility of leaders; it can also involve employees of the organization. While leaders may set the vision and tone of the organization and give validation to these principles, the power of a Purpose Reset also comes from the collective input, commitment, and alignment of all employees. When employees from frontline workers to executives are involved, the purpose becomes a shared endeavor that drives connection, engagement, and motivation. This inclusive approach ensures that the reset is not just a top-down directive but a meaningful transformation that resonates at every level, fostering a culture of collaboration and shared responsibility.

KPMG's Higher Purpose initiative is an illustration of how a Purpose Reset does not have to be a top-down directive imposed by leadership alone. Instead, it is a good example of a collaborative effort that engaged employees at all levels, fostering a shared sense of ownership and commitment. By involving both leaders and employees in the process, KPMG ensured that the new purpose was not just a statement on paper but a lived reality reflected in daily actions, decisions, and operations.

CASE STUDY: KPMG
Leaders and Employees Working
Together to Create a Purpose Reset

In 2014, KPMG launched the Higher Purpose initiative to address a growing need among employees for a stronger connection to their work's broader impact.

Though the initiative was spearheaded by human resources, it was the employees who were invited to take ownership. According to former KPMG Partner and Vice Chair of Human Resources and Communications groups Bruce Pfau, "Most importantly, we recognized that just telling people from the top down about their higher purpose would not succeed. We encouraged everyone—from our interns to our chairman—to share their own stories about how their work is making a difference."[13]

The program aimed to instill a sense of purpose by highlighting the meaningful outcomes of the firm's services. This was achieved through several key strategies:

- **Storytelling Campaign:** KPMG encouraged employees to share personal stories about how their work positively impacted clients and communities. These stories were shared internally and externally, creating a narrative that emphasized the firm's role in driving positive change.
- **Purpose Workshops:** The firm conducted workshops where employees could explore and articulate their own purpose and how it aligned with KPMG's mission. These sessions helped employees connect their personal values with their professional roles.
- **Leadership Engagement:** Leaders at all levels were trained to engage employees in discussions about purpose and communicate the firm's purpose effectively and to demonstrate how

each team member's work contributes to this purpose. Leadership involvement and its engagement of the full employee base was crucial in embedding the Higher Purpose initiative across the organization.

The results were striking: After launching the Higher Purpose initiative, KPMG's annual employee engagement survey showed that 90% of employees reported that the Higher Purpose initiatives increased their pride in KPMG. Scores on KPMG's employee engagement survey rose to record levels within six months of the launch of the Higher Purpose initiative, with 85% of employees saying that KPMG was a great place to work, and after a year of the Higher Purpose launch the scores rose to 89%. In that same survey, 76% of the employees said their "job had special meaning (and was not just a job)," which was six points higher than their industry counterparts.[14] Conversely, among those whose leaders did not discuss purpose, these figures dropped to 66% and 68%. Additionally, employees whose leaders communicated about purpose were three times less likely to consider looking for another job and were significantly more motivated to strive for continuous improvement and high performance. The year-to-date actual turnover rates for these groups were 9.1% and 5.6%, respectively, illustrating the profound impact of engaging employees in purpose-driven work.[15]

Though the Higher Purpose initiative was not without some challenges—including getting the initial buy-in and investment of the senior leadership team and overcoming (through training) the risk aversion and overly conservative and tentative approaches to the initiative by some managers—KPMG's Purpose Reset demonstrates how working across levels in an organization to align on purpose measurably increases morale, career satisfaction, and engagement in an organization.

THE PURPOSE RESET IS A JOURNEY, NOT AN EVENT

Undertaking a Purpose Reset within an organization is not a onetime event but an ongoing journey that requires the collective effort of both leaders and employees. It is a process that breathes new life into the company's purpose, ensuring that every action and decision is aligned with its core values and long-term vision. This alignment fosters a renewed sense of commitment, engagement, and meaning throughout the organization.

Leaders play a pivotal role in initiating and sustaining a Purpose Reset. They must first embody the organization's purpose with unwavering integrity and authenticity. By consistently demonstrating purpose-driven leadership, they set the tone for the entire organization. Leaders communicate the purpose clearly and compellingly, ensuring that it resonates with every member of the organization. This involves not only articulating the purpose but also living it out in their daily actions and strategic decisions. Leaders can foster an environment of transparency and openness, encouraging honest conversations about the company's impact and areas where it may have drifted from its purpose.

Employees, on the other hand, are the heartbeat of a Purpose Reset. Their engagement and commitment are crucial for bringing the organization's purpose to life. Employees can reflect on their personal values and how these align with the company's mission. By finding and nurturing this alignment, they can contribute more meaningfully to the organization's purpose and goals. Employees can actively participate in purpose-driven initiatives, bringing their unique perspectives and skills to the table. Their insights and feedback are invaluable in shaping a purpose that is both inclusive and impactful.

Ultimately, a Purpose Reset is about realigning the organization's actions with its core purpose, ensuring that it remains true to its values and aspirations. Even through challenging times and inevitable purpose drifts, a reset is always possible to start the process of realigning. Leaders don't have to get everything right; we will all have moments of being off purpose. That's why we think of purpose as a continuous journey that requires dedication, honesty, and collaboration. When leaders and employees come together to embrace and enact the organization's purpose, they create a powerful force for positive change, driving the organization toward a future filled with meaning and impact.

CONCLUSION
Responding to a Changing World

I n Kahlil Gibran's poem *On Work*, he poses the question: "And what is it to work with love?" He personalizes the labor, imagining weaving cloth as if it were for your beloved or building a house as if a loved one were to live there. His conclusion: "Work is love made visible."

The Purpose Reset focuses on how we can cultivate a greater sense of purpose and meaning for us as individuals, teams, and organizations. We truly believe in the power of purpose for you in your own life, and for building strong teams and successful organizations that people want to be a part of. And we believe that the impact of aligning with purpose goes beyond this. We described in Part I that living into our sense of purpose, *we should aim to love what we do, do what we love, and love who we are while doing it. We should also love the world that we are helping to bring into being.*

Writing *The Purpose Reset*, we've been keenly aware of both the challenges and the opportunities that we face today in the workplace and the world. We live in a time of unprecedented interconnection, from global supply chains to viral internet memes. In an era characterized by rapid change and uncertainty, we must navigate shifting landscapes, disruptive technologies, and evolving stakeholder expectations. This necessitates a high degree of resilience—a capacity to adapt, learn, and thrive in the face of uncertainty, change, and adversity.

We also live in a time of unprecedented opportunity, where we can access information about any topic with a few keystrokes, where science and contemplative traditions are converging, and where more people have more choices over livelihood than ever before. This creates an imperative for us to become more aware of how we work together and a chance for us to create lives, teams, and workplaces where we feel that our unique set of individual talents is contributing to a better whole.

There is so much the world needs more of, and your vision for this better whole will be your unique take. In *Recapture the Rapture*, author Jamie Wheal writes: "Go to the intersection of our trauma and our talent, where we most acutely feel the wound of the world and have the skills to do something about it."[1] You don't need to have a grand plan to solve climate change or create world peace. As you pay attention to your skills and interests and where you feel the pain of what is needed around you, you will find your unique expression of love. For some, it might be as simple as contributing to a world where managers are caring mentors and where parents are home for dinner, or being a part of an organization that pays employees well and treats everyone with respect.

This excerpt from *Letter to a Young Activist During Troubled Times* by Clarissa Pinkola Estés, PhD, states this idea beautifully:

> Ours is not the task of fixing the entire world all at once, but of stretching out to mend the part of the world that is within our reach. Any small, calm thing that one soul can do to help another soul, to assist some portion of this poor suffering world, will help immensely.[2]

We believe each of us has a unique blend of strengths, interests, and experiences to bring to the world—and that it will evolve with us and as the world changes around us. As technology, societal needs, and priorities change, we as individuals and our organizations must periodically reassess and redefine our purpose to remain relevant and impactful.

When I (Steph) wrote myself the "ladder to love" note that became the seed of this book, I wrote on the back of the note to myself: "The struggle is the purpose!"—it's hard to change. Letting go of the ladder and shifting toward love was a major reset. There were growing pains and much to learn, yet the resistance and challenges were part of the process. As I mentioned earlier in sharing my story, when I wrote myself this note in 2015, it was one evolution of purpose. I deviated from this orientation, especially as my role at SIY evolved. I was inspired by my colleagues and what I was learning. I grew to see the depth of need for emotional intelligence and connection in the workplace and was inspired by our clients, teachers, and the impact of the work. In other words, my purpose evolved as I gained new perspectives on what the world needed, on my interests, and on how I could contribute. We expect that your sense of purpose will continue to change and evolve too.

For this reason, throughout *The Purpose Reset*, we've emphasized purpose as a process. This idea alone is a reset and shift in perspective and helps us build a stronger and more resilient purpose-oriented mindset. A Purpose Reset is a transformation that may need to be renewed, reoriented, or revived as we learn new information about ourselves and the world. It is easy to drift out of alignment, slip back into old autopilot habits, or have new insights about ourselves or changes in the world throw us off course, but we always have an opportunity for a reset. Always.

Unlike a drift in purpose, which is unconscious, allowing purpose to evolve is a deliberate response to new inputs. Being responsive to a changing world can leave us on edge, feeling vigilant instead of agile. It helps to think of this resilient and agile approach in terms of seasons. Seasons are the natural world's reminder that everything is constantly changing and that themes reemerge. Just like nature adapts to new weather patterns or plants constantly move toward sunlight, we, too, can make daily shifts toward what lights us up.

Similarly, evolutions of purpose will have different phases or seasons.

- **Spring** is a time of exploration and expansion. You might plant many seeds, test out new ideas, go through a number of different exercises, and allow what naturally grows to continue to blossom while weeding out anything that doesn't feel aligned.

- **Summer** is a vibrant time to live out your purpose. This season might show you where the organization and world around you are encouraging you to grow and what aspects of your purpose you might lean into. Summer often has a feeling of the wind at your back.
- **Fall** is harvest time. The outcomes of your purpose will be ready for picking, which may look like taking on a new purpose-aligned project or receiving glowing feedback from stakeholders and clients. Fall can be a time to become more aware of what bore fruit and what didn't.
- **Winter** is a fallow time to reset and reassess. There will be times in our lives when something overtakes purpose as a primary driver. Perhaps a health concern on a personal level, or a need to focus on financial sustainability on an organizational level. Wintertime often offers space to go within, enjoy shorter days to rest, or spend time in solitude for deeper reflection. Purpose can be simmering on the back burner, replenishing for the coming spring.

Understanding the seasons of purpose shows the beauty of each phase and helps us build resilience to move through the harder aspects of each phase as well. You might reflect on what season of awareness and action you are in.

- To build awareness, consider: What season are you in? Do you need to plant more seeds, build, harvest, or be patient? If something is off, what is it? What is needed?
- To create aligned action, consider: What actions might help you realign and reengage with purpose?

As you consider what phase you are in, you might also consider that we've presented many ideas and exercises throughout this book, and sometimes discovering your purpose will feel like throwing spaghetti on the wall to see what sticks. We hope you will take what works for you now, and either let that be enough or come back for more later when you've let this digest. In many ways, you're looking to fall into a moment of insight, and doing these exercises and bringing purpose and meaning to the forefront of your mind leaves you more insight-prone.

Introducing the idea of purpose at the beginning of the book, we described it like steering a car. There will be many micro-adjustments as you drive to help keep you heading in the right direction. Just in the course of writing this book, we have each seen adjustments in our individual sense of purpose, and a significant Purpose Reset for the SIY Global team (as we shared in the previous section). During this time, Rich published a book of poetry (near and dear to his heart and a part of what he sees as his calling), Carolina left her full-time job to start her own business and podcast focused on contemplative-based purpose and human flourishing (a total alignment of her strengths and interests), and Steph, after focusing on one-on-one coaching, is integrating more work with teams and organizations again (an exciting weaving back together of many meaningful, purposeful threads).

In this season of your life, your Purpose Reset might be a small adjustment, a mindset shift, or a new hobby or project. Or it might mean a big life or career transition. It might mean working to transform the place you work and/or the team or organization itself. Either way, we hope to leave you inspired to engage with the theme of purpose and see how you can bring more of it into your own life, your team, and your workplace. We know that this book and its many exercises might feel hard to implement and that the process of aligning with your deeper purpose isn't always a rosy one. We hope to encourage you that this is a good struggle; the struggle of becoming more and more yourself as you create meaning and connection around you. We deeply believe that this leads to a more purposeful, intentional, and kinder world.

Together, let's create workplaces, organizations, and a world that fosters love and fulfillment. Let's make our love visible in our work.

AFTERWORD

I looked around the room of international high school students gathered for my talk on how to start and fund a company. They were a notably attentive, well-dressed, and curious bunch. Not a phone in sight, I had their full attention, a rarity in high school settings these days.

When I asked "How many of you are here because you want to be a start-up founder?" every single student raised their hand. Curious to hear their motivations (the entrepreneurship journey is a tough one!), I followed with "Why?" and went around the room to hear their one word answers: "Money." "Success." "Money." "Money." "Change." "Money." "Achievement." "Money." It was a stark reminder of what drives so many to the entrepreneurial path and, frankly, why so many struggle to succeed. Starting and building a company is extremely challenging work, especially absent a passionate purpose and mission—outside of financial gain. *A tough road ahead for this group*, I thought to myself.

Yet, these responses evoked empathy as well. Our global cultures nudge us toward materialism over service, individuality over collectivism, and personal achievement over impact. It's no wonder that our youth is blinded by the appeal of financial gain and so many organizations often feel rudderless from the inside, lost in a sea of pressure driving infinite achievement, efficiency optimization, and ruthless competition. Yet, it is clear that these shallow themes will not serve our systems or species long term. To survive and thrive individually and collectively, we must prioritize work rooted in meaning, broader impact, and the advancement of our individual and collective well-being.

It is no small feat to take on the challenge of transforming how organizations work from the inside out and then capture a simple set of tools to scale such impact. Yet, the authors, Steph, Carolina, and Rich have done just that. As a long-time supporter and admirer of their work at SIY Global and beyond, I know that the insights and frameworks captured within these pages can be as transformative for you as they have been for the many clients they've served, organizations they've steered, and leaders they've impacted along the way, including me.

Reading through *The Purpose Reset*, I'm struck by how deeply its message resonated with my own journey—both personal and professional. Like many of you, I've struggled with a sense of aimlessness, deep fatigue, and a fear of regret while navigating the journeys of motherhood, executive leadership, and even as a founder. In each case, more deeply connecting with purpose sparked a flurry of new energy and positive, sustainable change. In motherhood it's been a shift from "because I told you to" to "because I love you and I want you to be safe." In leading teams I've evolved "our company depends on hitting these numbers" to "if we can scale as planned, we will have a broader impact and more sustainable path to democratizing industry access." As an investor, the shift has been from "the investment is good if we will get a return" to "let's invest in this founder because they're building value *and* are so passionate about driving impact via their mission, we're certain they won't give up." And most recently, as an author and movement leader, my internal dialogue has shifted from "I hope people will appreciate what I am doing" to "if even one human is touched and inspired by my work, that is enough" (and mean it).

In each case, discovering and choosing to abide by a deeper purpose followed extensive trial and error, humbling missteps, and extended time investments. You hold in your hands a guide, a set of tools, an invitation to simplify and clarify your own path to purposefulness that will support a deep and practical connection in ways I wish I'd had along my own journey.

Perhaps it is frustration with what is starting to feel like "the old way" of leading, building, or working that inspired you to pick up this book. Maybe you are experiencing burnout or your own sense of rudderlessness. You might even be working to educate or coach members of a future generation of entrepreneurs. In a time when so many of us seek alignment with a deeper meaning and reason for our efforts, these authors have given us a gift. Having the tools and framework to both prioritize and realize purpose has never been more timely or essential. In deepening our capacity for compassionate, humane, and sustainable work, we'll serve not only ourselves, but humanity as a whole.

Be well, and onward.

—Cecily Mak
Autumn 2024

ACKNOWLEDGMENTS

This book would not be possible without the incredible support and contributions of so many.

First and foremost, to the amazing staff (past and present) at SIY Global and the Search Inside Yourself Leadership Institute—you show us what it looks like to work with love and purpose. Being part of the team is nothing short of a life-transforming experience, and it's being among you that makes this true. We're inspired by your dedication to spreading the power of mindfulness, leadership, and emotional intelligence, and we learn from you as we aim to embody what we teach.

To our SIY Certified Teacher community and our amazing clients, thank you for your passion, trust, and partnership. You've been our companions on this journey, sharing your wisdom, challenges, and triumphs as you bring more purpose to your work, your lives, and your communities. We are deeply grateful to everyone who trusted us with their stories—your experiences brought this book to life and will undoubtedly inspire countless others.

To our board members and key supporters, Cecily Mak, Jayesh Goyal, Thomasina Williams, Ryan Moore, Elizabeth Koch, Zach Goren, and Lisa Gregorian, who have provided steadfast guidance, support, and gentle nudges in the right direction, thank you for believing in this mission and for bringing your expertise and challenge. Special thank-you to Cecily Mak and Chip Conley—exemplars of what it means to do what you love with crystal-clear purpose and effusive joy. Thank you for lending your stories to bookend our words.

A huge thank-you to the publishing team at BenBella/Matt Holt Books, who guided us through this process with patience and expertise. Deep gratitude to Matt Holt for taking us on, to Katie Dickman for your insightful editing, helping us discern what to leave on the cutting room floor and what to embellish, and to the entire team for your support to keep us on track and bring this book to the world. Thank you, Jesseca Salky and Eryn Kalavsky, our incredible and determined agents. Without you, this book would still be a messy Google doc of ideas we're just kicking around.

To our partners, families, and friends, thank you for tolerating our long hours hunched over laptops and endless conversations about purpose, and for pretending to be fascinated by the latest article we read. Your love and support kept us afloat, especially when we were drowning in research and struggling to get to a first draft.

Finally, to everyone around the world who refuses to stay on autopilot—who instead seeks to connect and reconnect with your purpose despite the messiness and uncertainty of life—thank you for being our hope and inspiration. Keeping you in mind as the audience we were writing for guided us back to our purpose again and again. Your courage to live with intention and create positive ripples in the world is what makes this work so meaningful.

NOTES

INTRODUCTION

1. Steve Crabtree, "Worldwide, 13% of Employees Are Engaged at Work," Gallup, 2013, https://news.gallup.com/poll/165269/worldwide-employees-engaged-work .aspx.
2. McKinsey, "Employee Burnout Is Ubiquitous, Alarming—and Still Under-reported," 2021, https://www.mckinsey.com/featured-insights/coronavirus -leading-through-the-crisis/charting-the-path-to-the-next-normal/employee -burnout-is-ubiquitous-alarming-and-still-underreported.
3. PwC, "Putting Purpose to Work: A Study of Purpose in the Workplace," 2016, https://www.pwc.com/us/en/about-us/corporate-responsibility/assets/pwc -putting-purpose-to-work-purpose-survey-report.pdf.

CHAPTER 1

1. *Merriam-Webster*, under "purpose," https://www.merriam-webster.com /dictionary/purpose. Accessed October 7, 2022.
2. "Q&A with Erin Cech, author of *The Trouble with Passion*," University of California Press, 2021, https://www.ucpress.edu/blog/57580/qa-with-erin-cech -author-of-the-trouble-with-passion/.
3. As quoted by Gil Bailie in *Violence Unveiled: Humanity at the Crossroads* (Herder & Herder: Frieberg, Germany, 2021 [1995]).

CHAPTER 2

1. R. Pendell, "Stressed, Sad, and Anxious: A Snapshot of the Global Workforce," *Harvard Business Review*, 2022, https://hbr.org/2022/06/stressed-sad-and -anxious-a-snapshot-of-the-global-workforce.

2. WHO, "Mental Health and Substance Use: In the Workplace," World Health Organization, https://www.who.int/teams/mental-health-and-substance-use/promotion-prevention/mental-health-in-the-workplace.

3. Jake Herway, "Increase Productivity at the Lowest Possible Cost," Gallup, October 15, 2020, https://www.gallup.com/workplace/321743/increase-productivity-lowest-possible-cost.aspx.

4. Ben Wigert and Sangeeta Agrawal, "Employee Burnout, Part 1: The Five Main Causes," Gallup, July 12, 2018, https://www.gallup.com/workplace/237059/employee-burnout-part-main-causes.aspx.

5. "Burn-Out an 'Occupational Phenomenon': International Classification of Diseases," World Health Organization, May 28, 2019, https://www.who.int/news/item/28-05-2019-burn-out-an-occupational-phenomenon-international-classification-of-diseases.

6. Ibid., 7–8.

7. Tammy Erickson, "Meaning Is the New Money," *Harvard Business Review*, March 23, 2011, https://hbr.org/2011/03/challenging-our-deeply-held-as.

8. Andrew Reece, Gabriella Kellerman, and Alexi Robichaux, *Meaning and Purpose at Work* (Toronto, Ontario, CA: BetterUp, 2018), https://grow.betterup.com/resources/meaning-and-purpose-report.

9. Hu Jing and Jacob B. Hirsch, "Accepting Lower Salaries for Meaningful Work," *Frontiers in Psychology* 8, no. 1649 (2017), https://doi.org/10.3389/fpsyg.2017.01649.

10. Roula Amire, "Purpose at Work Predicts If Employees Will Stay or Quit Their Jobs," Great Place to Work, 2022, https://www.greatplacetowork.com/resources/blog/purpose-at-work-predicts-if-employees-will-stay-or-quit-their-jobs.

11. *Putting Purpose to Work: A Study of Purpose in the Workplace* (New York: PWC, 2016), https://www.pwc.com/us/en/about-us/corporate-responsibility/assets/pwc-putting-purpose-to-work-purpose-survey-report.pdf.

12. Claudine Gartenberg, Andrea Prat, and George Serafeim, "Corporate Purpose and Financial Performance," *Harvard Business School*, October 11, 2016, https://hbswk.hbs.edu/item/corporate-purpose-and-financial-performance.

13. Amire, "Purpose at Work Predicts If Employees Will Stay or Quit Their Jobs."

14. Shawn Achor, Andrew Reece, Gabriella Rosen Kellerman, et al., "9 Out of 10 People Are Willing to Earn Less Money to Do More-Meaningful Work," *Harvard Business Review*, November 6, 2018, https://hbr.org/2018/11/9-out-of-10-people-are-willing-to-earn-less-money-to-do-more-meaningful-work.

CHAPTER 3

1. Bronnie Ware, *The Top Five Regrets of the Dying: A Life Transformed by the Dearly Departing* (Hay House, 2012).

2. "Employees Seek Personal Value and Purpose at Work. Be Prepared to Deliver," Gartner, January 13, 2022, https://www.gartner.com/en/articles/employees-seek -personal-value-and-purpose-at-work-be-prepared-to-deliver.

3. Cortland J. Dahla, Christine D. Wilson-Mendenhalla, and Richard J. Davidson, "The Plasticity of Well-Being: A Training-Based Framework for the Cultivation of Human Flourishing," *Proceedings of the National Academy of Sciences* 117, no. 51 (2020): 32197–32206, https://www.pnas.org/doi/10.1073/pnas.201 4859117.

4. PERMA™ Theory of Well-Being and PERMA™ Workshops, University of Pennsylvania, School of Arts and Sciences, accessed on May 20, 2024, https://ppc.sas .upenn.edu/learn-more/perma-theory-well-being-and-perma-workshops.

5. Brian D. Ostafin and Travis Proulx, "Meaning in Life and Resilience to Stressors," *Anxiety, Stress, & Coping* 33, no. 6 (2020): 603–622, https://doi.org/10 .1080/10615806.2020.1800655.

6. *2015 Workforce Purpose Index*, Imperative and New York University, 2015, accessed on June 3, 2024, https://www.imperative.com/wp-content/uploads /2023/04/Imperative-2016-Workforce-Purpose-Index.pdf.

7. A. H. Maslow, "A Theory of Human Motivation," *Psychological Review* 50, no. 4 (1943): 370–396, https://doi.org/10.1037/h0054346.

CHAPTER 4

1. Mindful Nation UK, Report by the Mindfulness All-Party Parliamentary Group (MAPPG), 2015, https://mindfulnessinschools.org/wp-content/uploads/2017 /09/Mindfulness-APPG-Report_Mindful-Nation-UK_Oct2015-1.pdf.

2. Ever Forward Website, accessed on October 26, 2023, https://everforwardclub .org/the-ever-forward-club.

3. Roz Savage, *The Obituary Exercise*, https://www.rozsavage.com/the-obituary -exercise, accessed on November 5, 2023.

CHAPTER 5

1. Herminia Ibarra, "Working Identity—Nine Unconventional Strategies for Reinventing Your Career" from Harvard Business School's Working Knowledge, February 10, 2003, https://hbswk.hbs.edu/archive/working-identity-nine -unconventional-strategies-for-reinventing-your-career.

2. Shankar Vedantam and Maggie Penman, "How to Build a Better Job" on the *Hidden Brain* podcast, March 29, 2016, https://www.npr.org/2016/03/28 /471859161/how-to-build-a-better-job.

3. L. Fosslien and M. W. Duffy, *No Hard Feelings: The Secret Power of Embracing Emotions at Work* (New York: Portfolio, 2019), 59–60.

CHAPTER 6

1. Sarah Arthur, "Laying Bricks or Building the Kingdom?" University of Northwestern St. Paul, February 17, 2022, https://unwsp.edu/blog/laying-bricks-or-building-the-kingdom.

2. Edward L. Deci, "Effects of Externally Mediated Rewards on Intrinsic Motivation," *Journal of Personality and Social Psychology* 18, no. 1 (1971): 105–115, https://selfdeterminationtheory.org/SDT/documents/1971_Deci.pdf.

3. Edward L. Deci and Richard Flaste, *Why We Do What We Do: The Dynamics of Personal Autonomy* (New York: G. P. Putnam's Sons, 1995), https://psycnet.apa.org/record/1995-97872-000.

4. RSA Animate, "Drive: The Surprising Truth About What Motivates Us," YouTube, April 1, 2010, https://www.youtube.com/watch?v=u6XAPnuFjJc.

5. Tom See, "Going the Extra Miler," Iowa Now, April 27, 2015, https://now.uiowa.edu/news/2015/04/going-extra-miler; N. Li, H. H. Zhao, S. L. Walter, X.-a. Zhang, and J. Yu, "Achieving More with Less: Extra Milers' Behavioral Influences in Teams," *Journal of Applied Psychology* 100, no. 4 (2015): 1025–1039, https://psycnet.apa.org/record/2015-04971-001.

6. "Case Study: Search Inside Yourself Micropractices in a High-Stress Environment," SIY Global, https://www.siyglobal.com/resources/mindfulness-practices-in-a-high-stress-environment.

7. Valerie Keller, "The Business Case for Purpose," *Harvard Business Review*, 2015, https://assets.ey.com/content/dam/ey-sites/ey-com/en_gl/topics/digital/ey-the-business-case-for-purpose.pdf.

8. Richard M. Ryan and Edward L. Deci, "Self-Determination Theory and the Facilitation of Intrinsic Motivation, Social Development, and Well-Being," *American Psychologist* 55, no. 1 (2000): 68–78, https://selfdeterminationtheory.org/SDT/documents/2000_RyanDeci_SDT.pdf.

9. Christian Jarret, "Increase the Meaningfulness of Your Work by Considering How It Helps Others," British Psychological Society, September 5, 2017, https://www.bps.org.uk/research-digest/increase-meaningfulness-your-work-considering-how-it-helps-others.

10. "Acts of Kindness Are the Key to Happiness: Study," CBC, December 15, 2022, https://www.cbc.ca/documentaries/the-passionate-eye/acts-of-kindness-are-the-key-to-happiness-study-1.6682912.

11. Charles Duhigg, "What Google Learned from Its Quest to Build the Perfect Team," *New York Times Magazine*, February 25, 2016, https://www.nytimes.com/2016/02/28/magazine/what-google-learned-from-its-quest-to-build-the-perfect-team.html.

12. "reWork: Understand "What Is an Effective Team?," Google, accessed March 31, 2024, https://rework.withgoogle.com/jp/guides/understanding-team-effectiveness #introduction.

13. Cortland J. Dahl, Christine D. Wilson-Mendenhall, and Richard J. Davidson, "The Plasticity of Well-Being: A Training-Based Framework for the Cultivation of Human Flourishing," *Proceedings of the National Academy of Sciences* 117, no. 51 (2020): 32197–32206, https://www.pnas.org/doi/10.1073/pnas.2014859117.

14. "Strategic Growth & Innovation, Achieve the Unimaginable," McKinsey, https://www.mckinsey.com/capabilities/strategy-and-corporate-finance/how-we -help-clients/Strategic-Growth-and-Innovation.

15. Sonya Mann, "Brené Brown: Being Vulnerable Is a Key to Innovation," INC .com, October 11, 2017, https://www.inc.com/sonya-mann/brene-brown-being -a-brave-leader-means-being-vulnerable.html.

CHAPTER 7

1. "reWork: Understand "What Is an Effective Team?," Google, accessed March 31, 2024, https://rework.withgoogle.com/jp/guides/understanding-team-effectiveness #introduction.

2. "reWork: Team Effectiveness Guide," Google, accessed March 31, 2024, https://static1.squarespace.com/static/596a07c029687fd47a2d41cc/t/597 47c1cdb29d6a05c593a18/1500806173410/reWork+Team+Effectiveness+ Discussion+Guide.pdf.

3. David A. Garvin, "How Google Sold Its Engineers on Management," *Harvard Business Review*, December 2023, https://hbr.org/2013/12/how-google-sold-its -engineers-on-management.

4. S. J. Prins, L. M. Bates, K. M. Keyes, and C. Muntaner, "Anxious? Depressed? You Might Be Suffering from Capitalism: Contradictory Class Locations and the Prevalence of Depression and Anxiety in the USA," *Sociology of Health and Illness* 37, no. 8 (2015): 1352–1372, https://doi.org/10.1111/1467-9566.12315.

5. Aaron Kay, "Love Your Job? Someone May Be Taking Advantage of You," Duke Fuqua School of Business, April 24, 2019, https://www.fuqua.duke.edu/duke -fuqua-insights/kay-passion-exploitation.

6. B. T. Litz, N. Stein, E. Delaney, L. Lebowit, W. P. Nash, C. Silva, and S. Maguen, "Moral Injury and Moral Repair in War Veterans: A Preliminary Model and Intervention Strategy," *Clinical Psychology Review* 29, no. 8 (2009): 695–706, https://pubmed.ncbi.nlm.nih.gov/19683376/.

7. H. G. Koenig and F. Al Zaben, "Moral Injury: An Increasingly Recognized and Widespread Syndrome," *Journal of Religion & Health* 60, no. 5 (2021): 2989–3011, https://www.ncbi.nlm.nih.gov/pmc/articles/PMC8270769/.

CHAPTER 8

1. Niki Lustig, "Find Your Team's Purpose," Medium, March 202, 2015, https://medium.com/@nikilustig/finding-your-team-s-purpose-3a672773ed93.

2. Brad Wolfe, "Can Higher Purpose Help Your Team Survive and Thrive?" *Greater Good*, March 10, 2015, https://greatergood.berkeley.edu/article/item/can_higher_purpose_help_your_team_survive_and_thrive.

3. Brad Federman, *Cultivating Culture: 101 Ways to Foster Engagement in 15 Minutes or Less* (Dallas: Matt Holt Books, 2022), 23–24.

4. Claire Hastwell, "The 3 Biggest Predictors of Employee Retention (Especially Millennials)," Great Place to Work, July 16, 2021, https://www.greatplacetowork.com/resources/blog/3-keys-to-millennial-employee-retention.

5. Kim Scott, *Radical Candor: How to Get What You Want by Saying What You Mean* (London: Pan Books, 2017), 51.

6. Ibid., 44–47.

7. "What Is the RBSE?," Center for Positive Organizations, https://reflectedbestselfexercise.com/about.

8. Adam M. Grant, Justin M. Berg, and Daniel M. Cable, "Job Titles as Identity Badges: How Self-Reflective Titles Can Reduce Emotional Exhaustion," *Academy of Management Journal* 57, no. 4 (2013): https://journals.aom.org/doi/abs/10.5465/amj.2012.0338.

9. "Creative Job Titles Can Energize Workers," *Harvard Business Review*, May 2016, https://hbr.org/2016/05/creative-job-titles-can-energize-workers.

10. Adam M. Grant, Justin M. Berg, et al., "Serious Play at the Make-A-Wish Foundation," Center for Positive Organizations, October 2009, https://wdi-publishing.com/product/serious-play-at-the-make-a-wish-foundation/.

11. Federman, *Cultivating Culture*, 23–24.

12. Scott, *Radical Candor*, 50.

13. "What You Need to Know About Team Purpose (Plus Examples of Team Purpose Statements)," Saberr, September 17, 2021, https://blog.saberr.com/the-foundations-of-great-teamwork-purpose.

14. Mark Bonchek, "Purpose Is Good. Shared Purpose Is Better," *Harvard Business Review*, March 14, 2013, https://hbr.org/2013/03/purpose-is-good-shared-purpose.

15. Indeed Editorial Team, "8 Steps for Writing a Purpose Statement (With Examples)," Indeed, February 3, 2023, https://www.indeed.com/career-advice/career-development/purpose-statements#:~:text=Purpose%20statement.

16. Bonchek, "Purpose Is Good. Shared Purpose Is Better."

17. Dan Cable, "Helping Your Team Feel the Purpose in Their Work," *Harvard Business Review*, October 22, 2019, https://hbr.org/2019/10/helping-your-team-feel-the-purpose-in-their-work.

18. Blake A. Allan, "Task Significance and Meaningful Work: A Longitudinal Study," *Journal of Vocational Behavior* 102 (2017): 174–182, https://www.sciencedirect.com/science/article/abs/pii/S0001879117300702.

19. Christian Jarrett, "Increase the Meaningfulness of Your Work by Considering How It Helps Others," British Psychological Society, September 5, 2017, https://www.bps.org.uk/research-digest/increase-meaningfulness-your-work-considering-how-it-helps-others.

20. R. F. Baumeister, E. Bratslavsky, C. Finkenauer, and K. D. Vohs, "Bad Is Stronger Than Good," *Review of General Psychology* 5, no. 4 (2001): 323–370, https://doi.org/10.1037/1089-2680.5.4.323.

21. Mike Robbins, "Why Employees Need Both Recognition and Appreciation," *Harvard Business Review*, November 12, 2019, https://hbr.org/2019/11/why-employees-need-both-recognition-and-appreciation.

22. Brené Brown, "Adam Grant and Simon Sinek on What's Happening at Work, Part 1 of 2," Brené Brown, October 23, 2022, https://brenebrown.com/podcast/whats-happening-at-work-part-1-of-2/#transcript.

CHAPTER 9

1. Ashley Reichheld and Amelia Dunlop, *The Four Factors of Trust: How Organizations Can Earn Lifelong Loyalty* (Hoboken, NJ: John Wiley & Sons, 2022).

2. Monitor Deloitte, "The Purpose Premium: Why a Purpose-Driven Strategy Is Good for Business," Deloitte, 2021.

3. Edelman Trust Barometer, "Trust, the New Brand Equity," 2021, https://www.edelman.com/sites/g/files/aatuss191/files/2021-07/2021_Edelman_Trust%20Barometer_Specl_Report%20Trust_The_New_Brand_Equity_1.pdf.

4. T. Irwin, *Aristotle's First Principles* (Oxford: Oxford University Press, 1988).

5. Leigh Gallagher, *The Airbnb Story: How to Disrupt an Industry, Make Billions of Dollars . . . and Plenty of Enemies* (London: Penguin, 2018).

6. "What Makes Airbnb, Airbnb," Airbnb Newsroom, December 8, 2021, https://news.airbnb.com/what-makes-airbnb-airbnb/.

7. "About Google," Google.com, retrieved from the Google company website, 2024.

8. *Harvard Business Review*, Employee Engagement Survey, 2022.

9. "Human Capital Trends Report," Deloitte Insights, 2024, https://www2.deloitte.com/content/dam/insights/articles/glob176836_global-human-capital-trends-2024/DI_Global-Human-Capital-Trends-2024.pdf.

10. "State of the Global Workplace Report," Gallup, 2023, https://web.archive.org/web/20240409123548/https://www.gallup.com/workplace/349484/state-of-the-global-workplace.aspx#ite-506924.

11. Merck Pharmaceuticals, "Who We Are," retrieved from the company website, 2024.

12. D. Wainer, "What a $200 Billion Drug Reveals About Big Pharma's Playbook," *Wall Street Journal*, February 5, 2024, https://www.wsj.com/health/pharma /what-a-200-billion-blockbuster-drug-reveals-about-big-pharmas-playbook -e8d917c3.

13. "Vision and Mission," Procter & Gamble, retrieved from the company website, 2024.

14. "Purpose: Sifting from Why to How," *McKinsey Quarterly*, McKinsey & Co., 2020.

15. Ashley Reichheld and Amelia Dunlop, *The Four Factors of Trust: How Organizations Can Earn Lifelong Loyalty* (Hoboken, NJ: John Wiley & Sons, 2022).

16. "About Us," Lego, retrieved from the Lego company website, 2024.

17. Johnny Davis, "How Lego Clicked: The Super Brand That Reinvented Itself," *The Guardian*, June 4, 2017, https://www.theguardian.com/lifeandstyle/2017 /jun/04/how-lego-clicked-the-super-brand-that-reinvented-itself.

18. B. Tabrizi, "How Microsoft Became Innovative Again," *Harvard Business Review*, February 20, 2023, https://hbr.org/2023/02/how-microsoft-became-innovative -again.

19. Satya Nadella et al., *Hit Refresh: The Quest to Rediscover Microsoft's Soul and Imagine a Better Future for Everyone* (New York: Harper Business, 2017).

20. "About," Microsoft, retrieved from the company website 2024.

21. R. Durand and I. Ioannou, "How Leaders Can Create a Purpose-Driven Culture," *Harvard Business Review*, November 7, 2023, https://hbr.org/2023/11/how -leaders-can-create-a-purpose-driven-culture.

22. H. Joly, "Creating a Meaningful Corporate Purpose," *Harvard Business Review*, October 28, 2021, https://hbr.org/2021/10/creating-a-meaningful-corporate -purpose.

23. "From Me to We: The Rise of the Purpose-Led Brand," *Accenture Strategy Research Report*, Accenture, December 5, 2018, https://www.accenture.com/content/dam /accenture/final/a-com-migration/custom/_acnmedia/thought-leadership-assets /pdf/Accenture-CompetitiveAgility-GCPR-POV.pdf.

24. "People Prefer Brands with Aligned Corporate Purpose and Values," World Economic Forum, Stakeholder capitalism report, December 17, 2021, https:// www.weforum.org/agenda/2021/12/people-prefer-brands-with-aligned -corporate-purpose-and-values/.

25. Eric Almquist, Kelly Edwards, Philip Dowling, and Ashley King, "Does a Purpose Help Brands Grow?" The Visionary CEO's Guide to Sustainability, Bain & Company, November 13, 2023, https://www.bain.com/insights/does-a-purpose -help-brands-grow-ceo-sustainability-guide-2023/.

26. L. Foster, "The 100 Most Sustainable U.S. Companies Right Now," *Barron's*, March 3, 2023, https://www.barrons.com/articles/most-sustainable-esg-us -companies-1b5f70fd.

27. T. Swallow, "Top 10: Most Sustainable Global Brands," *Sustainability Magazine*, March 31, 2022, https://sustainabilitymag.com/sustainability/10-most-sustainable-global-brands.

28. Institute for Sustainable Investing, Morgan Stanley, "Individuals' Interest in Sustainability Is on the Rise," January 26, 2024, https://www.morganstanley.com/ideas/sustainable-investing-on-the-rise.

29. D.F. Larcker, et al., "2024 Institutional Investor Survey on Sustainability," Stanford Business School, 2024, https://www.gsb.stanford.edu/faculty-research/publications/2024-institutional-investor-survey-sustainability.

30. A. Goldberg, "The Power of Partnerships: How Adobe and Microsoft Deliver for Digital Businesses," *CIO Magazine*, March 31, 2020, https://www.cio.com/article/193209/the-power-of-partnership-how-adobe-and-microsoft-deliver-for-digital-businesses.html.

31. "About Us," Starbucks.com, retrieved from Starbucks company website, 2024.

32. G.V. Milano et al., "A Deeper Look at the Return on Purpose: Before and During a Crisis." *Journal of Applied Corporate Finance* 33, no. 2 (2021): 95–111, https://doi.org/10.1111/jacf.12460.

33. "Human Capital Trends Report," Deloitte Insights, 2023, https://www2.deloitte.com/us/en/insights/focus/human-capital-trends/2023.html.

34. "Our Story," Warby Parker, retrieved from the Warby Parker company website, 2024.

35. "Warby Parker: Dave Gilboa & Neil Blumenthal," from the *How I Built This* podcast with Guy Raz, 2016, https://www.npr.org/2018/03/26/586048422/warby-parker-dave-gilboa-neil-blumenthal.

CHAPTER 10

1. B. Hook, "Start with Values," Values Institute, 2023.

2. "Our Purpose," Apple, retrieved from the Apple company website, 2024.

3. "Our Vision," Apple, retrieved from the Apple company website, 2024.

4. "Our Mission," Apple, retrieved from the Apple company website, 2024.

5. "Our Values," Apple, retrieved from the Apple company website, 2024.

6. B. Merchant, *The One Device: The Secret History of the iPhone* (Little, Brown, 2017).

7. S. E. Needleman and A. Tilley, "Apple Changes Its App Store Policy. Critics Call the Moves 'Outrageous,'" *Wall Street Journal*, January 17, 2024, https://www.wsj.com/tech/apple-changes-its-app-store-policy-critics-call-the-moves-outrageous-7c023e0c.

8. T. S. Buda et al., "Two Edges of the Screen: Unpacking Positive and Negative Associations Between Phone Use in Everyday Contexts and Subjective Well-Being," *PLoS ONE* 18, no. 4 (2023): e0284104, https://doi.org/10.1371/journal.pone.0284104.

9. Ashley Reichheld and Amelia Dunlop, *The Four Factors of Trust: How Organizations Can Earn Lifelong Loyalty* (Hoboken, NJ: John Wiley & Sons, 2022).

10. C. Doherty and J. Kilney, "Americans Have Become Much Less Positive About Tech Companies' Impact on the US," Pew Research Center, July 29, 2019, https://www.pewresearch.org/short-reads/2019/07/29/americans-have-become-much-less-positive-about-tech-companies-impact-on-the-u-s/.

11. Accenture Strategy, Research Report, "Generation P(urpose): From Fidelity to Future Value," February 2020, https://www.accenture.com/us-en/insights/strategy/generation-purpose.

12. "CVS Caremark Announces Corporate Name Change to CVS Health to Reflect Broader Health Care Commitment," CVS Health, September 3, 2014, https://www.cvshealth.com/news-and-insights/press-releases/cvs-caremark-announces-corporate-name-change-to-cvs-health-to.

13. Carol Cone, "What Does a Purpose-Driven Company Look Like?" Salesforce, August 5, 2022, https://www.salesforce.com/blog/what-does-a-purpose-driven-company-look-like/.

14. "Tobacco-Free for Five Years," CVS Health, accessed September 21, 2022, https://www.cvshealth.com/news-and-insights/articles/tobacco-free-for-five-years.

15. "CVS Health Follows a Profound Purpose Prescription," Purpose 360, Eileen Howard Boone, accessed September 21, 2022, https://purpose360podcast.com/episodes/cvs-health-follows-a-profound-purpose-prescription.

16. Ed Catmull and Amy Wallace, *Creativity, Inc.: Overcoming the Unseen Forces That Stand in the Way of True Inspiration* (New York: Random House, 2014).

17. J. Woolf, "How Pixar Fosters a Culture of Vulnerability at Work," *Harvard Business Review*, 2024, https://hbr.org/2024/03/how-pixar-fosters-a-culture-of-vulnerability-at-work.

18. Adam Grant, *ReThinking Podcast: The Psychology of Self-Persuasion with Elliot Aronson*, 2023, https://www.ted.com/podcasts/rethinking-with-adam-grant/the-psychology-of-self-persuasion-with-elliot-aronson-transcript.

19. Shawn Tully, "How Boeing Broke Down: Inside the Series of Leadership Failures That Hobbled the Airline Giant," *Fortune*, February 22, 2024, https://fortune.com/2024/02/22/boeing-stock-crash-history-737-outlook/.

20. B. George, "How Boeing's Problems with the 737 Max Began 25 Years Ago," Harvard Business School, Working Knowledge, January 24, 2024, https://hbswk.hbs.edu/item/why-boeings-problems-with-737-max-began-more-than-25-years-ago.

21. "How We Act," Boeing, retrieved from the Boeing company website, 2024.

22. George, "How Boeing's Problems with the 737 Max Began 25 Years Ago."

23. L. Wayne, "Boeing Chief Forced to Resign in Ethics Dispute," *New York Times*, March 8, 2005, https://www.nytimes.com/2005/03/08/business/boeing-chief-forced-to-resign-in-ethics-dispute.html.

24. "About Us," Etsy, retrieved from the Etsy company website, 2024.

25. Etsy employee experience ratings and reviews, retrieved from Glassdoor, 2024; Indeed.com, 2024.

26. "Our Mission," Patagonia, retrieved from the Patagonia company website, 2024.

27. Y. Chouinard and V. Stanley, "The Future of the Responsible Company: What We've Learned from Patagonia's First 50 Years," Patagonia Works, 2023, https://www.patagonia.com/product/the-future-of-the-responsible-company -paperback/BK235.html.

28. "Our Mission," World Central Kitchen, retrieved from the World Central Kitchen website, 2023.

29. K. Severson, "How José Andrés and His Corps of Cooks Became Leaders in Disaster Aid," *New York Times*, 2024, https://www.nytimes.com/2024/04/02 /dining/jose-andres-central-kitchen-disaster-aid.html.

30. "Our Company," eBay, retrieved from the eBay company website, 2024.

CHAPTER 11

1. R. Durand and I. Ioannou, "How Leaders Can Create a Purpose-Driven Culture," *Harvard Business Review*, November 7, 2023, https://hbr.org/2023/11/how -leaders-can-create-a-purpose-driven-culture.

2. Seth Stevenson, "Marvel's Most Superhuman Feat Was Saving Itself," Slate, 2021, https://slate.com/business/2021/03/marvel-comics-history-bankruptcy -cinematic-universe.html.

3. S. Kumar, "Marvel Studios: The Juggernaut Rolls On," LinkedIn Learning, 2018.

4. B. Fritz, *With Great Power: The Rise of the Superhero Cinema*, podcast series, *Wall Street Journal*, June 2023, https://www.wsj.com/podcasts/the-journal /introducing-with-great-power-the-rise-of-superhero-cinema/3f8af98c-13e6 -4160-acb8-c24c73ce0496.

5. Stevenson, "Marvel's Most Superhuman Feat Was Saving Itself."

6. Kumar, "Marvel Studios: The Juggernaut Rolls On."

7. Stevenson, "Marvel's Most Superhuman Feat Was Saving Itself."

8. *Beyond Zero*, written/directed by Nathan Havey (Denver: HaveyPro Cinema, 2023).

9. Simon Mainwaring, "Purpose at Work: Lessons from Interface on How to Lead with Purpose," *Forbes*, 2021, https://www.forbes.com/sites/simonmainwaring /2021/06/11/purpose-at-work-lessons-from-interface-on-how-to-lead-with -purpose/.

10. Ibid.

11. Marc Benioff and Carlye Adler, *Behind the Cloud: The Untold Story of How Salesforce.com Went from Idea to Billion-Dollar Company—and Revolutionized an Industry* (Hoboken, NJ: Wiley-Blackwell, 2009).

12. *IKEA Sustainability Report FY23*, Inter IKEA Group, 2023, https://www.ikea
.com/global/en/our-business/reports/sustainability-report-fy23-240125/.

13. B. N. Pfau, "How an Accounting Firm Convinced Its Employees They Could
Change the World," *Harvard Business Review*, October 6, 2015, https://hbr.org
/2015/10/how-an-accounting-firm-convinced-its-employees-they-could-change
-the-world.

14. Ibid.

15. Ibid.

CONCLUSION

1. Jamie Wheal, *Recapture the Rapture: Rethinking God, Sex, and Death in a World
That's Lost Its Mind* (New York: HarperCollins, 2021).

2. Clarissa Pinkola Estés, *Letter to a Young Activist During Troubled Times*, Maven
Productions, https://www.mavenproductions.com/letter-to-a-young-activist.

INDEX

ABOUT THE AUTHORS

Photo by Sarah Deragon

Rich Fernandez, PhD, is the CEO of SIY Global, a global professional development organization that originated at Google, where it was known as Search Inside Yourself. Rich has dedicated his career to building more purposeful, mindful, and high-performing workplaces. Rich draws on his past experience as Head of Executive Education at Google, as well as senior leadership roles at eBay, JPMorgan Chase, and Bank of America. He is a frequent contributor to the *Harvard Business Review*, among other publications. Rich received his PhD in counseling psychology and MA in organizational psychology from Columbia University. He has been a featured speaker at the United Nations, Dreamforce, and the Association for Training and Development, among other renowned organizations. Rich is a poetry and meditation enthusiast and lives in San Francisco, where he finds sources of renewal and inspiration in long hikes on the coast and in the nearby redwood forests.

Carolina Lasso is the author of *The Path to Flourishing*, founder of the human flourishing academy Plenari, and the creator of the *Plena-Mente* podcast. She served as the Global Head of Marketing at SIY Global and is a certified Search Inside Yourself teacher. She's passionate about creating practical tools to help organizations and individuals align with their purpose and flourish, by combining her business background with her experience as a personal development facilitator. She holds a bachelor's degree from the University of Maryland and an MBA from New York University. She worked as a marketing leader at Google, American Express, and Telemundo/ZGS. Carolina is a speaker, certified mindfulness, emotional intelligence, resilience, and leadership teacher, purpose coach, marketing and entrepreneurship consultant, and bilingual meditation narrator. She enjoys oil painting, Latin dancing, spending time with her family in her native Colombia, and discovering new places around the world.

Steph Stern is a transformational coach and facilitator with a passion for helping people find more purpose and fulfillment in their work and lives. Steph served as a director and key member of the leadership team at the Search Inside Yourself Leadership Institute for several years. There, Steph worked directly with many organizations, including Google, SAP, Disney, Salesforce, and MIT, to bring mindfulness and emotional intelligence into how people and organizations work. She has over 10 years of experience working with individuals and organizations to develop greater awareness and compassion for themselves and for others. Previously, she worked for more than a decade on environmental policies and programs in both the public and private sectors. Steph is a Certified Internal Family Systems practitioner, and holds a master's in city planning from MIT and a bachelor's from Wellesley. She lives in Oakland, California, where she loves to hike and dive into creative projects.